TERROT REAVELEY GLOVER

TERROT REAVELEY GLOVER

H. G. WOOD

TERROT REAVELEY GLOVER

A Biography

CAMBRIDGE

AT THE UNIVERSITY PRESS

1953

CAMBRIDGE
UNIVERSITY PRESS

University Printing House, Cambridge CB2 8BS, United Kingdom

Cambridge University Press is part of the University of Cambridge.

It furthers the University's mission by disseminating knowledge in the pursuit of
education, learning and research at the highest international levels of excellence.

www.cambridge.org
Information on this title: www.cambridge.org/9781107594494

First published 1953
First paperback edition 2015

A catalogue record for this publication is available from the British Library

ISBN 978-1-107-59449-4 Paperback

VIRI INSIGNIS CONIVGI
TOTIVS VITAE CONSORTI DILECTISSIMAE
ET FILIIS ET FILIABVS
NECNON EIVSDEM SORORI
HOC TANTILLVM AMICITIAE DOCVMENTVM
AVCTOR DEDICAT

CONTENTS

INTRODUCTION

Some six months after Glover died in 1943, Harold Laski contributed to the *New Statesman and Nation* a most generous and discriminating tribute to him, in an article entitled, 'On not having known T. R. Glover'. Laski never actually met Glover. He had passed him in King's Parade and seen him in Heffer's bookshop, but when he was staying with W. H. R. Rivers and dining at St John's College, his host could but lament Glover's absence. 'You ought to know him,' he said, 'a fine combination of Dr Johnson and Charles Lamb.'

Though he never knew Glover in the flesh, Laski was aware of many common interests, such as a lively interest in the New World across the Atlantic, great skill in the art of combing a second-hand bookshop, and an obvious love of young people.

'All of these are qualities by which he is endeared to me,' wrote Laski. 'I do not mind the presence in him of obvious gusts of ill temper. I find no resentment at the fact that he seems rarely to have been capable of understanding views he did not share....I even agree that any careful reader of his books will find in them, first, a pretty obvious set of prejudices that he had never stayed to examine, and a mass of ideas which are, however scholarly their expression, ideas seen through other men's eyes. All this, as I turn over the pages of the neat score of volumes he wrote, seems to me completely devoid of importance. What makes him a friendly writer is first, that he has so great a gusto for living and second that like Charles Lamb he is always inviting you freely into the inner chambers of his mind.'

A friendly writer! A W.E.A. student who read *The Jesus of History* said, one reason it gripped him was that Glover seemed to be so interested in his readers!

If Laski regarded Glover as first and foremost a superb popularizer of other men's ideas, he realized that 'he had always seen them freshly for himself, as if their meaning was seen for the first time'. In this there is something of the power of poetic imagination, especially as we find it in Wordsworth—the power to reveal the wonder of the familiar.

Glover had the great gift of making the past come alive. He had it, I think, because his stout common sense was set in the perspective of an imagination that never stopped working. He wanted not only to know why people did things, but why they did them in a particular way. He always asked himself what he would have done in the same situation. So that, whoever it was, Herodotus or Alexander,...Horace or Augustus, he seemed to write about them from inside themselves and not aloofly: he makes them contemporaries whom one might easily have gone to see drive down Constitution Hill or who might publish a new work which made critics pleased or angry.

As you read 'you always discern the figure of T. R. Glover, tremendously alive asking this man questions, telling another how things have changed since his day, eager and vigorous, perhaps a little too self-confident, but adorably insatiable in his enthusiasm and his curiosity'.

That Laski was so warm and just in his appreciation of Glover as historian is not surprising. More remarkable is his understanding of Glover as a religious teacher. He follows up his tribute to the historian and literary critic, by recalling

another Glover whom I must not forget. There is the classical scholar, the superb popularizer, the ardent traveller to whom new places and new faces are the elixir of new life. But there is also Glover the mystic, a God-intoxicated man who wrote, indeed, books to communicate his joy in the faith he held to others, but in whose religious volumes one always feels that the book behind the book is, somehow, ten times more important and impressive than the book he managed to write. This Glover is a man with a message to deliver which obviously transcended in its significance all the historical learning, the classical lore, the technical insight into scholarship, that he possessed: I think he did not deliver his message, because he felt too deeply about it. He left only the impression of one who has caught a glimpse of some vision splendid and falters when he seeks to fulfil the task of conveying to others any sense beyond the passionate declaration that in this vision only is the truth to be found.

This too is a discerning critique, though it calls for two qualifications. The books he wrote, especially *The Jesus of History*, did communicate to many his joy in the faith he held. Archibald Marshall wrote to Glover in 1930,

I have just re-read your *Jesus of History* and you are now firmly established as one of my major prophets, along with Inge and F. W. Robertson who have done more for me than anybody of late years, the first having got me back to the Faith, the second constantly establishing me in it. It is a wonderful book, yours, and apart from its very deep spiritual value, I can appreciate how a lifetime of study and hard thought has flowered into so clear and apparently easy an impression. It is simply full of meat and a chapter of it more than fills one's mind for the day.

Some part of the message did get over to the readers of his books, but it lay in the nature of the message that it could not be fully expressed in books, just as Plato's philosophy could not be exhaustively presented in his dialogues. Glover delivered his message more effectively as preacher than as writer. Yet Laski is right. The book behind the books is ten times more important and impressive.

It is not within the power of a biographer to write this book behind the books, but he should be able to fulfil a simpler task. In his closing paragraph, Laski wrote:

I never knew T. R. Glover, and I have no idea of the thousand and one intimate habits which go to the making of a personality. What this big burly tutor was like as a teacher: whether he held a lecture-room as entranced by speech as he holds our reader by his pages: what happened to transform the gawky sixth-form boy at Bristol Grammar School into a man who lived every line of the classics he knew so well: why those years at Queen's University [Kingston, Canada] set the New World for him in the background of perpetual sunlight: who his intimates were at Cambridge: what for instance would have happened when he encountered agnosticism serene and pacifism urgent as in Lowes Dickinson, or atheism militant and militarism passionate, as in McTaggart: to questions like these, I have no answer.

To questions like these, some answers can, of course, be given. In answering them, I may make the book behind the books more difficult to discover. Glover would wish his biographer to be sympathetically critical, not adulatory. I must not pass over his limitations. But Bradley's sentence on Shelley, which Glover was fond of quoting, is a safe guide to follow. 'Always we get most from the genius in a man of genius and not from the rest of him.' Glover would not wish me to suppress the rest of him. I hope I shall not so dwell on it as to obscure the genius.

H. G. W.

Chapter I

BRISTOL, 1869-1887

Early days : boyhood and youth : Home, Church, and School

Terrot Reaveley Glover was born on 23 July 1869, at 10 Belgrave Road, Cotham, Bristol. Towards the end of his life, he would sometimes say, 'I have only two regrets: the first that Oxford refused to elect me to a scholarship before I went over to Cambridge; and the second that my father migrated from Scotland to England some months before I was born.' Neither regret should be taken too seriously; there were disappointments and sorrows in his life that cut deeper. Though he would have liked to go to Oxford, he was proud of being a Cambridge man. Though he would have liked to be born in Scotland, he was proud of his birthplace and glad to be a Bristolian. But his regret focuses his delight in his Scottish ancestry. His names came to him from his father's side. His paternal grandfather, Terrot Glover, belonged to Scotland and his paternal grandmother, Anne Reaveley, was a north-country woman. His mother hailed from Glasgow, and through her he could claim many Scottish relatives.

His father, Richard Glover, was the youngest of eight brothers. Born on 6 January 1837, Richard Glover was a year older than his wife, Anne Finlay, whose birthday fell on 6 February 1838. They were married in Glasgow on 27 March 1866. Early in 1869 they moved to Bristol, Richard Glover having accepted the call to become the first minister of the newly formed Baptist Church, which met in the chapel in Whiteladies Road, known as Tyndale. The young minister preached his first sermon in Tyndale on 11 April. He was to spend his whole long and honoured ministerial career as pastor of the same church. A few months after their settlement in Bristol, their first child and only son was born.[1] Two years later, on 10 October 1871, a daughter,

---

[1] Late on in life, reflecting on the date of his birth, and stimulated by listening to an address on shipbuilding, Glover described himself as 'Clyde-built and Bristol-launched'.

Elizabeth, was born, to be followed in 1875 by a second daughter, Dorothy Finlay.

In physique and temperament, the boy's inheritance was plain to see. His younger sister once said she knew no two people more alike than her mother and her brother. Perhaps the resemblance was more in temperament than in physique, but one who knew them well said to Glover in 1888, 'Your mother looks out of your mouth', and he himself assumed that his high cheek-bones, which often suggested to observers the physiognomy of a Highlander or a Red Indian, were a link with his mother. In stature and build, in his forehead and in his expressive eyes, he took more after his father. If his mother looked out of his mouth, his father looked out of his eyes.[1]

In one of his diaries, he suggests that he derived from his mother the uneasy temperament which included a tendency to be over-anxious, and a nervous impatient irritability. In so far as it was an inheritance, this uneasy temperament came to him from his mother's side, but it was accentuated in Glover by his ill-health and by the undue weight of responsibility which is often assumed by the first-born in a family. In his early days at the Bristol Grammar School, teasing might sometimes reduce him to tears, and this not because of any physical cowardice but because he possessed an almost feminine sensibility. Later on his outspoken children would warn him against becoming senti-mental—'soupy' they called it—in sermons and addresses. For the most part such warnings were quite unnecessary. Few preachers were more manly than Glover. Yet there was in him this streak of emotional sensitiveness. With regard to irritability and over-anxiety, his elder sister Elizabeth once advised him to learn to play Patience, and more than once rallied him for crossing his bridges before he came to them. But the advice he did not take and his nervous apprehensiveness he could never shake off.

In another of his diaries Glover recalls that his mother 'did things honestly, not living wastefully and was strict in keeping to her father's religion'. He inherited or imbibed her Scottish thrift, her hatred of waste and her care in the use of money. If she had something of Martha's carefulness, she also exhibited

---

[1] A Scottish friend, Mrs McCrie, described him as 'a beautiful combination of parents'.

Martha's grace of hospitality. It was said of her by her daughter that

she belonged to a generation not trained to speak, preside, take meetings or classes. But hospitality was her strong suit. Morning, noon and night, an ever open door and an ever spread table. Callers, visitors and friends, and sometimes those whom we children called 'strays'. People who were lonely, people without family, people in sorrow, people in perplexity, the strangers in a strange land, people who wanted a few weeks nùrsing or feeding up, people on the eve of marriage, sometimes the poor that are cast out,—she was always there and they were always welcome.

Her son shared both her pleasure in company, and her sympathies. If he shared her caution about the use of money, like her when he gave, he gave generously and unostentatiously.

A staunch loyalty to religious conviction was instilled into him by both his parents. Not only in certain physical features, but also in his intellectual ability, in his gifts of self-expression by speech and the written word, in his power of imagination and in his humour, above all in his unusual spiritual vitality, he took after his father. The direct influence of his father went deep, and remembrance and gratitude drove it deeper. He sketched the character and interests of his father in one of his Saturday articles in the *Daily News*. No name was mentioned, but all who knew Dr Richard Glover recognized the portrait and appreciated the truth and the charm of his son's tribute. I recall it here, as it is much the best way of indicating his debt to his father. If T. R. Glover ·had written *Father and Son* it would have been a very different book. The article was entitled 'A generation ago'; it should have been called 'My Father'.

In the first place he was good to look at—an apt illustration of Spenser's belief that 'soul is form and doth the body make'. For his hair was for forty years a gleaming white and there was plenty of it to the very end; his beard was white and well-trimmed; he had a good complexion, and great, brown, smiling eyes, capable of fun and sympathy, and telling of a nature, too, that you would not wish to trifle with, though you could readily be at home with it. The eyes told true. He was a man of wide range, nowhere a specialist, but at home in all sorts of things and with all sorts of people to a degree that you might not expect. He could never pass a tool-shop without a good look at it: he loved machinery; and he bought books as his means allowed. Books, not editions; for he had not the money, and, then, like Charles Lamb, he did not care very much about the externals of a book, so long as the author and the printer made reading possible. He would buy a book on Science or on History; the poets he had gathered in his youth, and in middle life he added Browning to them and read him till he knew him intimately.

In his old age it was more to History that he turned. Properly speaking, you would have expected him to read more Theology than he ever did, and to keep abreast more conscientiously of Philosophy; but he preferred perhaps what men did, and what they felt, to what others speculated about them. He just escaped being a mathematician; and, though he never was technically a scholar, he read in his college days a fair amount of Homer and St Augustine in the original. He liked people, too, as well as tools and books, and was at once a shrewd judge and a very gentle critic.

He was one of a great bunch of brothers, bred in a home where thrift and good temper and the sea were real factors. Most of them turned in one way or other to the sea, and he began his voyaging when a student. It was a long voyage, and he had plenty of leisure on the sailing ship of the fifties, and he used it in teaching sailors in the forecastle to read and in learning navigation himself. Ever afterwards St Paul's voyage appealed to him; many things drew him to St Paul, but the voyage was irresistible.

He was always fond of children, and made friends with them by cutting out of envelopes splendid railway trains and even more wonderful animals; and he could make up fascinating stories. Servants liked to wait on him, he was so gracious; and, if some shocking piece of domestic plumbing called him away from his sermons the cook was glad to leave the kitchen to hold the washer or to fetch the screw-driver, for he had the plumber's own knack of never having quite all the tools he wanted. His study was full of handy but terrible contrivances made of biscuit tins, clock springs, cocoa boxes, and the like. He loved singing. Hymns and Scottish psalms and Scottish songs never lost their appeal. Day by day for many years he had, in the old Scottish way, a psalm or (later on) a hymn at family prayers, as long as he had family enough to sing them. Eventually, when, as reported to an absent member, 'Your father sang a solo to the cook at prayers', the singing was reluctantly given up.

He held his opinions very strongly; he had what someone

called a 'gracious stubbornness'. The fact was that he had left the church of his parents, for the ministry of which he had started to prepare himself, because he found he could not sign its formularies. An elder brother had strayed before him, and trying to argue him in again, he argued himself out, and stayed out with his eyes open to what he was doing, never regretting the change, always rejoicing and believing in the freedom he had found, and always loyal both to the church he had left and the church he had joined.

He never went to Keswick or to any convention for the 'second blessing', or for holiness, or even for the deepening of the spiritual life; but he seemed to have a larger conception of God than many who frequent such gatherings. He confessed that he could not read other men's sermons, and he did not; but he was frankly interested in Darwin, and it never seemed to occur to him that you could not be friends at once with Darwin and St John. As to Higher Criticism, the older sort looked askance at him, but again he was tranquil and reasonable. He conceded the critic's central position; of course, you had the right to weigh evidence, to learn, and to know—or rather it was your duty; but you had also to make good your conclusions by sufficient argument and evidence; neither critic nor old school should carry it off with mere dogma. He saw plainly enough that the Love of God could not depend on the verbal inspiration of a supposed divine command to kill Canaanites; and if Darwin and Genesis did not altogether agree, well, both might be wrong here or there, and both might be right, Genesis as to God being the Author of all things and Darwin as to God's procedure. Evolution no more implied a Godless universe than Creation.

You could not live near him, frequent his church, meet him on committee or even on the tram, without becoming more and more conscious that here was a man for whom God was real and Christ central. One man, who heard him preach for many years, said he always gravitated to the Love of God. He believed in God—pessimism, he said, was an orthodox form of unbelief. From his experience came his love of the great evangelical hymns, of St John, of St Paul; an enthusiasm for preaching, for helping others to preach, for foreign missions. He could not understand how anybody who knew the Gospel could do anything but try to make it available for everyone.

Unruffled courtesy, playfulness, kindness, a large interest in everything human, and at the centre a passion for Jesus Christ—he made it difficult to doubt the reality of the best things; he made it seem natural to believe in God.

It will be readily understood that the life of the home was interwoven with the life of the Church. The minister's son will be regular in attending public worship on Sundays. As he grows older, he will attend the week-night service also. He passes through the Sunday School, entering as a scholar and becoming a teacher. Family worship and public worship combine to place habit on the side of religion—to use a phrase of Gladstone's which Glover entered in one of his commonplace books. Writing to his eldest son, Gladstone said, 'You cannot depend upon your tastes and feelings toward Divine things to be uniform: lay hold upon an instrument which will carry you over their inequalities and keep you in the honest practice of your spiritual exercises, when but for this they would have been intermittent.' This instrument was put into Glover's hands as a boy. He never lost his hold on it and never ceased to be thankful for it.

The Church was the centre of a vigorous social life. Apart from bazaars which were always occasions of interest, not to say excitement for young people, there was a regular Christmas party for the children of the congregation, when a deacon 'with a long beard and a droll whimsical voice' would entertain them with a magic-lantern. From time to time there were soirées which brought the younger folk together. The Church was attracting a number of families—Robinsons, Sargents, Garaways, Jenkins and many others.

As a boy Terrot Reaveley seems to have been more interested in his girl contemporaries than in the boys in the church-circle. When he taught in the Sunday school, he was given a class of young girls to teach. He early felt the attraction of feminine society and early developed his ideas of what constituted excellence in women. His schoolboy diaries contain many references to his impressions of girls he liked. Thus on 15 January 1886 he finished Tennyson's *Maud*. 'It is very beautiful, and so is Maude—too.' He regrets that Tennyson left off the last letter of Maude's name. Ethel—too is very pretty. 'She has more mind than any girl I know.' There is, however, only qualified approval. 'Ethel is very fine, but should not be so vehement. I am that, but she, being a girl, should not. Still I admire her.' This youthful admirer of many of the girls he met was to grow into the man, who, as his friend Dil Calvin said, 'was not ready

to accept any woman, still less, women as a whole'. His commonplace books record rather more epigrams which are witty at the
expense of women than sayings or stories appreciative of or
sympathetic with them. His hasty generalizations about women
provoked his friend J. C. Carlile into telling him that it was
wonderfully condescending of him to have had a mother. But at
least in his teens, admiration for youthful members of the opposite
sex tended to outrun cautious discrimination. Ethel, whose
intelligence he rated so high, said of him, 'he is a nice sort of
boy, but too fond of girls', and when his first attempt to win
a scholarship at Oxford failed, the father of one of his school-
fellows rather unfairly accused him of not working, and told him
that he could not go running after petticoats and get scholarships
too!

The social influence of Tyndale was not, of course, confined
to Glover's friendships with young people of his own age. The
stream of visitors to the home brought contacts with interesting
people, including as it did ministers, missionaries, lecturers and
occasionally politicians. The boy early learned the attractions
of serious well-informed conversation. He took full advantage
of his contacts with his seniors.

His religious convictions owed everything to the combined
influence of home and church. On 27 February 1883, when he
was fourteen years old, he was baptized and joined the Church.
The date is remembered with thankfulness in every succeeding
diary. Baptism by immersion on one's responsible public confession of faith in Christ involves a personal commitment of some
intensity.[1] The main idea of the sacrament for Glover would be
the original meaning of the word, *sacramentum*, as the Roman
soldier's oath of loyal obedience to his commander. That he took
the step, conscious of his need of Christ, and of his debt to Him
as his Saviour, is obvious, and he may well have been aware of
the symbolic significance of baptism by immersion as uniting
him with Christ in His death and resurrection. But the confirmation hymn, 'O Jesus, I have promised to serve Thee to the
end', expressed the dominant note of the rite. He was irrevocably

---

[1] Cf. what Glover wrote of Tertullian: 'Like men who are baptized of their own
motion and understanding he was greatly impressed by baptism' (*Conflict of
Religions*, p. 328).

committed to Christ's cause, and he had made the personal commitment, which was to shape and control all his thought and action.

From the time of his baptism onwards, the claims and the romance of the missionary enterprise of the Christian Church appealed to him. This interest came to him in the first instance from his father. It was deepened by visits and addresses from missionaries. Bristol Baptists were closely associated with the development of the mission in the Congo, the starting of which in the 'eighties involved the sacrifice of many lives. An address by T. J. Comber stirred the schoolboy and, when J. H. Shindler was accepted for the Congo in March 1886, he wrote, 'Lucky fellow! I am glad for him!' A year later, both Shindler and Comber had fallen victims to the pestilential fevers endemic on the Congo. But Glover's enthusiasm for missions was not confined to a particular field. In 1886, he writes, 'I should like to be a missionary, I think, but where to?' He was attracted by the personality and outlook of Timothy Richard, one of the most original and vigorous of the minds devoted to evangelizing China. On 28 May 1886 he records, 'Mr Timothy Richard was at dinner. He left for London and I saw him off from Clifton Down. He is a splendid character. May I be like him.' Timothy Richard was to be an exponent of the new evangelism which presents the Gospel as preserving and fulfilling all that is best in the cultures of those to whom the message is addressed. Whether he could have influenced Glover in that way in 1886 is doubtful, but it is noteworthy that the boy's mind was already moving in that direction. On the same day, he records: 'Finished Sir Edwin Arnold's *Light of Asia*: I admire Buddha', and 'I would like to be a missionary, I think.' Glover, however, was not destined for the mission-field, and when he spent a year abroad with the Y.M.C.A. during the first World War, he went to India, where the cultural background was less congenial to him than the Chinese tradition and atmosphere might have been.

The missionary interest so well sustained at Tyndale did not engender indifference to conditions nearer home. From very early on Tyndale was responsible for a mission church in a poorer part of the city and Glover took an active interest in the work there. Above and beyond this special activity, through the life of its members Tyndale contributed to the life and well-being of the city. It is often wrongfully alleged that people who care for missions ignore and overlook the needy at home. The same ardent women workers ran the Dorcas Society which assisted institutions and individuals in Bristol, and the working party which furnished the wonderful annual missionary sale. Like Carrs Lane in Birmingham, Tyndale in Bristol contributed many fine men to the Magistrates' Bench and the City Council. Four men took the initiative in a move to celebrate Queen Victoria's second Jubilee by founding a convalescent home for the poor of Bristol. They were the minister of Tyndale and a leading deacon, Mr Edward Robinson, an elderly Quaker chocolate manufacturer, no doubt Joseph Storrs Fry, and a prominent brewer. Edward Robinson once told Glover, 'Your father taught me to give, and it's been a great blessing to me.' As a member of Tyndale, the youth could not be unaware of or indifferent to the claims of social service.

Through home and Church, Glover found his first and ultimate loyalty to Jesus Christ, and he learned something of the ways in which that loyalty works out in evangelism and social service. His fundamental Christian convictions were nurtured in the setting of orthodox Dissent, marked by the emphasis on individual responsibility characteristic of the Baptists. Glover grew up a convinced Dissenter and a Baptist. He was much impressed by a lecture on the Claims of the Free Churches, given by R. F. Horton at Highbury Congregational Church in November 1886. Horton indeed became one of his heroes and exemplars, for had he not, as a young Oxford don with a brilliant academic career before him, given it all up for the sake of the ministry among the Congregationalists? Glover took full notes of the lecture which outlined the debt of gratitude which England owes to non-episcopalians, and which ended by insisting that 'men are not ashamed of dissenters till dissenters are ashamed of themselves'. Nonconformity is an absurd name, according to Horton, since the Dissenter stands for great positive principles, such as progress in religion, the importance of individual choice and decision, simplicity in worship and organization, and a refusal to identify the truth of Christ with the outlook and standards of any visible church. These principles Glover never forgot and never abandoned. The importance of this last principle was to be tested in his lifetime in connexion with the Baptist denomination to which he was deeply attached. While he was still in the Sixth Form at school, C. H. Spurgeon precipitated the 'Down-grade' controversy among the Baptists. Not without reason Spurgeon believed that many of his fellow-ministers were slipping from the standards which had hitherto been regarded as essential. They no longer believed in the verbal inspiration of the Bible or in eternal punishment in the literal traditional sense. They were, he said, on the Down-grade. He would not make specific charges of heresy against individuals, and this the Council of the Baptist Union regarded as unsatisfactory. On 16 January 1888 Richard Glover went up to a special meeting of the Council to consider Spurgeon's resignation. When he returned two days later, his son learned that the resignation had been accepted. This unhappy controversy raised for Glover the question whether the traditional Calvinistic standards of the Particular Baptists can be identified with the truth of Christ, and even as a schoolboy he felt convinced that they could not. There is little doubt that Dr John Clifford was the arch-heretic whom Spurgeon would not name, and Clifford was becoming one of Glover's heroes. On 23 April 1888 he goes down to the Free Library to read Dr Clifford's article in the *Contemporary Review* on 'Baptist Theology'. On returning home, he writes, 'Think I am a Restorationist'. It is clear where his sympathies lay.

Next to home and church, his school was naturally the most important formative influence in his life. For reasons which are not very clear, his father decided to send him to the Bristol Grammar School rather than to Clifton College, to which most boys from his preparatory school went on as day-boys. The fees for day-boys at Clifton were not appreciably higher than those at the Grammar School and certainly Dr Glover could have afforded them. At the Grammar School, Glover was to be under a headmaster, R. L. Leighton, who was a layman and a strong Liberal in politics. However when Glover first went in 1881, Leighton had not yet been appointed and the school was not very flourishing. 'It had less than 300 boys, and the Governors were seriously crippled by the expense of building the new school premises in Tyndalls Park. The teaching in Classics and Mathematics was good, but too narrowly conceived: little attention was paid to history or English literature, and the scientific side was farcical.' But after Leighton was appointed in 1883, the numbers and the quality of the education steadily improved. When the new headmaster arrived, Glover was already in the Lower Sixth and came at once under his influence. During the many terms he spent in the Sixth that influence went deeper. It was not, however, his headmaster who first awakened the boy's interest in the Classics, and before estimating the influence of R. L. Leighton, I must mention his debt to the Classics master, J. G. S. Muschamp, a thick-set little man whom the boys called 'Stumpy', and who had the reputation of being a martinet.

Muschamp was 'an old Peterhouse man who narrowly missed a first class in the Classical Tripos, an excellent teacher of Latin and Greek, and a man of fine taste and appreciation of literature', and Glover was never weary of acknowledging his debt to him. His little book on Horace contains a charming tribute to his old master, but perhaps even more striking is the opening paragraph of a paper on Conversion which he wrote as an article for the *Daily News*.[1]

When I was a boy at school, about fourteen years old, I was promoted to a new form, to be under the care of a master of whom I was very much afraid. So far on my course I had found that Greek and Latin came easiest of all my work; and possibly, if you had asked me, I might have said, in the dialect of that day, that they were 'the least beastly of all the lessons'. One term with J. G. S. Muschamp and Horace's *Odes*, book III, altered all that; Muschamp and I were friends and allies for life; I bought the first book of the *Odes* myself and read it next holidays; and ever since I have been a classical man without looking back, and there I am still, impenitent in my adherence to the Classics, whatever people say. And Horace's *Odes* I read through again for the nth time, crossing the Atlantic and Canada last summer. One term at school with a new master, and a definite direction was given to life, a new enthusiasm and a new purpose.

R. L. Leighton was a Balliol man, and if there was any risk of the teaching of the Classics under Muschamp being too narrowly conceived, he countered it with a wider outlook. When Leighton died in 1928, Glover contributed an appreciation to the School

[1] *Saturday Papers*, p. 71.

Chronicle, and some sentences will indicate what he owed to his headmaster.

After I passed into the Upper Sixth and until I went up to Cambridge in 1888 I was in daily contact with him. I can best sum up what it meant by recalling that for years after I left school, whenever a subject of real interest came up—anything that involved broad issues or touched life—something germane said by Leighton would come into my mind, something that bore on it and might illumine it. With years I feel more and more the value to a growing boy of a Teacher who sees matters in their relations rather than isolated, and I am grateful to have been taught by such a man.

Like some other headmasters, R. L. Leighton dealt also ın a shrewd worldly wisdom. 'He advised me not to enter the ministry, on account of orthodoxy, but recommended business.' So runs an entry in the diary for 1888. Wisely perhaps, Glover followed the first part of this advice and as wisely ignored the second. But as a classical scholar, Leighton added something that Muschamp did not give.

Muschamp gave us his own zest for Verse Composition, the use of language and style. Composition with Leighton was another story—a much uneasier one. 'Glover,' he said one day, 'I don't know what to red-ink in your prose unless I red-ink the whole of it. It's all quite right and none of it Greek.' That was a little damping: but by now I sympathize more with him than I did just then. With 'Stumpy' as we called him, it was quite different. But Leighton did for us—at all events for me—something that Muschamp perhaps could not have done. You might say they fairly represented Oxford and Cambridge. My debt to both of them is great and I may as well say that both won an affection and loyalty which they kept till death.

Whenever a headmaster acts as Sixth Form master also, it often happens that administrative duties, urgent business calls, will compel him to leave the Sixth from time to time to their own resources. This is not always a disadvantage, but it frequently happened that after the mid-morning break when he was to take the form, the head did not appear for a quarter of an hour or longer, and the boys were left without direction more than was good for them. At one time somebody suggested the pastime of writing verses, serious or otherwise. 'Glover', says one of his contemporaries, 'was far the best at this game. Perhaps it helped to give him his facility in writing humorous verse for the *Granta* and the *Eagle* in his college days.' In a little pocket-book of memoranda for 1886–7, Glover copied out many of these Sixth Form verses. Several of them are passable translations from Latin poets, particularly Catullus. Such schoolboy exercises are scarcely worth recalling, but some verses about Glover by a school-fellow will at least show how he impressed his contemporaries.

> A many-sided polyglot,
>   in mathematics versed.
> 'Tis hard to say where he is best,
>   nor yet where he is worst.
>
> He dabbles in philology,
>   in Anglo-Saxon too;
> indeed we should not be surprised
>   to hear him speak Hindoo!
>
> In wit he far surpasses all
>   and not in wit alone;
> for in debate he carries weight,
>   as every one must own.
>
> But yet in spite of all his lore
>   it cannot be denied
> that (though his character is good)
>   he's rather giv'n to pride.
>
> His form is not remarkable
>   for beauty or for grace;
> but who can imitate the smile
>   that sometimes lights his face?
>
> In him is seen a kind of mean
>   (I do not wish to flatter).
> I should not like to call him thin
>   but he might well be fatter.
>
> Not like an alderman well-lined
>   with capon, teal or plover,
> but like to no one but himself
>   is Terrot Reaveley Glover.

We may elaborate some of the features of this portrait. First there are the references to his weight and a hint that his figure and his movements lack grace. He was tall and heavy for his years. He must have been eleven stone in his last year at school.

And he was not athletic. Until the new head raised a fund for new playing-fields, games were somewhat neglected. Glover was secretary of the School football club for one season. He played for the Sixth versus the School, and occasionally for the School. His weight secured him a place in the scrum, but he was not a skilful player. From very early on he found in walking his chief recreation, and he explored Bristol and neighbourhood with unflagging zest. In the next place, the rhymester describes him as a polyglot. The term 'polymath' would have been happier. He was steadily occupying the classical humanist's quadrilateral, Greek, Latin, French, German, but he was developing his taste for all kinds of history and travel, rather than concentrating on the acquisition of languages. His appetite for both history and travel had been whetted by two trips abroad in the summer holidays, to Paris in 1885 and to Switzerland in 1886.[1] That he was rather given to pride was due to his becoming conscious of his powers as he found himself head of the school. In one of the latest of his school reports, Leighton described him as good, but garrulous. He was always a ready talker, and sometimes aggressive and self-assertive in conversation. But his wit, his facility in speech and the widening range of his interests made him a vigorous and effective debater.

The debating society at the school was an unusually flourishing society. Glover was secretary in 1886 and president in 1887 and 1888. He had splendid opportunities of advocating his Liberal views. He was keenly interested in the Home Rule issue and was a devoted follower of Gladstone. In November 1886 he moved a resolution in favour of Home Rule for Ireland and challenges the claims of Ulster in the following rhyme:

> Loyal? Nay, Ulster, you for very shame
> Should cede your long monopoly of that name!
> Loyal to whom? to what? to power, to pelf
> To place, to privilege, in a word, to SELF!
> They who assume, absorb, control, enjoy all
> Must find it vastly pleasant to be loyal!

The motion was carried by 27 to 20. But a year later, when he sought to persuade the society to condemn the Irish Policy of the

[1] At a still earlier age, the boy had sailed with his father to the Baltic and visited St Petersburg.

Conservative Government the figures were reversed. He lost by 19 to 35! He had no difficulty in persuading the House to oppose any system of spelling reform, but when he opposed cremation and pleaded for burial, he was overwhelmingly defeated. He was a convinced total abstainer, and a motion preferring total abstinence to temperance was lost only by the chairman's casting vote.

Perhaps the two most interesting debates in which he took a leading part dealt with the following two motions: (*a*) that Elizabeth was justified in putting to death Mary, Queen of Scots; and (*b*) that Socialism is to be approved. That he opposed the first motion is to be explained by his bias in favour of all things Scottish. As a small boy, he wrote to his grandmother Finlay, 'Are you Royalists? I am. I have had several arguments with Papa and Ethel G.' His royalism did not survive his entry into the Sixth. Then he classifies himself as Republican, but he still champions Mary, Queen of Scots. His peroration carried the House. 'Now, gentlemen, I call on you, whoever of you value honour, whoever of you have pitiful hearts, whoever of you love liberty and above liberty, whoever of you hate cruelty and duplicity and love mercy, you I call on to vote for the opponent and to give your sentences that Elizabeth was not justified in her murder of Mary of Scotland!' (*Great applause.*) The motion was lost by 16 to 26. He moved the resolution in favour of Socialism and seemed to regard it as a moral victory for his side when the majority was not more than 16. He had prepared for this debate by getting a Clifton master, Dr Cecil Reddie, to coach him for it. He also persuaded another Clifton master, Holmes Gore, an old boy of the Bristol Grammar School, to speak for the motion. Glover probably took as his text a passage from John Stuart Mill, which he recorded in a note-book. 'No longer enslaved or made dependent by force of Law, the great majority are so by force of poverty. They are still chained to a place, to an occupation and to conformity to the will of an employer and debarred from advantages which others inherit without exertion and independently of desert.' He never lost his sympathy with Labour, but he did not long retain belief in Socialism as the remedy.

Bristol Grammar School did much for Glover, and it is doubtful whether Clifton College would have done more. J. M. Wilson, who was then headmaster of Clifton, would have liked to have Glover at College, and when Glover heard Wilson preach in the College Chapel, he wished his headmaster were more like Wilson. But manifestly, Glover was well taught by Leighton and Muschamp, and found himself among a stimulating group of boys. The Grammar School was attracting really intelligent lively boys who did it credit. In the autumn of 1887, he tried for scholarships. He sat first at Balliol, and then at Wadham. In neither examination did he succeed, and at Balliol he was competing with very able rivals, including such scholars as G. W. Steevens and W. M. Geldart. Failing at Oxford, he turned to Cambridge. On 17 December he learned that he had been elected to a minor scholarship of £50 for Classics at St John's College, Cambridge. It was the beginning of a lifelong association.

Chapter II

CAMBRIDGE, 1888-1892

A Dissenter among Anglicans : Lady Margaret Boat Club :
the Union Society : early classical studies

The abolition of religious tests for entrance to and office in the
older Universities may prove to have been one of the most
revolutionary changes effected in the Victorian era. An apparently simple measure of social justice, it has profoundly modified
the relations of Church and Dissent and has posed afresh the
problem of Christianity and culture. The representatives of
Church and Dissent thrown together in the student body and in
course of time sharing the responsibilities of College Councils and
University Boards, could not maintain intact their earlier
suspicions and antagonisms. The Ecumenical Movement owes
more than is often realized to the abolition of subscription to the
Articles as a test of fitness for study and for teaching at the older
Universities. Somewhat similarly, the mixing of the classes in
the modern University is changing still further the relations
of bourgeois and proletarian, and exposing the reactionary
character of the Marxist conception of class-war and class-
consciousness.

The reform, however, was not welcomed either by Anglicans
or Free Churchmen without misgiving. Anglicans like Dr Pusey
feared that it would mean the end of the Universities as avowedly
Christian institutions. His fears were not groundless. The
development of the scientific disciplines has favoured the growth
of a scientific humanism, which is often unaware of its debt to
Christianity. There were many Conservatives in Oxford and
Cambridge who sympathized still with Dr Johnson's view that
every Dissenter should be regarded as a rascal until he proved
himself to be an honest man. Dissenters were in any case
an uncomfortably disturbing element. On the other hand,
Dissenters might succumb to the attractions of the Anglican
traditions embedded in the life and customs of the older Universities, or perhaps might drift away from the Christian outlook

altogether. T. H. Green, writing to Dr Dale of Birmingham, soon after the tests had been removed, said,

the opening of the national Universities to Nonconformists has been, in my judgment, an injury rather than a help to Nonconformity. You are sending up here [i.e. to Oxford] year after year, the sons of some of the best and wealthiest families: they are often altogether uninfluenced by the services of the Church which they find here, and they not only drift away from Nonconformity, they drift away and lose all faith: and you are bound, as soon as you have secured the opening of the Universities for your sons, to follow them when you send them here, in order to defend and maintain their religious life and faith.[1]

This letter helped to convert Dale to the proposal to remove Spring Hill Congregational College to Oxford, which led to the foundation of Mansfield College.

When Glover went up to Cambridge in October 1888, he was not likely to abandon his Free Church inheritance for Anglicanism. He was more inclined to adopt the defensive aggressive attitude of many Dissenters, who expected to find the atmosphere of the University somewhat enervating. As G. M. Trevelyan has reminded us, at the time when Glover was an undergraduate, many of his contemporaries were 'more aggressively anti-clerical than it is worth the while of any one to be today.... The more intransigent attitude of Leslie Stephen's and John Morley's writings on compromise in these (i.e. religious) matters, still had charms.'[2]

While Glover found no attraction in the agnosticism of John Morley and Leslie Stephen, he accepted the anti-clerical implications of their repudiation of compromise. However, Glover did not start his University career as a violent anti-clerical. He took advantage of the opportunities provided by the University sermons to hear outstanding preachers. In his first term he was much impressed by Welldon. But naturally, his main religious associations were with the Free Churches in Cambridge. He kept in touch with the Baptist Church at St Andrew's Street, where T. G. Tarn was then minister, but his attendance there became irregular for two reasons. First of all, he came to know old Mrs Whibley, the mother of H. G. Whibley. The son will long be remembered for his public-spirited service both to the city and to the Free Churches, particularly the Congregational churches

---

[1] *Life of R. W. Dale*, p. 496.   [2] *An Autobiography and other Essays*, p. 22.

in Cambridge. His mother holds a unique place in the affections and the memories of many young men whom she quietly encouraged to undertake social and religious work. Either she or Lavington Hart, who was then at St John's, persuaded Glover to take up a class in the men's Sunday morning school at the Castle End mission. For two years he was a regular teacher, and he continued to stand in as a reserve teacher for emergencies, after he had graduated. This Sunday morning class kept him away from regular attendance at public worship in the mornings. Too late for St Andrew's Street, he would more often than not stroll down from Castle End to the Union and write letters. In the second place, he was attracted to Emmanuel Congregational Church, at first by the preaching of W. S. Houghton, and later by the ministry of P. T. Forsyth and, for the greater part of his undergraduate days, he rented a pew there and attended the evening service with some regularity.

Soon after the tests were removed, some of the first Nonconformists to be admitted formed the Cambridge University Nonconformist Union in order to defend and maintain their life and faith. It was not narrowly conceived, and it opened the minds of many students to wider issues. Indeed Glover's first impression was that its programme was rather secular in character, but he joined it in the course of his second year and became secretary early in his third year. Some indication of the range of his interests as well as of the interests of the Union may be found in his contributing a paper on Ibsen, which subsequently appeared as an article in the St John's College magazine, the *Eagle*. The paper offers some shrewd criticism and sound appreciation of the Norwegian dramatist. After noting a lack of humour in Ibsen, Glover adds, 'His characters are oftener mad than is usual in most books. Moreover there is a sort of nudity about their spirits, which is a little perplexing to those who see chiefly what I may call the clothing of actions. You see too far into his characters to be able to feel that they are quite real people after all.' He admits that this may be the reader's fault rather than Ibsen's, but he clearly suspected a realism that claims to penetrate the ultimate mystery of individual character. Glover must have read most of the plays available in English and it is interesting that he advised readers to start with *Emperor and*

Galilean. Glover's mind is already grappling with the problems of the fourth century A.D. and with the conflict of religions in the Roman Empire. A play concerned with the Emperor Julian naturally attracts him. But he also sees rightly that the conflict between Christ and Caesar and the search for a third empire in which it may be resolved, lie at the heart of Ibsen's thinking and constitute his importance as interpreting the crucial issue in the cultural tensions of his time and ours.

While the main religious influences in his life and thought were thus still Nonconformist, he was of course in touch with Anglicanism. Many of his closest friends, both at school and college, were Anglicans. Among his contemporaries at school was G. A. Weekes, who went up to Cambridge at the same time as Glover did. At St John's he came to know Peter Green and J. H. B. Masterman, among others. He belonged to an inter-denominational college circle that met for prayer and discussion of religious issues on Saturday evenings. Naturally from time to time he attended College Chapel, and in his first year he became interested in the College Mission in Bermondsey. Glover was no hard-shell Dissenter.

Before I write of his development as a classical scholar, it may be well to deal with some of his other interests. During his first two terms he was tried out on the river. Being tubbed brought the usual results of basic discomfort, but he continued to row until he was dropped by Lady Margaret Boat Club at the beginning of the May term 1889. His build and weight pre-destined him to row at thwart 'six', and I suspect that he had not really the stamina required for that position in the boat. 'A boating idyll', written in February 1889, suggests another possible reason for the decision to drop him from any of the May boats, but it is not to be regarded as history.

> Upon the bank I see thee stand
>   O Lilian, my Lilian!
> I see thee wave thy dainty hand,
>   O Lilian, dear Lilian!
> I fain would wave a quick reply
>   But O! the cruel fate
> That gave the coach his watchful eye
>   'Six! watch it! Six, you're late!'

It goes on for five verses, which make it plain, if that were necessary, that Lilian is only a figment of the poet's imagination. He was dropped for other reasons. In the summer he supplemented grinds (or walks) with tennis, and until the Tripos was over, the well-known Madingley and Grantchester grinds became his chief resources for exercise. In the autumn term of 1891 he took up rowing again but, after a week's tubbing, a slight physical ailment which persisted for years compelled him to desist. But he never lost his interest in the fortunes of L.M.B.C. and his boat-song—not the boating idyll—is still sung at bumpsuppers.

Glover joined the Union Society as a life-member in the first week of his first term, and spoke frequently in the debates. He made his maiden speech on 12 February 1889 in support of the motion, 'This House is opposed to granting any more "rights" to women.' The motion was carried, and if his speech was serious and not a debating *jeu d'esprit*, Glover had receded from his schoolboy Liberalism, for in the School debating society he had argued in favour of votes for women. In the College debating society, also, he opposed votes for women. At the Union, however, he spoke in favour of degrees for women. .His support of this reform never wavered. Still verging on the Conservative outlook, he appeared on the paper at the Union in the summer term 1889, as opposer of the motion that 'The House of Commons needs reform'. It was moved by his friend and contemporary at St John's, E. W. MacBride. The motion was carried and Glover admits that the poverty of his speech deserved his defeat. But he remained true to the Liberal policy of Home Rule for Ireland, and he did not conceal his sympathies with Labour. In the autumn of 1889 he spoke at the Union in favour of the right to strike. The motion was lost, but Glover remained impenitent. He went to hear Ben Tillett, one of the heroes of the dockers' strike, and thought he spoke well. However, he attended the famous debate on Socialism on 26 November 1889 when McTaggart overwhelmed H. M. Hyndman, who could muster only 27 votes in favour of his motion, while the Noes ran up to 227. Glover did not at once abandon Socialism, but he was well pleased that Hyndman's Marxist variety was so decisively rejected.

Glover was on committee at the Union. He never stood for the office of secretary, but he was on committee for some terms and eventually became a life-member of the committee, having been elected for three terms in succession. He was involved in the differences of opinion between the undergraduate officers and the treasurer, who is usually a don and who in the Lent Term 1893 was Oscar Browning. There was some criticism of the auditing of the accounts and also of the treasurer's dealing with some house property adjacent to the Union. In the course of the controversy, Glover and others waited on the O.B., who was 'spluttering and inconsistent'. Glover must have taken some part in the discussion and doubtless his contribution was forthright and uncompromising. It produced the following limerick.

> There once was a man called O.B.
> Who remarked 'in religion I see
>   No shadow of good
>   When a man is so rude
> As a person called Glover to me'.

Glover was not unappreciative of Oscar Browning, and this controversy did not permanently estrange them. He did not go back on this verse in the *Granta*.

AD O.B.

> The pious Monarch, when he founded King's
> Recked not of Charters and such idle things:
> By Cam's fair streams he saw the grassy lea,
> And King's *was* when he spoke the words 'O.B.'

As a writer of light verse Glover was a frequent contributor to the *Granta*, and R. C. Lehmann, at that time owner and editor, thought well of his verse. In the two years, 1892 and 1893, as many as twelve of his idylls appeared in the *Granta* and he received £18 for his contributions. He was present at the dinner held at the Reform Club on 16 December 1892 to celebrate or anticipate the 100th issue of the *Granta*. He sat between Barry Pain and R. C. Bosanquet. Most of the regular contributors to *Punch* seem to have been present, E. C. Burnand, Linley Sambourne, E. T. Reed, Toby M.P. (H. W. Lucy) and Arthur à Beckett. The guests also included F. Anstey (Guthrie), A. Conan Doyle, and Anthony C. Deane. Glover enjoyed such company and retained his interest in many whom he met in this way. He continued to write for the *Granta* throughout his first period in Cambridge. He was trying his hand at many forms of verse, triolets and limericks on the lighter side and sonnets in the more serious vein. He was also writing Latin and Greek verse, and translating epigrams from Martial and the Greek Anthology into English verse. Perhaps he was most successful with the simple ballad form. Both the Latin and the English of these verses in praise of the bachelor's life are from his pen.

Nil praestat caelibe vita	*When a man's single, he lives at his ease*

Ave vita caelibis!
  Salve sors Bohaemi!
Melior divitiis
  Nulla potest emi.
	Blest is the Bohemian
	  And the wifeless chappy!
	Gems nor gold nor silver can
	  Purchase lot more happy.

Quam securo tempore
  Potest ille frui,
Quam beate vivere
  Totus potens sui.
	Blissful in the life he lives
	  He dreads no disaster,
	Him no care, no trouble grieves,
	  He's his only master.

Quaere apud Bibliam;
  Vitam angelorum
Praedicat simillimam
  Vitae esse horum.
	In the Holy Writ we read
	  (Ne'er that Writ dissembles)
	That the life the Angels lead
	  More this life resembles.

Quippe semper nesciunt
  Nuptialem facem,
Ergo magnam sentiunt
  Et aeternam pacem.
	For the nuptial torch is not
	  In the home supernal:
	So there falleth to their lot
	  Peace profound, eternal.

Huic me vitae dedico
  Nec infidus ero:
Caelibum sic numero
  Semper esse spero.
	Here's the life that I would choose,
	  In this throng I mingle:
	Ne'er will I its blessings lose:
	  I'll be always single.

The Latin poem in the style of Walter Mapes appeared in the *Eagle* in December 1891, the English version in the *Granta* of 8 March 1892.

For his development as a classical scholar, Glover was singularly happy in being awarded an exhibition at St John's College. Among the younger dons was the historian, J. R. Tanner, who came of Bristol stock and who welcomed him as a Bristolian. As it happened, a popular lecture by R. F. Horton had already aroused his interest in Wordsworth, and Glover was delighted to find himself a member of Wordsworth's College. But most important was the wealth of classical scholarship which was at once at his disposal. Seldom can the Classics have been more impressively represented at the high table of St John's than they were when Glover went up in 1888. The veteran J. E. B. Mayor was still lecturing. Sir J. E. Sandys was Public Orator. Graves, Haskins, W. E. Heitland, W. F. Smith and H. R. Tottenham were all actively engaged in the teaching and study of the Classics. Glover has drawn their portraits in his own inimitable way in his charming *Cambridge Retrospect*. W. E. Heitland was his tutor and became one of his truest and closest friends. His early communications with his tutor, however, were rather unfortunate. His friend, G. H. Leonard, who became Professor of History at the University of Bristol, happened to be in Cambridge in July 1888 and thought he might do Glover a service by calling on Heitland and negotiating with him about the assignment of rooms. As the following letters show, this only annoyed Heitland, and he took Glover to task for being over-anxious about his lodging arrangements.

My dear Sir,

A friend of yours came to see me about rooms in College for you yesterday morning just as I was off here by train. I had to get rid of him in a hurry and I trust gave no offence.

But I write now to say that such proceeding does not *save me trouble* (as he seemed to think) but *gives me trouble*. Will you in future kindly communicate *with me*. It is always best not to try indirect means till direct ones fail. If you write and say what sort of rooms you would like, I will suit you as near as I can.

Rents run about £6 or £7 a Term.

I am not well, and this sudden invasion did me no good, I assure you.

(*signed*) W. E. HEITLAND

T. R. Glover, Esq.

My dear Sir,

I will do what I can to meet your wishes. But most of the vacant rooms are on the ground floor. Some are over the river. Till I hear from you to the contrary I assume that you would prefer lodgings to either of these.

Please understand that your claim comes in a certain order, after some, before others. You cannot write and order such and such a set. The question is, do you wish for rooms in College or not? Do you wish them only under certain conditions? If lodgings, am I to take them for you as for others, or not?

Meanwhile, be sure that I shall not forget the claims of those who give little or no trouble.

Now do not ask for an appointment. I *hope* to be in Cambridge the 3rd Tuesday in August, but am not yet sure.

Please tell your father that personally I shall always be glad to make an appointment with him (not a third party) and if he wishes for Aug. 21 he has only to say so and I will do my best to arrange it so.

(signed) W. E. HEITLAND

The question of rooms was eventually arranged to the satisfaction both of Glover and his tutor. His rooms were on Staircase H in the First Court. His mother came up with him in September, to settle him in and to see that his rooms were adequately furnished, and Heitland entertained mother and son most courteously to lunch on 29 September, the day on which Glover slept in College for the first time.

Under Heitland's directions, Glover attended lectures by Sandys and Tottenham in his first term, and by Tottenham, Graves and Haskins in the Lent term 1889. Sandys took him for translation and composition in his first term, and was more critical of his English than of his classical accuracy. His answers are found to be 'correctly done but lacking in finish and elegance of style'. No doubt the lectures recalled Muschamp rather than Leighton, but Glover's experience was not as discouraging as that of his contemporary, A. C. Deane, at Clare. Deane says,

I went up...fully intending to take the Classical Tripos. My tutor provided me with a list of the classical lectures in Clare which I should be expected to attend, and to those lectures I went. They were simply horrible...classical study as interpreted at Cambridge or anyhow at Clare—meant conjectural emendations of the text by German professors and philology.[1]

Glover was well grounded in philology and in the art of emendation, but he was with scholars who had a lively interest in literature. He chafed at the limitations of Cambridge scholarship, but he certainly gained from the discipline. Years afterwards

---

[1] *Time Remembered*, p. 50.

in answer to a question put to him by Carnegie Simpson he wrote,

> You ask me of the Cambridge mind,
> What most distinctive there I find,
>   What traits or preferences;
>
> A sense of fact—sometimes aligned
> To love of truth, sometimes confined
>   To verifying references.

Though, as I have already noted, Glover thought an Oxford training would have been more congenial to him, yet he might have agreed with the Master of Trinity's verdict:

> The critical atmosphere for which Cambridge is celebrated was an astringent that served me well. My natural tendency to be hasty and superficial was kept constantly under correction. I often think that young men who are in danger of being flashy should go to Cambridge, and those who are in danger of being dull should go to Oxford: too often the opposite principle is adopted.[1]

Throughout his undergraduate years, he seems to have devoted a great part of his attention to the Greek dramatists and poets, and to Greek verse composition, though his Latin composition, particularly his prose, continued to be his best.

In his first year, he is making the closer acquaintance of Aeschylus and Euripides, and summarizing his impressions in sonnet form. For his guidance in composition he looks also to Theocritus. In the Lent term 1889, he sent in a set of verses for the Porson Greek Verse prize, and was honourably mentioned. Heitland 'though usually more inclined to find fault than praise, is extremely pleased'. This trial trip paved the way for his later successes. In 1890 and 1891 he carried off the Browne Medal for a Greek epigram. In the latter year he was awarded the Porson prize for Greek verse and was honourably mentioned for the University scholarships. It was not surprising that in the Classical Tripos, Part I, he was one of the four candidates in Class I, Division I. Naturally he stayed up for a fourth year, and read for Part II, concentrating now on the historians, Greek and Roman. He won the Senior Chancellor's medal in February 1892, and obtained his first class in Part II in the following June. On 7 November he was elected to a Fellowship at St John's.

---

[1] G. M. Trevelyan, *An Autobiography*, p. 14.

Chapter III

CAMBRIDGE, 1893-1896

College Fellowship : religious development : betrothal :
departure for Canada

His election to a Fellowship gave Glover a much-needed breathing space. He could supplement the Fellowship by private coaching and by invigilating for the Cambridge Local Examinations, and so keep himself while waiting for a more permanent appointment. He would at the same time have leisure for further studies in which he was interested.

As always happens, promotion to the high table brought him into fresh and more intimate relations with those to whom he had previously looked up as seniors and tutors. The classical dons to whom he owed most, W. E. Heitland and Sir J. E. Sandys, became closer friends than ever. He was to gain much from contacts with Fellows with other interests, of whom he had so far seen little or nothing. As time went on he came to know and appreciate mathematicians and scientists like Larmor and Bateson, Marr and Rivers. But immediately his circle of friendship was enlarged by his interest in early Christian literature and Church history. This formed a link between him and the Master, the Rev. Charles Taylor. He writes to his mother in January 1893,

I am getting very thick with the Master himself, and have had four notes from him in 48 hours. He has given me his book on 'the Witness of Hermas to the four Gospels', and I have read about half of it. He has also sent me the proof of a new article on the same subject to correct. Heitland told me I should find him a very good friend, if he learnt I was interested in Theology. 'For', said Heitland, 'he is interested in no party, or set, and so he is fair to all.'

While he is discussing the *Shepherd* of Hermas with the Master, he is studying other Apostolic Fathers under the guidance of Armitage Robinson, and following J. E. B. Mayor's lecture on Tertullian and Minucius Felix. He goes to H. M. Gwatkin for

Church history and to Rendel Harris for palaeography. The latter also interests him in the second-century apologists. In 1893 Mrs Lewis and Mrs Gibson found the early Syriac version of the Gospels in a palimpsest manuscript in the library at Mount Sinai. So Glover learns Syriac and in his diaries for 1894 and 1895 appear a few quotations in Syriac—the Lord's Prayer in Syriac and some citations from Afrahat. This interest brought him into contact with F. C. Burkitt, R. H. Kennett and A. A. Bevan. In these years 1893 to 1896 he laid the foundations of his knowledge of the Christian literature of the first two centuries.

Throughout this period, his health was somewhat indifferent. Among other things, he suffered in 1893 from acute dyspepsia and diarrhoea. In the Lent term W. E. Heitland had a serious illness, and Glover was particularly attentive in looking after him. Whether or no this aggravated his own troubles, when in the Easter vacation he went down to Hastings, where Heitland was convalescing, the latter became seriously alarmed about Glover's state of health and wrote to his father in the following terms:

I have seen a lot of your son in the last three months. He often visited me in my sickness. My nurses were both struck with his delicate looks and made him confess his frequent sufferings. They were both alarmed for him, and told *me* (when I was better) their fears.

Now he is here in a boarding house. How dreary life is there is shown by his constantly coming round here. How he is suffering inside is pretty clearly betrayed by his looks. I am in fact so uneasy about him that I venture to write even to his father. . . .

I doubt whether he, in his anxiety to spare you, tells you how wretchedly ill he feels. And I think you ought to know. I do not think you are the man to be unduly alarmed or to be annoyed with me for saying what I believe to be true, that he wants the best advice and liberty to act on it. I have indeed urged him to make sure of seeing his medical uncle in London, and, if Dr Glover thinks it necessary, a specialist in stomach complaints. . . .

I value him so highly that I watch him narrowly. Young men of his moral and intellectual qualities are very very rare. Let this excuse my anxiety.

Perhaps as a result of this letter, Glover consulted his uncle, Dr James Glover, in London, and decided to take the summer term off. He was away in Switzerland for some months and spent another month in Harrogate before going up for the autumn term. A letter to his father written on 19 November 1893, describes his real though still partial recovery.

I am keeping the Sabbath day (saving a wicked phrase) in my room. Yesterday was raw and rainy. I had to call on Mrs Graves, for after accepting her invitation to dinner on Wednesday I could not go as I had an important lecture to attend. I wrote at once, but naturally I had to go and get my forgiveness, which came very readily and kindly. They live near Bessie [his elder sister, then a student at Newnham] so I looked in there too. On coming out I found it sleeting which developed into snow. I had my window open in my bedroom however as Dr Bell bade, saying 'Foggy air is better than foul' and so on and took my cold bath and walk before breakfast in the snow. At breakfast I had diarrhoea, so I went up to W. L. Brown and asked him to excuse me to Mrs Keynes with whom I was to lunch. He thought I should not go. A year ago I was 'took bad' and turned colour and so on there one Sunday and I didn't want that again. Also I have to go to Castle End tonight in an endeavour to stimulate a rather sodden 'Evangelicalism' into a more redemptive piety. So I am husbanding myself and feeling like Benaiah or whoever it was slew a lion in a pit on a snowy day. Unfortunately my lion can't be run away from. Caelum non stomachum mutant qui trans mare currunt, has been my too true experience. But I don't worry. I am more equably well than before. My bad days are fewer and not so bad as formerly. Still it is amazing not to be better after so much time and expense.

He continued to be worried by ill-health, and in 1895 he had to undergo a slight operation, advised and performed by the distinguished surgeon, Sir A. Pearce Gould. But for many years, his general health was better than it had been in the early part of 1893. About this time, his mind was often preoccupied not only with disease but also with death. Deaths in both Cambridge and Bristol circles affected him. In October 1893 C. E. Haskins died, a loss to the College which Glover felt personally, and in November a young man in the Tyndale circle, Fred Townsend, died two months after his marriage. Glover was more deeply affected in the following year by the death of Amy Garaway, a close friend of his sister's who seemed almost like one of the family. She sickened with tuberculosis, and died on 2 June 1894 just nine days before her twenty-first birthday. As will appear from one of his letters, Glover was wrestling with the problem of mortality and seeking a sure ground of hope and consolation.

His religious convictions were steadily taking shape. He still believed in the future of Nonconformity. In his early days in the combination room, he disagrees with J. R. Tanner who thinks all is up with Nonconformity. He receives dubious support from W. E. Heitland who allows that there may be some future for the Baptists as a kind of spiritual gadfly! But Glover did not believe the Baptists would perform even that modest role, if they followed Spurgeon in affirming the verbal inspiration and inerrancy of the Scriptures and in denouncing higher criticism. Glover among the Baptists was to find himself very much in the position of Clement of Alexandria, as he described it in his Dale lectures later on. 'Clement has first of all to fight the battle of education inside the Church, to convince his friends that culture counts, that philosophy is inevitable and of use at once for the refutation of opponents and for the achievement of the full significance of faith.'[1] Substitute 'the higher criticism' for 'philosophy' and it describes Glover's position.

Early in 1893 he had been stung by a foolish paragraph in the Baptist journal, the *Freeman*, into writing a defence of higher criticism which appeared on 6 January. It runs thus:

Perhaps you might allow a layman a very little space for a few remarks on what you so constantly assail as the 'higher criticism'. As I am not a theologian, you will doubtless assign their right value to my words.

It cannot have escaped your notice that in recent years we have come into the possession of a vast amount of fresh knowledge concerning things Biblical. We are getting more deeply imbued with the spirit of antiquity, learning the sister-languages of Hebrew more thoroughly and thus gaining a truer knowledge of the Semitic mind. Besides this, we now know the peoples with whom Israel came in contact, more than ever before. Egyptians, Assyrians, Babylonians, Phoenicians, are as familiar to us as the French. The result is a change in our criteria. To-day in Greek history, we have left the methods of Mitford for those of Grote and in some matters we are advancing beyond Grote himself,

---

[1] *Conflict of Religions*, p. 276.

notably where archaeology is concerned. Similarly one feels entitled to apply new knowledge and new methods to the Bible.

Some are doubtful of the result. But if we believe in the Bible, surely our faith would be frail if we feared to test it. If our faith is found to be wrong (which I do not think will happen) it is better to be on the side of truth at all costs. Now, where I think your correspondents are unfair is in failing to distinguish between sound methods and unsound applications of those methods, and in arbitrarily choosing and rejecting results attained by the same means. For instance, if you condemn the 'higher criticism' root and branch for the sake of Belshazzar, it is doubtfully fair to accept Dr Sayce's testimony to the Hittites. If you distinguish, you have conceded my point, that method and application are very different matters.

This might fairly be described as Glover's opening shot in a long campaign. He spoke in this letter of 'our faith in the Bible', but he clearly understood it in a different sense from that in which most readers of the *Freeman* understood it. He was approaching the Bible as a historian and a literary critic. Its quality as literature and as historical record was to be assessed by the canons accepted in the study of any historical literature. He did not believe in the Bible from cover to cover, as the traditionalists professed to do. He was undergoing that process of testing his fundamental religious convictions, which Rendel Harris used to say resulted in one's having a shorter creed but a larger God. His father who believed that 'all hurry was wrong, since God gives every man all the time he needs', encouraged him to take his time and as he said, to be true to his darkness as well as to his light. Glover had been a little disappointed that his father did not appreciate all the lines of enquiry in which he was interested. At one time he presented him with Robertson Smith's *Religion of the Semites*, but his father did not care for it. However he was assured of sympathy and wise counsel from a father who would write:

Do not over-trouble yourself as to my disapprobation of any incompleteness in your views. You will come to find a place in your creed for everything the Church as a whole has accentuated. You are not under obligation to believe as I do. Your supreme obligation is to keep temper and character such as will let you see God and truth,—and consecutively to hold, utter and obey what is revealed to you.[1]

The centre of Glover's faith was not the Bible but Christ. He had been much impressed by a sermon he heard as an undergraduate on the text, 'What think *ye* of Christ?' The preacher had urged the duty as well as the right of private judgment. 'It is not enough to repeat an orthodox creed or to echo some scholar's opinion. Read the gospels for yourself and form a judgement of your own.' Glover never forgot this. He wanted to see Jesus and he determined to see him with his own eyes. Here he found his one sure anchor as this letter to his father reveals. It was written on 19 November 1893, when he had expected to have his father staying with him, an expectation frustrated by the death of Fred Townsend.

I am very sorry you are not coming—still sorrier for the reason. I wrote a short note to Mr Townsend last night. It is a very terrible thing altogether. This life is very real and the next is so very shadowy—a case of 'believing where we cannot prove'—with no evidence whatever except the common hope or perhaps longing of man and the word of one. I must say that the more one reads the Fathers and realizes their futile methods of argument, the more a priori unlikely does all Christianity become, but arguing a posteriori from its effects and from the personality of Christ himself it is too strong to disbelieve. It seems to me that we must base our religion on something other than the common bases. The Old Testament won't do at all. I have had too much of it in Justin and Tertullian. You can't prove Christianity out of the O.T. If you say you can, so can you prove Home Rule or anything else to be prophesied. For instance the Metrical version, 'A man was famous and was held in estimation, according as he lifted up his axe thick trees upon' is just as much a prophecy of Gladstone, as 'All day long have I spread out my hands to a rebellious people' is of Christ. Yet the latter is a mainstay in some sort of the Fathers of the Church. Nor will Greek Logos-philosophy do. It has too much figment and too little fact. You would scarcely attempt to defend Christianity with quotations from Confucius and the Sanskrit books, except as showing that it contains all the best in them. Yet this is what we do with the O.T., Plato and Philo. Then comes the question, what basis is there at all? One's constant endeavour is

[1] Letter, 2 April 1892.

to get a basis that will not give way like the O.T. and will not rest on such guesswork as Philo's. It seems to me very like fairy tales to separate off a quality and make it into a personality. Can you base Christianity somehow so? It has met the need and fulfilled the wants of mankind at its best, and as the universe seems generally well contrived with a complement for everything, it is not improbable that here too need felt and need met are in a line with things generally and therefore what commonly appeals to most men at their best is probably as true as anything else. It is unsatisfactory, but is hardly perhaps so demonstrably fanciful as making Christianity the fulfilment of the latent prophecy in the posture of Moses when he 'stood with arms spread wide'. Judging too from his character and personality Jesus seems more likely to be right and reliable than ordinary teachers. Where he does speak of what is beyond our proving, he does not give himself away as others do. In any case his own attitude toward the unproveable is sounder than that of any of his expositors. And it seems to me that all one can do is to take up his position as far as possible. Also his view of God, whatever he was himself, is the only thing that can make life tolerable. But as I said before we have to take most things on trust from him as resurrection, a future life, his relations with God and perhaps even more. Knowing then that the Galilean saw and acquiesced in the order of the universe, in life and death and bereavement, and wished nothing changed and found nothing to regret for all his appreciation of man's mind and feeling, I think we must be content too.

This letter does not contain his final valuation of the early apologists or the Logos-Christology, but it shows clearly the foundation of his personal religious faith.

The year 1896 was marked by two of the happiest events of his life, his engagement to Alice Few and his appointment to the Professorship of Latin at Queen's University, Kingston, Ontario. Naturally, both at College and at Emmanuel Church Glover found himself a member of new social circles. Particularly through the Church he came to know well Mr and Mrs H. G. Few and their family. They showed him great kindness, and when he was taken ill in February 1895, persuaded him to come to their home 'Berrycroft' in Grange Road, where he could be more effectively nursed and where he would be less lonely than in his rooms in College. He accepted the invitation, which in fact W. E. Heitland had engineered for him, and found at once the benefit. Naturally, he saw a good deal of the Few family including Alice, who helped to nurse him and with whom he read Homer and Livy to help prepare her for the entrance examination for Girton. As it happened, Alice Few did not go up to Girton in the autumn of 1895. Instead she went to study music in Berlin.

The close of the summer term, 1896, found Glover also in Berlin. The ostensible reason for his journey was to fulfil a commission for F. C. Burkitt. He was to transcribe three pages of the Curetonian Syriac manuscript of the Gospels, which were in the Royal Museum of Berlin. His major purpose was to ask Alice Few to be his wife. They became engaged on 31 May and certainly Glover deserved all the congratulations of his friends on this happy event. A short note from Mrs J. N. Keynes was typical of many. 'My husband and I were both very glad indeed to hear of the successful issue of your visit to Berlin. We think you did well not to confine your attention exclusively to old manuscripts and congratulate you upon having made a discovery more interesting even than a missing page of Ecclesiasticus.' He duly transcribed the pages from the Curetonian Syriac on 8 June, though he was inclined to begrudge the time spent on it. 'Worked hard for some four hours at the 3 leaves of Cureton's Syriac for Burkitt. Found it interesting work though I was writing against time, and really enjoyed doing—or *having done it*.' Mind and heart were deeply engaged elsewhere.

Soon after their return to Cambridge, on 26 June, Glover received a letter from Principal Grant of Queen's University, Kingston.

MANSFIELD COLLEGE, OXFORD
Thursday, 25 June 1896

Dear Sir,

May I call your attention to an advertisement in the *Spectator* and *Athenaeum* of June 17th for a Professor of Latin in Queen's University, Canada? Speaking of it last night to my friend Principal Fairbairn, he called my attention to you in a way that made me feel that you would suit us, that the post would be congenial to you, and that you might possibly entertain the consideration of it. If I am correct in this last opinion, allow me to say that I am to be in London for the next ten days, and that it would give me a great pleasure to see you, at any time that we might arrange between us, at the Royal Colonial Institute, Northumberland Avenue, to discuss the subject.

Sincerely yours,

G. M. GRANT,
Principal of Queen's

The salary offered was 2000 dollars and Glover was in doubt what to do. Grant's letter was supported by one from Dr Fairbairn who had suggested Glover's name as a suitable candidate. As will be seen from the terms of the letter, Glover could hardly set the proposal on one side. Fairbairn wrote:

I thought that the opening at Queen's University was on the whole a very good one and likely before very long to lead to better things. I will tell you all I know about it. It was founded in 1841 very much under Presbyterian auspices and has remained (while largely supported by the State) predominantly Presbyterian, Principal Grant being a very active member of the Presbyterian Church of Canada. In the University there are several very good men including Professor Watson whose *Kant and his English Critics* you will know. The University has also a very good Medical School. The town is beautifully situated just at the point where Lake Ontario ends and the St Lawrence begins, i.e. at the entrance of what is known as the Thousand Isles. A man there would have opportunity to cultivate not only Classics but Theology and many opportunities of service in connexion with the various Churches. On the whole I think it a good opening for a young man, but Grant will himself give you a fuller account of what is both possible and actual.

Of course, I am not able to judge as to the comparative chances of success here and success there. I would like for my own part to keep you on this side but you know how slow and painful the process is of getting work at Cambridge. I would prefer, I frankly confess, to see you working at Theology in England and I wish it were possible to plant you down in one of our Colleges or in a Baptist College to carry on your studies and help our pulpits by training the men in higher scholarship and fuller light. But we have not, of course, always the power to do what we would like, and this seems to me the next best thing and I have thought that as a very happy event had happened recently the prospect of permanent office would not be unwelcome.

On 1 July Glover went up to London to the Royal Colonial Institute, and saw 'Principal Grant, a nice old man, and

Chancellor Sandford Fleming of Queen's University, Canada'. He also met Sir Mackenzie Bowell, not realizing at the time that he was meeting a former Premier of Canada. However, a talk about Queen's with these distinguished Canadians much impressed Glover and though naturally he was reluctant to be parted so soon from Alice, he decided to send in a formal application. He had no difficulty in securing strong testimonials in his favour. While he was on holiday in Glaisdale on 29 August, he received Grant's wire, 'Appointed come'. A few days later, he had the official intimation from the Secretary-Treasurer of the University. On 17 September he joined the S.S. *Numidian* at Liverpool, where he said goodbye to his betrothed and to his father, who came to see him off. The ship sailed on the 18th and he reached Quebec on 26 September.

Chapter IV

CANADA, 1896-1901

Professor of Latin : the Pitt Press *Olynthiacs* : marriage : admiration for Canada : politics : Church-life in the Dominion : Canadian friendships : return to Cambridge

According to Heitland, Glover took to Canada like a duck to green peas. He did not, however, escape all the difficulties of the Englishman in adjusting himself to life in Canada, nor when making inevitable comparisons did he always give the preference to Canada over the homeland. Indeed during his five years at Queen's University, Kingston, he was often homesick, and at their close he was eager to return to Cambridge. It was only after he had left Canada that he realized how much it had done for him, and discovered an affection for the Dominion which grew with the years. From the first he was attracted by land and folk. The climate, the scenery, and the history of Canada alike appealed to him. 'The sweep of the country and the vigorous climate delighted him; Lake Ontario—"The Lake"—was almost an idol.' The long spells of skating he much appreciated. He enjoyed his work at the University. He met and became firm friends with some of his colleagues. Besides John Watson, the Professor of Philosophy whom Fairbairn had commended to him, he came to know John Macnaughton, the Professor of Greek, a Highlander whose *perfervidum ingenium* was a constant joy. James Cappon, the Professor of English, he also liked and admired. To these three he dedicated his first considerable work, *Life and Letters in the Fourth Century*. Nor were his friendships confined to the University circle. Among Baptists he came to know Hiram Calvin, whose business included shipbuilding for traffic on Lake Ontario. Hiram Calvin's son, Dil, was a student at Queen's during Glover's last year or two, and Dil Calvin became one of his closest friends. Whenever he crossed the Atlantic, he tried to fit in a short visit to his friends Dil and Eleanor Calvin, and he corresponded with them almost to the end of his life.

The years he spent in Kingston were among the happiest of his career. Here after his marriage in 1897, he and his wife made their home for four years. Here their two older daughters, Mary and Anna, were born. At Queen's, Glover found himself as a lecturer and teacher, and entered upon his literary career.

Arriving at Kingston, after a rough passage on the S.S. *Numidian*, he was almost at once plunged into his work as Professor of Latin. Within a month he is feeling settled down and happy in his work—'catching on well, I think, and making a good start, and feel simply loads better than I did. I think I shall have more scope every way here, though rather far from the English learned world.' A postcard addressed to Mrs Keynes gives his early impressions of Canadian education.

I have been here now for three weeks, 'co-educating' and find the system rests on an enormous substructure of common primary and secondary schools and even common playgrounds. So for Canadian purposes it answers fairly well. Tell it not in Newnham—but when I told my class (incidentally, not as an item of education) that the Cambridge undergraduates voted four to one against women—the sudden applause of the men took my breath away. One argument against co-education not yet quoted is that the women here *will* chatter. I can stop the men but——. The work is interesting me thoroughly and though they lack the six years' drill in Classics of the English School they mean business and like their work.

About the same time, he writes to his mother,

I am liking this—liking it perhaps more than you would wish me to. The folk are not from so high strata because there aren't so high strata in Canada as in England. They are badly, very badly trained in school, for there is a state-system which they worship in Canada, but which is merely systematized smattering and deliberate dabbling and leaves men knowing something ill about lots of things and nothing well. But it is a government system and a fine broad culture, so it is quite right even if very shallow.

A little later (1 November 1896) he writes,

The classes progress favourably, the seniors especially making headway. When they are called on now, they translate instead of fumble as they did at first. I think I have got a hold of them. I see Machiavelli or Lorenzo de Medici said, 'A ruler must make himself felt in the first four days.' We began (tho' I did not know of this saying) with strict business habits coupled with graciousness, the hand of iron and glove of velvet, and the result is that in the first month the iron hand has only been used once or twice with the utmost gentleness, and class and Professor get on famously.... So I am very happy in my work.

If the students tended to be mediocre in ability and lacked the training of an English grammar school education, yet Glover was impressed and attracted by their grit and seriousness of purpose. He writes with warm approval of a man who took on the job of furnace-stoker in the Principal's house, to help finance his University career. 'In many ways I am better off here than in Cambridge. I have more men to deal with and men seemingly with less conceit and more earnest—a big generalization. Rather, men of less means and more respect for their dons and more friendly feeling to them.' This last happy relationship between dons and students was favoured by the traditions and the limited size of Queen's University. Glover writes to his father:

From all I hear of surrounding Universities there is more freedom and good comradeship at Queen's than in any of them. Queen's is one big family and they say wherever a Queen's man goes he can count on Queen's men rallying round him in any time of need. As we have only 500 or so undergraduates and post-graduate B.A.s, etc., they get to know the Professors as they cannot at the Scotch Universities, and when you reflect that I am one of the Professors, you will see what a stimulus that must be.

He adds in the same letter,

The work as I have said before is congenial and I gather I am not unpopular with the 'boys' or (tell it not in Gath) with the 'girls', but they all know you are engaged. It is six months since we were engaged, which makes the next six months seem very long when one rehearses the enormous amount that has happened in the last.

Among other attractions which Queen's and Canada possessed for him were the strength of the Scottish element and the absence of an established church. He is no longer a dissenter, with a small 'd'. 'I miss the English Church so much, that this miss and the climate give one perpetual satisfaction.' This is one of the factors which inclined him to purchase a house and stay on indefinitely. 'I am enjoying the work and the students and the surroundings and the freedom from the English Church and its lethal atmosphere and all things weighed I can't do better than stop, I think. Of course, there is the winter to come, but everybody says it is not so trying as November with its changes.' But to decide to settle after two months and before he knew what the winter was like and still more before he knew whether Canadian life and climate would suit his wife, seemed premature and the house was not bought.

As Dr Fairbairn anticipated, and Glover realized, he had more scope for his religious interests than he might have had in Cambridge. Principal Grant was glad of his help in the Department of Divinity and invited him to lecture on the beginnings of Christianity in England. He was also encouraged to offer a series of talks to students on Sunday afternoons on the Apostles' Creed. He writes to his father on 29 November 1896,

My Creed class is getting on very well—60 or 70 the first time, about 80 the second. To-day it is 'Et in Jesum Christum, Filium ejus unicum, Dominum nostrum'. Have you read Watson's *Mind of the Master*? He has a fancy creed mapped out in his second paper as thin and meagre as anything I ever saw. Aren't you surprised at me in my new character of Athanasius? An Evangelical Catholic Independent is, I think, the nearest I can come to my denomination.

During his first year at Kingston, Glover was occupied in seeing through the press an edition of Demosthenes' *Olynthiacs*, which he had been asked to undertake at the close of 1895. This contribution to the Pitt Press series was his first published work. The introduction gives evidence of his power of appreciating and describing the political and social background of events. Heitland would have had him give more attention to grammar in a text edited for schools, but Glover, with a better understanding of a schoolboy's interests, followed his own bent and concentrated on the historical and political aspects of his subject. As his letter to the *Freeman* indicated, he was a disciple of Grote rather than of Mitford. He would have printed the three speeches in Grote's order, II, I, III, but the Syndics of the University Press would not sanction so daring an innovation. Though he took note of the work of Beloch and so realized the strength of the case for Eubulus and the Peace-party, the opponents of Demosthenes, Glover retained Grote's approval of the orator as statesman and patriot. There was no surrender to the view that Droysen was to make popular, that the rise to power of Philip of Macedon was inevitable and necessary and that it was short-sighted folly for Demosthenes to resist it. Glover never truckled to the idolatrous worship of success and power. Schooled by R. L. Leighton, in his notes he drew attention to modern parallels. When Demosthenes announces his lofty intention of avoiding 'empty abuse' (*Olynthiacs* II, 5), Glover observes:

Attic orators were not generally so squeamish. If Mr Asquith's suggested 'Golden Treasury of Political Billingsgate' were ever compiled, Demosthenes himself could supply a good many elegant extracts. We must suppose statesmen to know their audiences, and if we allow this we find that though every age has solemnly said that abuse is not argument, every age has enjoyed it notwithstanding.

On a passage in the first *Olynthiac* (section 5), καὶ ὅλως ἄπιστον, οἶμαι, ταῖς πολιτείαις ἡ τυραννίς, ἄλλως τε κἂν ὅμορον χώραν ἔχωσι,[1] Glover comments as follows:

For the tyrant's view, cf. Hdt. VII. 156 (Gelon) νομίσας δῆμον εἶναι συνοίκημα ἀχαριτώτατον.[2] Both are quite right. Republican France in 1792 was much too near monarchical countries either to be left in peace herself or to leave them in peace. Demosthenes' view of Macedon is very like the view good patriots in the Balkan States today will take of a great power to their North.

This comment is still to the point though the patriots in question are liable to be liquidated if they do not keep their mouths shut! Note after note in Glover's edition of the *Olynthiacs* exhibits this stimulating character, and we may regret that though Heitland's rather pedantic criticism was offset by the warm approval of Macnaughton and others, Glover decided that marketing classical texts was not his forte. In a letter dated 6 January 1901, he writes:

I have been looking over the letters dealing with my *Olynthiacs* and the reviews of it. I think I would give the 30 guineas never

[1] A despotism, I take it, is as a rule mistrusted by free constitutions, especially when they are near neighbours.
[2] The dictator judges a democracy to be a most unpleasant or undesirable neighbour!

to have touched it. Yet I did a lot of work at it and some of it is good work though I say so. But the preface was a great mistake. My next one is much more chastened. Some people cannot bear anything in the least degree diverging from the solemn.

He may have been well advised to concentrate on ancient history and on classical literature in its broader aspects, but a few more commentaries like his edition of the *Olynthiacs* would have done much to commend the classics to Sixth-Form boys.

A further example of his lighter and still effective manner of handling the Classics may be found in a letter he wrote to his sister Elizabeth when she was preparing a paper or perhaps school-lessons on the function of the chorus in Greek plays. He is contrasting the Greek chorus with the lyrics in Shakespearean drama:

Shakespeare's lyrics more or less bear on the plot, at least a character sings them, if I remember, with a view to something. Also are they not generally in the comedies? In a Greek play the chorus merely represents what you may call current opinion and makes conventional reflexions.

Hero.   So then the dye is cast and I am lost.
Chorus. Who casts a dye will thenceforth coloured go.
Hero.   To some far land it now behoves me turn.
Chorus. Whose life the Gods insure will travel safe.
Hero.   I travel, whether life-insured or not.

Then Choric Ode:

STROPHE A

Blest is the man with prudence and with wits
Who pays a penny for a pink Tit Bits,
    Secure of life
He travels, though the engine leave the track,
    His children and his wife
Will see him with his policy come back,
    Be it at daydawn when cocks crow
Leaving the high nocturnal pole
Where sit contented with the sleepers' role
    The hens in row;
Or in the dusk when the suburban trains
Draw from old London all her cash and brains.

Woe worth the day, thus spake an ancient wight,
When the eclipsed sun brings back the night.
    Erewhile the wife
Of one, that delved and digged not over-nice,
    Drew forth the carving-knife
Untailing longicaudal sons of mice,
    Thenceforward tail-less must they fare;
So one that leaves his home to range
Throughout the ringing grooves of idle change,
    Behind leaves care.
Care killed insooth that feline quadruped
That on the derelict rodent tails had fed.

Then follow Strophe and Antistrophe B.

This is not exactly a translation—say an adumbration of the real thing—quite as relevant to the issue of the drama as many of Euripides' choric odes which are often quite disconnected. The chorus is graven by art and man's device and line balances line. It relieves the intensity of the action. The chorus thus fulfils the part of the silly porter in *Macbeth* or the clowns in *Hamlet*. This must content you. Remember the Greek play had only three speaking characters on the stage at one time. It was played in the open air in an enormous theatre where facial expression would be lost. So masks were used and speaking trumpets or something of the kind in their mouths. The motive is rather simpler or rather there is much less bye-plot than in William, unless you come to Euripides who has more of it than Aeschylus and Sophocles. Less rested on the actor than on the writer—if he could only be heard.

This letter is typical of the zest which characterized his first year at Kingston. Of course he missed old friends. He would have given much for a talk with R. H. Kennett or J. S. Tucker. Of course, his mind was taken up with the thought of his approaching marriage, and happy expectation was shot through with high seriousness. He writes to his father at the close of 1896:

As I get older and realize more and more the meaning of the new relation 1896 has added to my life, I feel more and more I have been too much, as mother used to joke, 'lacking in natural affections'—and I wish I had done more in the three decades which I have overlapped in the way of giving you 'aid and comfort'. I can never undo the past, but I hope the future may be better and that I may fail less as a husband than as a son. All these relations grow more mysterious and sacred with time and have an awe and terror about them. 'Terrible as an army with banners' is a true bit of description I think.

But when he starts to discuss the wedding arrangements, he writes about them to his mother with mingled banter and perversity. If Mr Few gives his daughter away, then his mother should give him, Reaveley, away. But the most lively discussion took place on the question of whether or no he should wear a frock-coat at his wedding. He fought a long and ultimately losing battle on this issue. His father came down on the side of the womenfolk in this matter. He wrote in April 1897, 'I have no doubt you will find your life much enriched by marriage, and possibly if there are any such things about you as wilfulness or oddities of an obstinate character, they may find a gracious solvent in her gentle influence. Conventionalism as Shakespeare or Bacon or somebody remarked is the Servitude of the Dull but the Salvation of the Brilliant.' The diary for 1897 records his surrender to conventionalism. On 11 May, Terrot Reaveley Glover, suitably attired, and Alice Few, were married, his father and Dr P. T. Forsyth officiating.

After a passage, not fortunately as stormy as his first, Glover and his bride reached Kingston in good time for the opening of term in October 1897. They spent two rather uncomfortable months in lodgings but moved into a house of their own, 78 Barrie Street, in November, and at the close of 1898 they made their home at 134 King Street. Naturally they were delighted to start housekeeping in earnest, though housekeeping in Canada has difficulties. The art of managing the furnace for central heating is not learned in a day. To keep it in and to keep it at the right heat are distinct and indispensable lessons. Then domestic servants were as difficult to get and to retain at that time in Canada as they are in Britain to-day. Within a week of settling in at 78 Barrie Street, Glover writes to his mother, 'Here we are in our house and in the very thick of our troubles. Our servant bounced off suddenly after three days and the furnace is a nuisance to work.' However, he can report that his wife is 'more cheerful, happy, active and herself than she has been since she came to Kingston'. If satisfactory domestic help was hard to come by, the kind and active assistance of friends and neighbours meant much to them. Canadian hospitality was richly bestowed on them.

Though they had only just settled in, when a vacancy in the Professorship of Greek at the University of Liverpool was advertised early in 1898, Glover decided to apply for it. Presumably he felt clear that he would not wish to make his home permanently in Canada and so took the first chance that offered of returning to England. Rendel Harris was doubtful of the wisdom of his application. He wrote, 'Naturally I will do anything to help that comes in my way, but I think thee a duffer to leave Canada so soon, before having got the real good out of the sojourn or made thyself a solid name in the colony.' Glover saw the wisdom of this counsel and though he did not withdraw his application, he was not disappointed when it was turned down. He set himself the more seriously to get the real good out of his time in Canada.

His interest in things Canadian steadily deepened. He liked the surroundings of Kingston and appreciated Canadian scenery, though colour-blindness prevented him from enjoying to the full the rich colours of the autumn. His early impressions of both politics and religion were by no means favourable, but in politics he changed from being almost a little Englander and a Radical to something of a Whig and Liberal Imperialist. In November 1896 he wrote to his father:

This is a queer country—very loyal because they loath the Yankees, but 'Canada First' was the watchword of a party which collapsed because it included everybody.... In fact Canada's loyalty to Britain is loyalty to Canada. Sentiment keeps her from annexation to the U.S.A., partly sentiment of origin, more still hatred of the Yankees. The young men have a way of going to the States as they command good wages and get good work, for the Yankees trust them more than their home-grown specimens. They are not so keen on the dollar and are reckoned to average honester. Still the atmosphere even here is dollarific and they don't read. Their grandchildren may, they hope, which doesn't help me.... They are abominably proud of their country, which but for the Canadian Pacific Railway's possibility of being of use to us in case of Eastern war might be chucked into the Yankees' hands for all the harm it would do us, that I can see.

Imperial Federation is pure rot—they don't want any legislative connexion with us. If we will secure their shipping by our navy they to a man will fight for themselves against the Yankees, *but no one else.*

A few years later, the Boer War revealed to Glover the hastiness of this misjudgement. He also realized later that he had accepted uncritically Canadian views of the U.S.A. However, as he reads Parkman's histories—histories, which, as he says, should be of more interest to Britons than Prescott's *Mexico* and *Peru*—he begins to appreciate better the British achievement in the Dominion. In another home letter (6 December 1896) he says:

I am reading Parkman's Canadian histories with interest. If I had now to launch a colony, I would send the good folk out with a good stock of supplies, tools, grain, etc. and then try to forget their existence. The French kept meddling here and the Jesuits ruling everything to such an extent that the place never throve till we took it. Parkman (*an American*) says: A happier calamity never befell a people than the conquest of Canada by British arms....Two of your [his mother's] prophecies are fulfilling themselves. I am losing some of my admiration for America— the U.S.A. I mean, and I am beginning to feel *very* shaky on Irish Home Rule, after studying Quebec Province so far....Unless it can be demonstrated to me that it won't mean so much priestly rule as I see there, I am no longer a Home Ruler. However, I think the English electorate is tired of that plank and will go for others.

As he studied the early history of the Dominion he came to appreciate better the strength of the sentimental tie between Canada and Great Britain. 'It is 110 years', he writes in December 1896, 'since the King's loyalists came to Ontario, leaving the States for conscience sake and bringing here some of the best elements of the country.' To help in strengthening and developing some of these best elements through training young minds in the best classical tradition seemed to Glover to constitute a call of duty. There was in Canada a respect for law and an interest in tradition which it seemed were lacking in the U.S.A. As Glover saw it, there was a danger in Canada of the French Catholics and Celtic Irish exerting too great influence, and it was

important to strengthen the Anglo-Saxon element. He writes
to his father:

> If I never thanked you before I do now for the fact that tho'
> you do not leave me wealth or place or any bauble of that kind
> you gave me Anglo-Saxon blood and above all the Protestant
> faith. Much against my previous tendencies I am coming round
> to believe you want some sort of Aristocracy in a land—define
> the word aright—you want the best elements to rule, and I don't
> believe the ignorant Paddy . . . is the best person to rule a com-
> munity honestly and intelligently. . . . There are many adver-
> saries, obscurantist priests, skindeep theorists on educational
> systems, dollar-hunters and other 'practical' people—and is all
> this a call to stay or to return home? I see no church I am drawn
> to join and will retain my membership of Tyndale as long as
> I can, but I believe I can affect men who are going out all over
> the province—to some degree. I believe I am doing so a bit
> already. Now, go or stay?

At least for the next few years he was to stay.

He did not allow his feelings about Celts and Catholics to be
the finally determining factor in his attitude in local politics. He
writes to his mother in January 1899:

> To-day is the town Council election. We have four candidates
> in our ward for three seats, one only I gather worthy of a place.
> The worst of the four sits across the aisle from me at church.
> Three men running for Mayor, one keeps a little candy store,
> two are doctors, one of them a homoeopath, the other an Irish
> Catholic—the man they say who was called in to see Archbishop
> Cleary some years ago and said, 'Enlargement of the liver'
> (Cleary drank), whereupon the Archbishop said it could not be
> so, and when he protested on and on, Ryan (the story goes)
> rejoined, 'Well, go to hell your own way.' I think of voting for
> this man because he is neither a fool nor workman's candidate.
> He is also a professor in the Medical College—a Conservative.
> So when you find me voting for Celt, Catholic, and Conservative,
> you won't call me hidebound, prejudiced and narrow-minded
> any more.

Glover's reactions to the Boer War show how far he had
travelled from his youthful Gladstonian Liberalism. He writes
to his father in November 1899:

> I am inclining to think with some of our men here that the
> remarkable readiness of the Transvaal for war against us, coupled

with the rather large name 'South African Republic', which
looks as if designed for more than it at present covers, would seem
to prove that Chamberlain was not after all very much to blame
for the war, that it was in fact inevitable and that it is a good
thing Morley's views do not rule in Downing Street. I think that
Cromwell, if he were still with us, would hold it time to stop the
Dutch trouble for good, and that peace and hope lie in undivided
British supremacy.

A month later he writes:

I don't know about others so much, but the home-bred on the
staff are all pretty well unsettled by the Dutch War, not so much
by fears for the ultimate result as worried by blunders and
accidents that occur. . . . Consequently Cappon and I somehow
find ourselves meeting at Watson's about it all and a sort of
under-current of restlessness damps the ardour for work. One
can't do anything. However some things are clear to me. (1) That
Gladstone made a terrible blunder in 1882, which in view of this
war will injure his fame for long to come; (2) that no government
is to hold power in England for a while yet that can shew any
slightest symptom of a willingness to compromise any more
about this; (3) that Chamberlain, be his methods rough or
smooth, saw (and all honour to him for it, though I don't like
him) the truth that the ambitions of the Boer were not limited to
the Transvaal and that in the end Britain must rule the Transvaal
or see one big Dutch republic in South Africa. The last of these
points may admit of dispute but it looks very much like truth in
view of everything.

In adopting this interpretation of the conflict in South Africa,
Glover may have been influenced by his friend James Cappon
who ably expounded this view in a book later. But he may also
have become convinced that just as the substitution of British
supremacy for French rule had been a boon to Canada, so the
subordination of Dutch rule to British would be a boon to South
Africa. Glover was reading several of Rudyard Kipling's works
at this time and finding them congenial, though he was stirred
to write a poem trouncing Kipling for so often depicting colonials
as loose-living and foul-mouthed. His comments on the 'khaki
election' of 1900 contain his most violent repudiation of Gladstone and his closest approach to the Conservatives.

I have been following the English elections as well as I can in
the Canadian papers, but they are not always clear as to the

gains and losses of the parties. Still my impression is that while the Government will go back with much the same majority as before, the opposition will be rather stronger by its losses, e.g. Stuart, G. B. Clark, Wilfrid Lawson and Co. (i.e. the pro-Boers!). Oom Paul has nothing to hope for from Westminster. Some papers seem to say that Chamberlain is a menace to the peace of Europe....I don't see how the Government could have done anything but stand up at Fashoda and fight Oom Paul....My criticism would be that Salisbury was flabby abroad and dangerous at home, letting foreign interests slide and damaging freedom at home. I am not a Radical[1] and I don't want change, and if only the Conservatives would not ram the Church down our throats and could be relied on to hold to something—not the Church, but principles or our interests abroad or our general effectiveness—I should have no quarrel with them. As it is I am ashamed to have been one of a party misled and ruined by Gladstone. I don't want to exhume him from the Abbey, but if we could bury most of his ideas with him—the Transvaal and Soudan wobblings, the Reform Bill of 1884, the Home Rule Alliance! We could keep his tariff reform and the Irish Church disestablishment.

Before passing from his politics, I may add his account of a visit of Winston Churchill to Kingston early in 1901. Glover in thanking his mother for a Christmas present says:

We may spend some of it on Winston Churchill's lecture here, to which we are invited by a flaming poster which says Lord Wolseley said the story of his escape was an epic poem and that Julian Ralph predicts he will be prime minister of a federated Empire. So on the first score it is our duty to ourselves to enlarge our theory of epics and on the second our duty to posterity to see who is to rule it or them, as posterity and grammar chooses.

So early in the New Year they went to hear

that lively youth, Winston Churchill. I should differ, if I may, from Lord Wolseley, for I do not call the story of his escape 'an epic poem' or anything like it. He got over a fence, walked unmolested through Pretoria, clambered into a train and rode eastward, dropping off unnoticed. After a day in hiding, he

---

[1] A year before he had written: 'I am afraid I am growing more and more Whiggish and less and less Radical as I grow older, liking less and less the interference with individual freedom that seems to be the vogue and the one-House-of-Parliament idea.'

found an Englishman who hid him in a coal pit for some days and sent him to Lorenzo Marques in a freight of new wool—uncomfortable travelling. So he came back to the front. Watson met him at dinner and found him a lively jaunty youth. His lecture had these characteristics—it was very conversational, with suggestions of Corney Grain in its studied offhand 'you know the sort of thing' style. But Watson does not anticipate his being a prime minister, as advertised, for he did not form a high idea of his statesmanship. He seemed to think a 10 % duty on non-British corn in England was possible and desirable.

Church life in Kingston and the Dominion proved rather disappointing. The absence of an establishment did not ensure the progressive vitality of the churches. Denominational loyalties were rather hard and narrow. Social activities were often more in evidence in the churches than serious spiritual concerns. Services were bright and emotional rather than devout and intellectual. 'Sunday is the weak spot in Kingston, what with choirs hypertrophied and divines atrophied.' 'If on occasion the divine faithfully sows the word, then cometh the choir and taketh away that which is sown.' As a known Baptist, Glover felt obliged to attach himself to one or other of the Baptist churches in Kingston. Unfortunately, the worthy minister at the church he chose to attend had no humour or imagination. 'Yet I feel he needs support, so we go—a weariness to us both.' At one time he suggests that there must be a passage in Ecclesiasticus which says a live Presbyterian is better than a dead Baptist! He continues his regular churchgoing but oh! what churches!

A week of prayer began the year [1898]—then three weeks of special services at the Baptist Church—mission, revivals, evangelists, the welkin fairly ringing with them and after all?...One does feel so dead and so alone. We both long for Bristol or Cambridge on Sundays. We have no friends like J. S. Tucker, Rendel Harris, Forsyth, Gwatkin, Kennett.

From time to time he would go to the Methodists or the Presbyterians, when there was more prospect of a good sermon. He liked the Presbyterian minister, Macgillivray, and on occasion his colleague John Macnaughton would preach, and such occasions were not to be missed. Glover's tribute to 'John' may be read in chapter VII of *A Corner of Empire*. He treasured 'John's' epigrams. But even the Presbyterians might fail him. On 5 December 1897,

I foolishly took Alice to Chalmers Church this evening though I knew the St Andrew's Society was to be there, but I had liked Macgillivray. Things began with voluntaries, I recognized an air and lo! it was Annie Laurie! followed by others of the kind. One was 'Flowers of the Forest', Alice said. I waited for the Hundred Pipers and Duncan Grey but up to the time of our leaving they had not come. We had the 100th Psalm and 'O God of Bethel' and then—Rudyard Kipling's great hymn given by the choir! Shades of Richard Cameron! I nearly went out. More in the same vein. Macgillivray forgetting 'whose I am and whom I serve' gave out his text Ps. 73, v. 26[1] and left it stranded and neglected, to jest about Scotchmen brought up on porridge and the Shorter Catechism....A Scotch hymn followed the sermon, to be followed in its turn by the prayer and something from the choir: but covered by Horatius Bonar (whose spirit must have wondered what he was doing in that galley) we came out, and they may have had Duncan Grey and Willie Brewed and all that to their hearts' content.

Reflecting on this experience, he adds, 'I feel like Elijah in one way. They have profaned the church with choirs, bazaars, ten-cent teas, revivals (they are never done with them), Jubilees, secular recitals, and I feel that I only am left. A little more and we will start a Friends' Meeting in this room and touch the unclean thing no more.' It is not surprising that in another letter he says,

What ministers really need over here is to keep reading fresh matter. The primrose path of meetings and social duties leads to the desert of mental and spiritual sterility. Too many meetings. It may do elsewhere but for this world we should sing

> Where congregations rarely meet
> And quickly homeward wend.

With a footnote,

> Twice on the Sabbath we should meet
> To hear the word of grace,
> Then sit no more and talk no more
> But run our heavenward race.

[1] My flesh and my heart faileth: but God is the strength of my heart and my portion for ever.

In April 1899 he made a casual contact with a special form
of revivalism. He writes to his mother on 9 April:

About a week ago out for a walk I passed a Hornerite meeting-
house. These people are disciples of one Horner who has grown
dissatisfied with a corner of Methodism and seceded. The faith
is one of physical exhibition of the Spirit. As I passed there was
a noise, a wailing as of the wind and I was moved to look in. At
the desk end sat an unmoved irrelevant-looking clergyman and
round him rough old men moving about on their knees and
waving clasped hands, while women and children sat and looked
on, and this wailing sound went on and on—a most peculiar sight.
A man tells me he was at an open-air meeting once and there were
strange manifestations. A man suddenly jumped up and making
in a straight line for a tree, swarmed up it. Women threw themselves on the ground and kicked, and then the clergyman got up
and prayed 'Oh! Lord! Thou hast sent down a pop-corn
blessing!' A very appropriate metaphor! St Paul I think would
have prayed for a more solid kind.

Contacts of this kind led Glover to judge the Anglican form of
worship more sympathetically. During his time in Kingston,
St George's Cathedral was burnt down, and he and his wife
attended a service in the rebuilt cathedral in January 1901.

When we entered it was lit only from the dome and I really
felt I was in a church—high roof, cruciform with a choir. The
turning up of the general lights took off some of the effect. The
service was very musical, but I was in a mood to enjoy the
symbolism of Catholic tradition after the Americanized amphi-
theatres I have worshipped in so much of late. Really the
English Church believes in the text 'decently and in order'. Prof.
Clark preached with great simplicity and earnestness on John ii.
'Whatsoever he saith unto you, do it.' I enjoyed it very much.

Like St Augustine, whose *Confessions* he was studying in 1900,
Glover was dissatisfied with any preaching that was not associated with the name of Christ. He notes with regret that addresses
at Queen's on Sunday afternoons seldom allude to the author of
our religion. Many years later he observed of many American
preachers that they seemed to be curiously Christ-shy. It was
always a joy to him when a preacher spoke feelingly of Christ.
Writing to his mother on 21 October 1900 he says:

To-day we had the new minister of the other Baptist Church instead of our own pastor—such a change. Here was a young man nervous and positively with something to say which he had really felt and made his own instead of. . . pickings from American weeklies! He took the text about foxes having holes etc. and dwelt on Christ's loneliness in this world. A sermon which makes one realize a new (or anew an old) view of Christ's personality is a real boon, and here it was. . . . He certainly has a chance of usefulness here, for a man who has a conception of Christ having real feelings like a human being, is needed.

Through his five years in Queen's University, Kingston, Glover was preparing and being prepared to make his own contribution to meeting just this need. He realized that if he was to persuade students from farms and counting-houses to study Latin, it was essential to present classical writers as living personalities and to study literature as a criticism of life. He summarized his experience in the preface to the first edition of his *Studies in Virgil*, in the following terms.

I found when I was Professor of Latin in a Canadian University a system of 'options' in vogue which permitted a man, if he so wished, to drop the Classics altogether at a very early stage. . . . Latin. . .had to compete with all sorts of subjects and to stand on its own merits. A curious result followed. Not at all infrequently a student, in spite of woeful preparation and a persistent inability to translate with accuracy or to compose without elementary blunders in syntax would nevertheless realize something of the literary value of the poet or historian who was being read in class, and would persevere with an almost pathetic enthusiasm in a study in which he could hope for no distinction but which he could and did enjoy. He realized in fact that the old Scottish term 'Humanity' meant something.

Glover goes on to speak of the inspiration the presence of such men and women in his class was to him as a teacher. He gained confidence in the appeal of classical literature, 'only it was plain that classical study had to be primarily the study of literature and of life', with syntax, philology, composition and so forth clearly regarded as a means to an end. 'What the students may have gained from these courses they can best say: that the experience was of immense value to the teacher I record with gratitude.'

The students' view of the matter is given in a paragraph which no doubt Dil Calvin contributed to chapter VII of *A Corner of Empire* (pp. 147–8):

Senior Latin (Pass) was a new experience. For the first time, the dry bones of a 'dead' language were stirred; instead of continually construing and parsing, we heard of a Latin literature....Again and again, often within a very few moments after the class opened, formal questioning or construing ceased and we listened to a talk on ancient history or classic art or mythology, growing out of the Latin text. And the effect of it was not to decrease but to increase the amount of effort one was willing to make. To show us what could be done with a 'dead' tongue, we were given prose exercises from the daily newspapers to work into Latin. Again it was not enough to get the meaning of the Latin—it had to be put into idiomatic English. 'Oh my dear sir,—what an expression—I recommend to you the Authorized Version of the English Bible, it will improve your style.'

If the needs and interests of Canadian students confirmed Glover's conviction that life and letters must never be separated, he also owed much to his colleagues, particularly to John Watson and John Macnaughton. He belonged to a Saturday Club, in which he could listen to Watson's papers on Philo and Augustine and hear Macnaughton eulogize R. L. Stevenson. In the Saturday Club he could give trial runs to many of the studies which afterwards formed chapters in his *Life and Letters in the Fourth Century*. His colleagues enlarged the range of his thought and pruned his style. It was Watson who criticized the style of some of Glover's early essays as having too much of the combination-room quip about them and as being even slovenly in places. At the same time he thought the later essays showed more power in mastery and arrangement. Glover profited by such criticisms as his work on the fourth century advanced. A typical reference to the value of his contacts with his colleagues is given in a letter dated 9 March 1899:

I had a very nice chat with Cappon some days ago and I was with Watson last night. I think I have friends in them both. Watson says he thinks I have changed since I came, to a more philosophic and less external way of dealing with my Latin literature. He is likely to be right, for beside the dread of the Cambridge men and their test of accuracy hovering before my eyes I now have that of these Scotchmen and their questions about the interpretation of life. Watson said he thought I had gained this by being here. I agreed but thought I should need to leave soon, for in view of criticism of my methods by outsiders who don't understand, I am getting to have as canty a conceit of my Latin as Macnaughton of his Greek, and I think it may be a good thing for me to be with better men again though they are always in my mind. Three years or sessions of this have given me a standing-ground for the assertion that my Cambridge method of teaching classics answers in Canada as well as at home.

Another friendship which meant much to him was that of E. W. MacBride who had been Glover's contemporary at St John's and who was now Professor of Biology at McGill University. MacBride came to spend a few days with the Glovers each Christmas vacation. These were opportunities for vigorous discussion of all things in heaven and earth. MacBride was an omnivorous reader, and would tackle Harnack's *History of Dogma* one vacation and the works of Robertson Smith the next. Glover could stand by MacBride when he raised a hornets' nest of Montreal theologians about him by delivering a lecture on evolution, in which he believed. 'I have not seen the lecture but I know the man and while he may have hit hard and probably did for his biologic faith, to rank him with the Bradlaughs is absurd....I have known MacBride twice before simply bear down prejudice by simple worth.' The two had much in common, their memories of Cambridge and their hopes of getting back there, and their desire to accomplish some original work while in Canada. Glover had early formed the idea of writing a book on the writers pagan and Christian of the fourth century A.D.

I hope some day to bring out a luminous book on these old people and I think my present notion is a fairly fresh one, for I am approaching the time from the literary side and most go at it qua theologians or historians, and the men who write about literature only touch on my people in a perfunctory way because they have got to say something about them to make their books complete. Then of course I am interested in the theological and historical sides too and I hope to give a series of good pictures without bias. It will be a long long job however.

MacBride would talk to him urgently about pressing on with this special subject, mastering it, reading all about it and not

wandering away from it. For some three years Glover lived with
it. Some of the essays, as they were written, appeared in the
Eagle and others in the *Queen's Quarterly*. Besides the Saturday
Club, annual reunions of old students both at Queen's University,
Kingston, and at the University of Toronto, where he was a welcome guest-lecturer, gave him the opportunity of hammering
out these studies to his liking. He was finding his own line of
approach and becoming clear as to the distinctive task of the
historian. He found MacBride's scientific training was not an
adequate preparation for historical interpretation. The historian has to estimate and be content with probabilities, and
must often be more cautious, more ready to suspend judgement
than the natural scientist. On the other hand he is concerned
to grasp the particular character of each event, and has to bring
out that element of individuality which eludes scientific generalizations and philosophic systems.

It was at this point that Glover found himself dissatisfied with
John Watson's Idealism. He owed much to Watson as the
chapter on Augustine in the *Life and Letters* makes abundantly
clear. As time went on, he realized more fully how great his debt
was and indicated it in the charming dedication of his *Studies in
Virgil* to Dr John Watson, Professor of Philosophy in Queen's
University, Canada.[1] In actual discussion with his colleague, he
was conscious of a serious divergence of judgement and interest.
Writing to his father in December 1898, he says:

Apart from missing family and friends, the spiritual loneliness
is very great. I have no man likeminded. Men are either sub-
Unitarian or traditionalist. I was wondering last night whether
this did not in some way make me a missionary, but missionaries
ought to have better tempers than I have, and while mine is so
unchastened I don't feel I can preach to other people about anything. The alternatives to Nicene Christianity as given above

---

[1] The verses of the dedication are as follows:

> How many a time, dear Watson, the snowy road we'd pace
> With the frozen lake behind us, and the North wind in our face;
> But the sun was bright above us in the blue Canadian sky,
> As we walked and talked together of deep matters, you and I.
>
> It was snow and air and sunshine; and I look across the sea
> To those days of glorious winter, and the life they meant to me;
> For my mind and soul caught something, as of sun and snow and air,
> From the friend who walked beside me in those winters over there.

seem melancholy enough. I can't argue with men of philosophic training like Watson (nor with Dyde[1] who always sees two things where the microscope sees one) but I feel Watson, though he would not admit it, is quite divorced from history, and leaves out a great deal that a historical student sees cannot be left out. You can't work everything with pure thought—not regenerate masses nor minds I fear. The difficulties of the Incarnation are very great, but the difficulties of explaining everything since that date as based on nothing at all seem great too. The conclusion I reach is that there are things hard even for my mind to fathom. Of course, if you leave out a great body of facts, you can get an easier solution. I don't think 'Be a good boy' theology will work!

Though it is clear that he came to appreciate more and more Watson's philosophic outlook, yet he remained convinced that it left out things which the historian perceives cannot be left out. Nor is it only the unique claim of Jesus Christ which is involved in the historian's doubt of the adequacy of the idealist approach. Every character in history and literature claims respect and recognition in his or her individuality at the hands of the historian. In *Life and Letters of the Fourth Century* Glover was developing his skill in seizing on the illuminating detail which sets in relief the distinctive quality of each writer studied.

When some ten or a dozen studies were in hand, he submitted them to the Cambridge University Press, and to his great satisfaction they were accepted in November 1900, and, rounded off with an introduction and two or three further studies, the book appeared the following year. While Glover's book was on the anvil—when it was half written in fact—Samuel Dill's classical work *Roman Society in the Last Century of the Roman Empire* was published. It says something for the quality of Glover's contribution that the University Press accepted it, though the field had been so fully and so admirably covered by Dill. A comparison of the two books reveals how little they overlap and how fittingly they supplement each other. Glover always felt a peculiar affection for this, his first considerable book, and it gave him great pleasure towards the close of his life to find that it was still

[1] Dyde was Watson's colleague in the Department of Philosophy at Queen's. Years later, when his son called on the Glovers in Cambridge, the name puzzled Glover's boy Richard. When told that the guest's name was Dyde, Richard said, 'But if his name's died, what is it now?'

read and appreciated by some who were struck by the parallel between our age and the fourth century and who were interested and encouraged by these studies of the ways in which some leaders in the fourth century had faced the problems of a declining civilization. For Glover, it meant that he had enlarged the range of his reading of Greek and Latin authors beyond that of most classical scholars, and he continued his study of the Classics with a heightened awareness of their later influence and their permanent worth.

In his diary for 1900 under date 12 March Glover wrote, 'J. R. Tanner, it seems, said to mother, they [St John's College] would have me back some time, she writes in a letter to-day—an obiter dictum but I hope a true prophecy.' A year later the prophecy came true. On 18 March 1901 came 'letters from Sandys and J. R. Tanner to say the College wish me to return as Fellow and Classical lecturer in October. A great joy and thankfulness to God came'. Glover wrote his letters of acceptance the same day, as he had no hesitation about his decision. On 2 May, the Glovers left Kingston for Montreal and the following day sailed for England on the *Lake Champlain* and landed in England to settle on 14 May.

The reasons for his decision are obvious. A minor consideration might have been the fact that he was not altogether happy in working with Principal Grant. Grant seemed to him inclined to exact or expect too much from his staff and too little from his students. At one time he thought Grant was a trimmer, but he respected him for taking his stand against Prohibition. 'Grant' he wrote in December 1898, 'has come out against Prohibition— the man of many turns and some twists seems to be genuine now as it looks as if he had more to lose than to gain, for the Temperance people will be down on him for teaching young men to drink.' This tribute to Grant is the more remarkable because Glover himself was a convinced and lifelong total abstainer. But though he had his difficulties in working with the Principal, long before he left Glover had come to appreciate Grant's devotion to the interests of the University. His sketch of Grant's character and career in *A Corner of Empire* is drawn with admiration and affection. The real reasons for the decision were first his sense of isolation in the worlds both of scholarship and religion. I remember Kirsopp Lake contrasting his position in Leiden with life in Oxford. In Leiden he was the one man dealing with the New Testament and early Christian literature. When he had a new idea, he had to criticize and work it out for himself. In Oxford, he could have submitted it to half a dozen experts. Glover felt isolated as the one Professor of Latin in Queen's University. It was, after all, a restricted academic circle. He wanted and needed to be in contact with scholars of his own standing in his own field again. But second, both he and his wife were homesick, and he felt sure she would be happier in England. And third, they wanted their children to be educated in England, not in Canada. They left Kingston with real regrets, but the many friends in the University and in the town who were sorry to lose them, felt it was right for them to go.

Chapter V

CAMBRIDGE, 1901–1914

The Glasgow Chair : the education controversy : the classical
lecturer : *Studies in Virgil* : the Dale Lectures : Glover and the
Society of Friends : the S.C.M. : the Angus Lectures

When the Glovers arrived in Cambridge on 14 May 1901,
naturally their first preoccupation was house-hunting. In
October they settled in at 14 Downing Grove. Four or five years
later they moved to 57 Glisson Road. Finally, in 1911, they
transferred their home to 67 Glisson Road, where Glover lived
till the day of his death.

At first sight, the situation of his home might not seem to be
very convenient for a Fellow of St John's College, but probably
the walk to and from College at least once and often twice a day
meant much for his health. Most days in term-time he was to be
seen crossing Parker's Piece, proceeding down St Andrew's
Street and Petty Cury, to the market square, where David's stall
would often tempt him to break his journey, particularly when
homeward bound. He made many purchases from David, which
are duly recorded in his diaries, often with some lament for his
extravagance, to appease the spirit of Scottish thrift which was so
strong an element in his make-up. But he could never keep away
from second-hand bookshops, and he could seldom resist the
attraction of a first edition or a good library set of any author in
whom he was interested, and he was interested in many. Regrets
for extravagance are counterbalanced by regrets for bargains
missed.

He loved company on these walks between the College and
his home, as he enjoyed conversation, whether light and bantering or more serious. As he passed through First Court, when
setting out for Glisson Road, he would link his arm with that of
any acquaintance, don or undergraduate, who happened to be
about in the court, and in spite of protests, the captive would be
compelled to walk a mile with his captor. This was known as
'doing a Glover', but his lively conversation was usually felt to be

an adequate reward for any inconvenience and loss of time involved. W. A. Darlington recalls an occasion of this kind.

It was characteristic of Glover that once, meeting me in First Court, he turned me round without a word, slipped his arm into mine and bore me off into the town on some unexplained errand. I did not ask where we were going or tell him I had an appointment. Half an hour of T.R.G.'s company was something not lightly to be foregone and would be accepted anywhere in my circle as an excuse for lateness. I went willingly.

At a much later date, Hensley Henson in his autobiography records a typical meeting with Glover. The Bishop visited St John's in May 1940, and he writes,

After breakfast I walked and talked with the Master [E. A. Benians] in the College garden. Then he proposed to show me the College library, but as we passed through the Quadrangle, we encountered Dr Glover to whom the Master introduced me. He is powerful to look at with a brusque manner and decisive speech. He insisted on taking me into his room, where for about twenty minutes we had an interesting conversation.[1]

The Master proposed, but Glover insisted. It was characteristic.

When Glover returned to Cambridge in 1901, he little expected to be still there in 1940. He was glad to be back, but ready to move again if the right opening offered. He was not without ambition, and he felt himself to be qualified for a professorial chair and more likely to get such an appointment outside Cambridge than within it. In 1906 the Chair of Latin at the University of Glasgow fell vacant. Glover applied for it, and it was a great disappointment to him that his application was not successful. He had many links with Glasgow and its University. Frequent visits to relatives in Glasgow had given him an affection for the city. In 1901 the University celebrated the 450th anniversary of its foundation. Glover had written an address of congratulation from Queen's University, Kingston, and he was asked to represent Queen's at the festivities in June 1901, which he was delighted to do. His love for all things Scottish made him particularly eager to secure the Glasgow professorship.

---

[1] *Retrospect of an Unimportant Life,* vol. III, p. 99. *Apropos* of this interview, Hensley Henson is said to have expressed his surprise that so intelligent a man should be a Baptist.

Unfortunately for Glover's chances, the Latin Chair was filled in July by J. S. Phillimore vacating the Greek Chair. Like many other candidates, Glover then put in for the Greek Chair, only to be dismissed as a Latinist, on the intervention, he was told, of Asquith. It was true that up to that time his published work had been concerned with Latin literature. He had followed up *Life and Letters in the Fourth Century* with his *Studies in Virgil*, of which more must be said later. His power to appraise Greek historians and to interpret Greek life and thought had yet to be revealed. It was some compensation for his disappointment, that it brought many expressions of friendship. John Skinner of Westminster College was not the only one who was personally glad that Glover was not leaving Cambridge. John Macnaughton of Queen's, Kingston, wrote, 'I was sorry you did not get Glasgow, but there will be lots of things going in a few years.' As time went on, Glover was not destined to secure the professorial rank for which he was so well fitted. The chairs for which he applied he failed to get, and the offers which came to him between the wars he did not feel able to accept. At the time and later he found real consolation in a letter from Gilbert Murray, who wound up by saying 'affairs like this make as much call as anything on one's philosophy, but a man who can write as well as you carries his Chair with him'.

During the period before the first World War, Glasgow was the only possibility of a career away from Cambridge which seriously attracted Glover. But even in this first period of resi-dence, there was a certain ambivalence in his attitude towards the University. He loved Cambridge, both town and University, and yet he was critical of her. He liked living in Cambridge and he was deeply attached to St John's, and yet he was uneasy and restless and sometimes anxious to get away altogether. There were many reasons for this restlessness. The climate of the fen country did not suit him. The Lent term in particular tried him sorely. As his young son Richard observed one March, 'Father is awful at this time of the year.' In 1906 whooping-cough put him out of action for the whole of the Lent term, and his col-leagues, especially E. E. Sikes, were very good in relieving him of his duties. In this period he developed his life-long objection to any form of ventilation, except in the mildest weather. Girton girls who attended his lectures on Roman History and arrived early, would open the class-room windows for the pleasure of seeing the lecturer shut them all before starting his lecture.[1] Like many others, Glover found Cambridge enervating, yet it would have taken more than the muddy bleakness of the University town in winter to lower Glover's vitality. Physically, he was a strong man in spite of ailments induced in no small degree by worry. He was intensely alive, intellectually and spiritually, a rapid and almost omnivorous reader, and a writer who could work at very high pressure.

His capacity for work led him to work too hard. There can be little doubt that on his return to Cambridge he tended to over-work, and this added to his restlessness and discomfort. Always anxious about his ability to discharge his responsibility as a father to his growing family—as a Sixth-Form schoolboy he had despaired of ever being able to maintain a wife and family—he took on extra jobs, such as lecturing at Bedford College, London. This he found to be too tiring, and more wisely he limited himself to additional work as lecturer and coach at Newnham or Girton. Then his varied interests, political and religious, made inroads on his time and taxed his strength. Rather pathetically under date 18 May 1912, he records, ' I wish I had time really to read the classics', but he wrote this when his outside commitments were unusually heavy. The extent to which he was overworking in the years just before the first World War is evidenced by the extraordinarily kind suggestion made by Anne W. Richardson of Westfield College, London, in October 1911. Realizing how tired he was, she offered him £150 to enable him to take a term off. The offer was not accepted, but it was much appreciated, and the suggestion was acted on inasmuch as Glover resigned the praelectorship at St John's and so lightened his labours.

Both politically and religiously, much in the atmosphere of the University was uncongenial to him as a Liberal and as a some-what militant Dissenter. On his return, he found himself in sympathy with the Liberal Imperialists, Asquith and Sir Edward Grey, rather than with the Little Englanders. He could speak for the colonial point of view. He could even follow Chamberlain

---

[1] One of them writes, 'As soon as he came into the lecture-room he would wrap his gown more closely round him, seize the window-pole and shut all the windows.'

in the call to think imperially, but he had no use for Tariff Reform, and remained a staunch Free Trader. Naturally he welcomed the Liberal electoral triumph in 1906 and supported the Liberals in the controversy with the House of Lords in 1910. He notes with some misgiving the advance of Labour as an independent political party. There should be some understanding between Liberals and Labour, he is fully convinced. But College loyalty and personal friendship override party preference where the representation of the University is concerned. In February 1911 Glover votes for his friend, the Johnian and Conservative, Joseph Larmor, as M.P. for the University, and rejoices when he is elected by a clear majority over the Liberal, Harold Cox.

The Liberal revival of 1906 brought new hopes of peace, retrenchment and reform, which were to be wrecked by the events of 1914. But the period, if in some respects one of optimism, was also one of bitter controversy. Glover shared the expectation of a new era, and he also found himself involved in animated and sometimes more than animated controversy with colleagues at the high table. The chief bone of contention was the Education Act of 1902, which aroused and deepened Glover's dislike and distrust of the Established Church. Like the majority of Free Churchmen, Glover was blind to the very real merits of the Act as a measure of educational advance, partly because the Conservatives having obtained a majority to win the war were using and abusing their parliamentary advantage to pass controversial measures for which they had no mandate, and partly because the Act tended to strengthen and perpetuate the injustice to Nonconformists in the privileged position of the Church in one-school areas. This is a very real grievance, as William Temple frankly recognized when he was Archbishop of Canterbury, and though recent legislation and the improved relations of Church and Dissent have reduced its importance and its emotional heat, it has even yet not been removed.

But in 1902 and in the village schools round Cambridge, it was a very serious matter indeed. In far too many instances, the village schoolmaster or schoolmistress who, we are now told, is on the road to join the dodo, was under the domination of the rector or vicar of the village. Appointments did sometimes depend on the willingness and ability of the candidate to play the organ in the village church. Nonconformists found themselves excluded from employment in a large proportion of the schools of the nation, and young Nonconformist teachers were tempted and were sometimes under pressure to conform to the Church of England for the sake of securing the teaching post they desired. Even before the Act was passed, Free Church leaders in Cambridge like Rendel Harris and H. G. Whibley had been incensed by the high-handed action of a local vicar in dismissing the village schoolmistress because she refused to override the conscience clause. Glover supported the movement to enable this particular mistress to continue to teach in the village. It was not then surprising that he joined the Passive Resistance movement as the most effective protest against the injustice to Nonconformists involved in the Education Act.

He did not take this step without some hesitation. In October 1902 the autumn assembly of the Baptist Union was held in Birmingham, and the issue of Passive Resistance was the subject of heated discussion. Glover was attending the assembly, where he was to commend to the interest of the denomination the Robert Hall Society for Baptist undergraduates, which had been founded at St Andrew's Street Baptist Church the previous spring. He came in for this discussion of Passive Resistance, and heard his father move an amendment opposing the refusal of rates, the form of protest which the Union was asked to approve and adopt. Dr Richard Glover grounded his case on the unconstitutional character of such a form of protest, and on the wrongfulness of making such a protest before constitutional means of redress had been exhausted. He appealed to the attitude of Socrates as Plato depicts it in the *Crito*. The law must be respected, even when it miscarries. Dr Glover's plea was swept on one side by the impassioned oratory of Dr John Clifford. Nonconformity had been born of passive resistance and refusal to obey unjust laws. Once the Bill became an Act, protest might be too late. It is proverbially difficult to unscramble eggs. Clifford went on to rouse passion by denouncing Rome on the rates. Free Churchmen in this campaign did not confine themselves to their main grievance, but fought positively for uniformity in the school system of the State which is in doubtful keeping with their original protest against uniformity in the religious organization of the nation. At the time of this debate, T. R. Glover sided with his father. At least he admired him for taking his stand, and he appreciated the appeal to Socrates. The entry in his diary under date 8 October 1902, runs thus: 'P.M. meeting on Education Bill. Charles Williams good, Blomfield clever [the mover and seconder of the main resolution]. R.G.'s amendment against Refusal of Rates. He very good. John Clifford rhetorical and wild and wide. Amendment lost.'

Glover preserved a letter to his father from one of his few supporters in the discussion, Professor W. S. Aldis, who had retired to Kidlington near Oxford. The letter is of interest, not only for its comment on the discussion of passive resistance, but also for the writer's view of the position of Nonconformists at Cambridge and Oxford.

As one of the two dozen, or thereabouts, who stood up to support your amendment on Wednesday last, may I venture to send a word of congratulation on the stand you made. I am very doubtful of the righteousness of the rate refusal policy. I faced essentially the same problem in regard to the income tax raised for war purposes last year, and while I could not see my way very clearly one way or the other, the balance of right seemed on the whole to be in favour of paying. But I am quite clear as to the unwisdom and wrongness of pledging an excited assembly to adopt, under circumstances not yet arisen, a method which, to be of any use, requires the individual, personal, conscientious self-sacrifice of those who carry it out. 'Lord I am ready to go with Thee to prison or to death'—is only too likely to be followed in a very large proportion of the whole number of those who shouted on Wednesday by the actual record—they all forsook Him and fled.

So I thank you for giving us the opportunity of expressing our opinion.

May I also say how interested I was in your son's statement about the Robert Hall Society at Cambridge! Let him not be discouraged at being so few. When first I went up to Cambridge there were four other dissenters of all kinds—that is four who really acted as such in attending a dissenting place of worship. At that time and for some years after—till 1870—almost all of the increasing number attended St Andrew's Street, and it has been one of the minor griefs of my life that, since the death of my father-in-law, Mr Robinson, that old chapel has been so largely deserted by the nonconformist undergraduates. So I hope the Robert Hall Society will prosper. An attempt was made in Oxford to form something of the kind, but it collapsed after one session.

Mansfield College is not the help to the Oxford Nonconformists which your son seemed to imagine. Nonconformist undergraduates are content to attend the Sunday morning services at Mansfield and, with exceptions, do not get into touch with Nonconformist Church life, except perhaps in the case of the Wesleyans. But nonconformity is not so strong in Oxford University by a long way as at Cambridge.

When Glover returned from Birmingham for the opening of the Michaelmas term 1902, he found the situation locally becoming more tense. Free Church leaders in Cambridge endeavoured to secure some concessions in one-school areas from Churchmen but could make no headway as the Church was resolved to take full advantage of the new Act. So in 1903 Glover signed a manifesto in favour of passive resistance, and himself deducted the equivalent of the education rate, when the time came for payment of rates. He maintained this form of protest until the beginning of 1921.[1] He was often rallied at high table on his summons to appear in court for non-payment of rates and magistrates were not always civil. James Adam chaffed him vigorously, for generally the Scots and the Presbyterians were doubtful of this form of protest, as were also most Methodists. However, John Skinner, who would not refuse the school rate himself, said he was 'glad others will—the more the better', and rather unexpectedly Glover found a supporter in William Bateson, who announced in hall that it was 'only indolence and cowardice which prevented him taking the same line'.

In spite of restlessness and in spite of some disappointments, Glover, throughout this period, was becoming more deeply rooted. His family responsibilities were increasing. A third daughter, Elizabeth, was born in 1902, and seven years later a son, Richard. At the end of 1912, Janet appeared on the scene, and finally in 1917 a second son, Robert, was added to the family. The growth of the family made removal more difficult

[1] On 19 January 1921, he records, 'Paid rates in full after seventeen years of Passive Resistance, which has done nothing; I think the times require rallying to any kind of State.' So he had come round after all to something like his father's view.

and less desirable, and led Glover to seek further advancement within Cambridge rather than without. In 1906, after the disappointment at Glasgow, he was cheered to find his position at St John's College assured. He had been appointed in the first instance for five years. He was reappointed for fifteen years, with a pension at the close. This was really an appointment for life, if he cared to stay on for the remainder of his teaching career. Further evidence of the way in which he was appreciated in St John's College came in June 1907, when he was elected to the Council of the College for the maximum period of four years. J. R. Tanner in congratulating him, said that talking with men he heard nothing to suggest it was unwelcome, as Glover, who was very sensitive to criticism, might have fancied. For some years until he resigned it in 1911, he held the office of Praelector, and on the eve of the first World War, the College nominated him for Proctor.

The University was slower in according Glover recognition. When he returned in May 1901, the University lectureship in Ancient History fell vacant, and Glover put in for it. Not unnaturally, as a newcomer he was unsuccessful, and N. Wedd of King's was appointed. Ten years later, Glover stood for the Professorship of Latin, when A. E. Housman was elected, but in that same year, 1911, the Ancient History lectureship came his way. He was becoming more deeply rooted in the University as well as in his own College.

As a classical lecturer and tutor, he was making a name for himself. His conception of the duties of a Latin professor differed widely from A. E. Housman's. He attended Housman's inaugural on 9 May 1911, and Miss Jex-Blake and his Girton students were entertained to read the disapproval writ large on his face. He noted in his diary the worst of Housman's heresies. 'Of the duties of a Latin Chair, literary criticism forms no part.' 'It is none of his business to communicate literary appreciation to his audience, and he has no business to presume he knows more than they.' 'Why is the scholar the only man of science of whom it is demanded that he display taste and feeling?' So Housman espoused the standards beloved of Cambridge classical scholars, and became the textual critic and strict grammarian, who laboured on the text of Manilius and exposed the stupidities of German critics. He did little to inspire his hearers with an appreciation of classical literature. This Glover held to be his duty, nor was he content with Housman's aphorism 'the aim of literature is the production of pleasure'. Surely literature must aim at more than that. It should be a criticism of life, concerned with the quest for truth and righteousness, and not merely with the production of pleasure.

So Glover set out to communicate literary appreciation to his hearers and he did not conceal his taste and feeling. A German student who attended his lectures in 1912 rather surprised him by the warmth with which he spoke of them, as 'unlike Cambridge lectures in having personality'. Many of his hearers have re-corded their impressions and they agree in their witness to Glover's amazing capacity for digression and his equally amazing capacity for inspiring interest in the classics. W. A. Darlington writes of him:

Glover would have been accounted a great teacher at any time and in any company. He had little to do with us officially, for I think his regular work lay in a higher sphere, among the fourth year men who had taken their degrees and were working for Part II of the Classical Tripos. Unofficially we saw him often, for he was a friendly man with none of the aloofness which too many of our dons showed towards their pupils in off hours.... It was in my third year, when half a dozen of us went to his rooms for lectures on Thucydides, that his full quality became known to us. He did not lecture—he talked; and Thucydides was less a subject than a jumping-off place.

He would begin in ancient Athens and pass, with no sense of violent transition in time or place, to London or Paris, New York or Berlin where the men of our own day were encountering the same hopes or fears, achieving the same successes or facing the same failures as those old Greeks. We listened, and the classical world came alive for us. To Glover, Pericles and his contem-poraries were not simply figures in an ancient history, but human beings to be seen in the same perspective as their modern counterparts—the men whose doings Glover himself, when later he became Public Orator to the University, was to celebrate so often in sonorous Latin when honorary degrees were pre-sented.

Margaret Postgate (now Mrs G. D. H. Cole), who attended Glover's lectures about the same time as W. A. Darlington, bears a similar testimony. In her autobiography, *Growing up into Revolution* (pp. 39f.), she writes:

On the Roman side, I must pay a belated tribute to Terrot Reaveley Glover, afterwards Public Orator, whose first year lectures on Roman History were a revelation to one who had never known that history lessons could be anything but material for ten or twenty questions to be answered in writing 'with your books shut' and handed to the next girl to correct. Glover, that ugly and uncouth man, with the harsh voice, believed in relating the subject-matter to whatever happened to be interesting him at the moment. In 1911 he had just[1] returned from Canada, and his lectures contained a good deal of comparison of things Canadian with things Roman. Realizing this, he on one occasion observed in half-apology that 'it is a poor subject that will not get into a lecture on Roman History': when the remark was reported to Miss Katharine Jex-Blake, our Director of Classical Studies, she observed acidly, 'It is certainly a curious subject that does not get into Dr Glover's lectures on Roman History!' But he was a great teacher and whatever matter he introduced, he made ancient Rome a reality to us before he had done.

Miss M. G. Duff who was at Girton from 1923 to 1926 and who attended Glover's lectures on Classical History in her last year found them marked by the same characteristics.

They were of course mainly about Canada and the U.S.A. with occasional references to India, but in spite of this he was the first person to awaken my interest in Classical History.... His lectures were popularly supposed to be useless for Tripos purposes and most of my friends dropped off one by one to go instead to a lecturer who had the Tripos very much in view. I enjoyed T.R.G. so much and learned so much from him that I attended his lectures for the whole year, and, as it happened, found them most useful in the Tripos—though he was not an examiner that year. He certainly made me think more than most lecturers.

Miss Duff confirms and illustrates what W. A. Darlington says of Glover's readiness to get into touch with undergraduates. She relates an episode which she rightly describes as typical.

In the summer of 1926 he announced one day that he would not lecture the next day because he had to be in London—or

---

[1] Glover had been back for ten years when Miss Postgate attended his lectures. His impressions of Canada were still vivid.

rather typically, he said he would be glad to lecture if his class would meet him on the steps of the British Museum and, after waiting a moment for any response to this invitation, remarked, 'Not even three just persons?' I forgot this and went to St John's for the next lecture and on coming away met T.R.G. who had not been able to go to London because of the General Strike. He knew me by sight but we had never talked before and his characteristic greeting was: 'Come in, Miss Duff, and tell me how you live and what you think.' So I went in to his rooms and had a long and interesting talk. I told him truthfully that I was not much interested in Classical History, except odd periods, and I came away with the galley-proofs of his latest book because he thought, quite correctly, that I should find something of interest·in it.

These testimonies may suffice to illustrate the outstanding qualities of Glover as a lecturer, his gift of making ancient history live, his constant digressions to bring in modern parallels, his friendly interest in individual students. Some minor characteristics should also be noted. One student remarked, 'Dr Glover takes his own lectures seriously. He doesn't like you to be late. If you are, he stops, takes off two pairs of spectacles, looks at you and puts them on again. Such scrutiny is not sought a second time.' Glover was also in some matters a stickler for etiquette and decorum. Cecil Northcott writes, 'My memory of Glover at Cambridge (1924–9) was of him entering a lecture where there was a mixed audience and beginning his lecture with "Gentlemen".' Q. followed the same practice and was suspected of anti-feminism in consequence. Probably in both cases and certainly in Glover's, it was adherence to strict etiquette. University lectures are addressed to members of the University, and women at that time were not members of the University. Glover was in favour of degrees for women, even if he was doubtful about the franchise, and once told Miss Duff no woman should have a vote unless she had six children and five pockets! Again he liked women to wear hats at his lectures, and was inclined to insist on it when the usual convention was that women wore hats out of doors but took them off in lectures if they wanted to. Miss Duff successfully challenged his ruling. 'In the first lecture I attended I waited till he was looking in my direction, removed my hat and planted it firmly on the desk, gazing fixedly at him. He glared back but said nothing and never objected again.' Taking his lectures seriously and making a stand for decorum[1] did not mean that the lectures were heavy and sombre. Far from it. His bantering humour played round his subject and occasionally round himself. Did he not assure an audience of students that T.R.G. stood for tact, religion and grace? He liked, if he could, to draw his students out and was disappointed when they would not be drawn. 'He used to ask questions freely and was obviously delighted if the class would argue and discuss with him.' His mother-in-law, Mrs Few, who used often to follow his lectures on ancient history, would sometimes complain that the lecture had been either too thin or too frivolous, too many digressions and not enough solid history, too many light touches and weightier matters neglected. But his more serious asides were the more effective, because his humour was so often in evidence. A correspondent who went up to Newnham in 1912 and attended Glover's lectures on Greek History during her first year, writes:

I have never forgotten how, one morning, he stopped when he was talking about the large proportion of people in Ancient Greece who lived below the poverty line, and said, 'You, young men and women, have just come up to Cambridge and for many of you it is. your first taste of freedom, especially of freedom to spend your own money in your own way. You will have many temptations to run into debt: I would like to ask you this morning to remember that the little trades-people with whom you deal— I don't mean the big firms—are nearly all below or only just above the poverty line. Pay for what you buy from them when you buy it or as soon as the bill comes in.' This changed the 'professor' into a very fatherly man for me.

In reminiscences, Glover the lecturer, perhaps inevitably, overshadows Glover the classical tutor and coach, but many of the abler men would say they got much more from Glover in submitting Greek and Latin compositions to him than they did from attending lectures. Jerome Farrell, who went to him for Greek verse, writes:

There is little I can record of Glover from personal acquaintance except the feeling that he was kind and competent—so

---

[1] Even at Queen's, Kingston, he had insisted on men coming to his lectures properly dressed, and on one occasion, the students responded to his rebuke by all turning up in sweaters at his next lecture.

much so that I was more ashamed than gratified at what a prep-school boy would call 'scoring off the beak'. I used in a set of iambics the phrase πεῖραν ἁρπάζειν, at which Glover exclaimed as I think with every excuse, 'My dear boy, where did you ever see a phrase like that?' Of course I said, 'At the beginning of Sophocles' *Ajax*.' He dived for the *Ajax* and said, 'You're perfectly right', and did *not* add, 'It may be all right for Sophocles but doesn't come well from you.' From Glover I learnt never, when a schoolmaster, to try to cover up a mistake but frankly to admit error and ignorance.

Glover often professed a certain impatience with the niceties of grammar, and as time went on, he found coaching in composition very burdensome, but undoubtedly some of his best work as a teacher of the classics was done in private tuition.

If recognition within the University came somewhat slowly, his reputation as a scholar was enhanced outside by his *Studies in Virgil* which appeared in 1904, and by the invitation to deliver the Dale Lectures at Mansfield College, Oxford, in 1907 and the publication of these lectures in March 1909, under the title *The Conflict of Religions in the Early Roman Empire*. Glover submitted his *Studies in Virgil* in the first instance to the Cambridge University Press, hoping that as they had published *Life and Letters in the Fourth Century*, they would be willing to take his second book. To his intense disappointment, after keeping his manuscript for three months, the Syndics turned it down, owing, he was told years later, to the adverse judgement of Henry Jackson. On Charles Sayle's advice, the manuscript was offered to Edward Arnold who published it in 1904. Subsequently it was taken over by Methuen. It is now called simply *Virgil* and has reached a fifth edition.

Mr Vernon Rendall suggests that the book may have offended the strictly academic mind in two ways. First, Glover preferred the great French critics, such as Patin and Sainte-Beuve, to the German commentators on Virgil, for the very sound reason that 'the Germans do not enjoy the poetry of Virgil as the French do, and to be a sound critic of a poet it is necessary to enjoy him'. It is possible that those who read Glover's MS thought he was neglecting the work of the Germans in his chosen field. Second, Glover's use of English and modern illustrations may have shocked more academic minds. Did he drag in Carlyle, Lamb and his favourite Wordsworth too often? It is difficult to believe that such reasons determined the judgement of Henry Jackson, though they may have weighed with some more pedantic scholars. A simpler explanation may be suggested by an entry in Glover's diary under date 27 January 1903: 'Took 9 chapters of Virgil to Press in p.m.... If not accepted, I shall take it as sound criticism and let it wait and be mended with time.' It looks as if he submitted the first nine chapters as samples and asked for a decision on these specimen studies, before completing the book. *Life and Letters* had been judged and accepted on samples, and had been completed after acceptance, and he seems to have followed the same plan with his *Studies in Virgil*. If so, the first nine chapters, now constituting two-thirds of the book and occupying just over two hundred pages, may have seemed too slight a work for the Press to publish. The decision and the delay in arriving at it were both unfortunate.

Glover felt the rebuff keenly, but rightly did not take it as sound criticism, and persevered with publication. The originality and freshness of the book should have been clear from the chapters submitted. As John Watson, to whom the book was dedicated, said in acknowledging it, 'Like all you write it shows you are a voice and not an echo.' No considerable work on Virgil by a British scholar had appeared since Sellar's admirable monograph of 1876. There was room then for Glover's book and many discerning readers recognized and still recognize its merits. Mr Vernon Rendall characterizes those merits in the following critique.

The earlier part of the book is thorough and solid enough on the themes one would expect, The Age and the Man, Literary Influences, The Land and the Nation, but it is in the five chapters headed 'The Interpretation of Life' and 'Results' that Glover considers more disputable matter and gets to the heart of Virgil. What did the poet mean us to think of Aeneas and Dido and Augustus, who is introduced, one would say, as often as he can be? We are told that it is Virgil's way to draw characters who have been 'humanized by deep distress' [Wordsworth creeping in again!] and this applies most of all to the central figure of the *Aeneid*. There is something of the Oriental in Dido, who is always queenly, and Aeneas was definitely at fault in his treatment of her. He stayed too long at Carthage and he agreed to the proposals made by her in her weakness. But we do not see the whole of him. It was not the Roman way to show feeling. I may add that a study of the expression of the emotions in Rome, before Greeks and Orientals came to modify the national character, would reveal an extraordinary suppression of personal feeling as the ideal to be aimed at. Aeneas, Glover tells us, resembled Marcus Aurelius who sadly lacked any sense of gaiety.

What are we to think of Augustus, of whom two varying views are given by Tacitus? Was he, as Glover suggests, essentially the 'middleman' who comes in the train of genius, to use as far as he can its ideas and gains? He owes his success to his practical adroitness and his intellectual inferiority. Why then did Virgil make so much of him? Surely not just out of gratitude for the farm near Mantua, but from a real admiration for the Emperor as a patriot and man of peace. This is one of the disputable points in these interpretations of life, but they are profoundly interesting and the last chapter, 'Results', justifies Virgil's views of life and pain: 'Character, in Virgil's view, means achievement in the long run for the race and the individual, but quite apart from results, character is an achievement in itself and the righteous man does not look for rewards from righteousness.' Anchises joined his son with him in the admonition, 'Et dubitamus adhuc virtutem extendere factis?'.

His sympathetic interpretation of the character of Aeneas is among the outstanding merits of Glover's book. Mr R. W. Moore recalls a lecture on Virgil which Glover gave to a schools' audience under the auspices of the Bristol Branch of the Classical Association.

The large lecture-room at the Royal Fort was packed and he held his audience spellbound as much by his manner as by what he said. I remember his solemn and slightly detached cadences as though he were speaking with conscious restraint on a personality to which he was bound by the most affectionate of ties. When he spoke about Aeneas there was a measure of intimacy of tone in his relation to his subject and an impressive oracular, slightly remote tone as he gazed almost one would have thought without seeing at the solid rows of faces in front of him. I can recollect only one sentence and that imperfectly. He was speaking of Aeneas: 'He goes into the West and finds his Western land. And what does he find there?—just death....' Taken from its context this sentence will be misleading. I am sure that what he was trying to convey was the human anxiety of Aeneas and hinting that his long and epic pilgrimage was marked at many a turn by deep human sorrow and that what he was here referring to was the burial of Misenus, his first act on landing on the Italian shore; and soon there would be Palinurus.

The attitude of the lecturer reflects the appreciation of Aeneas in the book, and lovers of Virgil will continue to value and enjoy the book for this, if for no other, reason.

A letter from Dr D. S. Cairns to Glover in 1912 contained a most interesting appreciative reference to *Studies in Virgil*. Cairns wrote:

We had Lloyd George here [Aberdeen] tonight in full spate and a reception followed. I had a talk there with Gulland who told me that he had been the other day with Asquith and Birrell. Quoth Asquith to Birrell, 'Have you seen a book on Virgil by a man called Glover?' I rather think Birrell said he hadn't. Asquith went on to say that he had not thought that anything new could be said about Virgil, but that you had undeceived him, that he thought a lot of your book and that he was at present reading a couple of chapters every night before going to bed.

Critical reviewers at the time and since have questioned some of Glover's judgements on Virgil's contemporaries. Had he not dismissed Propertius too cavalierly as merely writing 'professoren-poesie', and was he not too contemptuous of Horace? So far as Horace was concerned, Glover was later to make ample amends. He did indeed reaffirm his adverse judgement, though obviously with growing hesitation in a sonnet which appeared in the *Westminster Gazette* on 23 August 1916. It was entitled, 'A Poet?' and runs thus:

A POET?

Horatius Flaccus, in my boyhood you
    Won me for Latin. But, of late, I own,
    You hardly 'make the heart beat', older grown:
Your *Dulce et decorum* scarce rings true;
Your Lydias seem lay figures; tune and tone
    Lack inspiration; all is of one hue,
    Mediocrity scarce golden; and you view
Life from a point too safe, too much alone.
Are you a poet, Horace? I confess
    Your loyalty to Maecenas, and your wise
    Old freedman Father, and the Sabine farm—
Noctes cenaeque deum—half-disarm
    My cooler judgment, as the memories rise,
And I could wish I still might answer Yes.

Sixteen years later, the Cambridge University Press published two charming lectures on Horace which Glover delivered in Bristol. It was a kind of palinode, as he himself said, and he called it *Horace, a Return to Allegiance*. But if he recovered his first love for Horace, he seems never to have changed his mind about Propertius.

No doubt Gilbert Murray had *Studies in Virgil* in mind when he said, 'A man who can write as well as you carries his Chair with him.' The invitation received in 1905 to give the Dale Lectures at Mansfield College, Oxford, in 1907, provided him with an opportunity of handling a still more important theme and of interesting a wider circle of readers. As far back as 1902, he had been thinking of a work on Tertullian and his opponents. He had even drawn up a scheme of four chapters: I, The World, as it appears in Philostratus, Lucian and others; II, Philosophy: Epictetus, Marcus Aurelius, Sextus Empiricus; III, The Heretics, particularly Marcion; IV, The Church and Montanism. It was a very tentative sketch, and when he was invited to give the Dale Lectures, he merged it in a more ambitious scheme. He would present the conflict of religions in the first two centuries of the Roman Empire, ending with Tertullian but not making the founder of Latin Christianity the centre of the picture. There were in existence histories of early Christianity and histories of the Roman Empire and its culture, but few had attempted to combine the two and this Glover proposed to do. He stated his aims in his preface in the following terms:

To see the founder of the Christian movement and some of his followers as they appeared among their contemporaries; to represent Christian and pagan with equal good will and equal honesty, and in one perspective; to recapture something of the colour and movement of life, using the imagination to interpret the data and controlling it by them; to follow the conflict of ideals, not in the abstract, but as they show themselves in character and personality; and in this way to discover where lay the living force that changed the thoughts and lives of men, and what it was; these have been the aims of the writer—impossible but worth attempting.

He began his preparation in 1905 by reading Dill, *Roman Society from Nero to Marcus Aurelius*, and not unnaturally he felt puzzled as to the wisdom of proceeding with his Dale Lectures.

'Dill is very solid and sound.' He has said all that needs to be said about Seneca, for example. Perhaps he is not so good on Plutarch. 'It might be said that there is little historical perspective in the book, not enough allowed for development of religious movement in the Empire.' But after all Glover was attempting something different from Dill; where they overlapped, Glover's presentation would still be his own and there was nothing in Dill corresponding to the lectures Glover hoped to give on the Founder of the Christian movement and his followers.

By the summer of 1906, the lectures were beginning to take shape, and he was ready to deliver them in the first half of 1907. The eight lectures delivered at Mansfield College, Oxford, in February, March and May of 1907 were expanded into ten chapters, and the book was published by Methuen in March 1909. The sales exceeded those of his previous books and the publishers were considering a third edition in July the same year. Chapter IV, which was devoted to 'Jesus of Nazareth', attracted most attention and most criticism, as the *Nation* in an advance notice had naturally anticipated. 'One of the signs of the times is the earnest effort now being made to pierce through the mass of *Aberglaube* which dogma and tradition have laid over the person of Jesus, and Mr Glover's book promises to be a fresh and interesting contribution in this direction.' Fresh and interesting, it certainly was. Glover had endeavoured to approach the central figure of the gospels in the spirit in which Seeley wrote *Ecce Homo*, accepting the standpoint and exercising the controlled imagination of the historian. Of Seeley, Dean Church wrote,

One thing is clear, wherever the writer's present lot is cast, he has that in him which not only enables him, but forces him, to sympathize with what he sees in the opposite camp. If he is what is called a Liberal, his whole heart is yet pouring itself forth towards the great truths of Christianity. If he is what is called orthodox, his whole intellect is alive to the right and duty of freedom of thought. He will therefore attract and repel on both sides.[1]

This might have been written of Glover. Many at once jumped to the conclusion that he was a Liberal—at best a Unitarian,

[1] R. W. Church, *Occasional Papers*, vol. II, p. 141.

perhaps not a Christian at all. E. E. Sikes drew Glover's attention to a notice of the book in the *Oxford and Cambridge Review*, which approved the 'terrible impartiality' of Glover as historian, but regretted that he was not a Christian. The reviewer in the *Tablet*, by quoting passages specially chosen and taken out of context, made the book to look like the crudest old Unitarianism, which was then saddled on to Nonconformity. In the same spirit J. S. Phillimore later referred to the book, and to this chapter in particular, as 'a bit of popular Arianism'. A highly appreciative reviewer in the *Times Literary Supplement*, who confessed that not a few passages in the book had moved him 'with a feeling of which praise is a less fit expression than gratitude', discerned rightly that Glover's affinities were with Ritschl and Harnack, that he was so to speak, orthodox with a difference.

Some of his most intimate friends were dissatisfied with the chapter on Jesus. His father much preferred the chapter on the followers of Jesus. John Skinner and John Oman both agreed in thinking chapter IV too Western and too modern, a judgement in which Kirsopp Lake concurred. Oman said it was too like Renan, whose influence gets outside his books. 'The chapter has a French lacquer.' Skinner thought it Unitarian in tendency, and Glover notes, 'He holds Unitarianism to be a mood and does not like it. Nor do I and would not wish to be associated with it.' If some scholars were doubtful about this presentation of Jesus, it made a wide appeal to students and to the serious reading public. The chapter was reprinted separately as a pamphlet in 1912, and Glover was delighted to get a letter from Keir Hardie, who said, 'Don't spoil by enlarging it or applying it to modern problems or anything else. Send it forth as it is, and like the grain of mustard seed it will grow.' Many who with Keir Hardie would have deprecated the intrusion of modern applications, yet wistfully desired an enlarged portrait such as Glover gave them later in his *Jesus of History*.

That chapter IV could be printed as a pamphlet was typical of Glover's method. Almost any of the chapters might have been treated in the same way. As Edwyn Bevan said in the *Quarterly Review*, we were invited to look out of various windows, one by one. 'As a series of individual studies, a sort of spiritual iconography of the first century [? first two centuries] Mr Glover's work is a contribution of a very valuable kind to the study of the field.'[1] In some ways the most successful of these portraits were the masterly studies of Clement of Alexandria and Tertullian, with which the book concludes. Kirsopp Lake liked the study of Clement best, and certainly it would not be easy to find a more sympathetic or more attractive portrait of that discursive Christian gentleman and scholar. But perhaps the study of Tertullian is the finer achievement. The reviewer in the *Times Literary Supplement* at least held this view.

The concluding chapter on Tertullian is perhaps the one where the quality of cleverness is most prominent, because Mr Glover had here to contend with a prepossession on the part of the ordinary reader, and the two sins of overstrained rhetoric and polemical harshness are ones which our comfortably charitable age finds it particularly hard to forgive. That Mr Glover does not shrink, in spite of this, from the task of making this great man attractive is to give proof of some bravery; and he shows his skill as an advocate by setting the dreadful passage quoted by Gibbon undaunted in the forefront of his argument. Even those readers who may pronounce Mr Glover's last chapter a piece of special pleading must admit that it is pleading governed by an extraordinarily quick sense for the susceptibilities of his audience.

No one can read this chapter and be content thereafter to dismiss Tertullian as a possibly sadistic fanatic on the strength of Gibbon's superficial judgement or Matthew Arnold's passing reference to 'the fierce Tertullian' in a well-known sonnet.

Glover's portraits of Clement and Tertullian are successful because he had affinities with both subjects. He shared Clement's wide-ranging literary interests and kindly human sympathies. He shared Tertullian's hasty impatience. If ever a sermon was addressed first to the preacher, this is true of Tertullian's treatises, *De Patientia*. As a younger friend of Glover's said to him later, when supporting a request to him to translate Tertullian, 'You ought to do it. You are just as much a beast as Tertullian and the same kind of beast.' At least, he was sufficiently like the African advocate to understand and sympathise with him.[2]

---

[1] *Q.R.* (July 1910), p. 217.

[2] J. T. Sheppard discerned the real difference between Glover and Tertullian, when he said to him, 'Oh no, you are not like Tertullian. Your curses are on your lips; his were in his heart.'

The Conflict of Religions established Glover's reputation as a writer and a scholar. An appreciative notice in the *Theologische Literatur-Zeitung* by no less an authority than Paul Wendland was a clear recognition of the quality of his work. His position as a historian of culture was now assured, though whether he should concentrate on the history of the Greco-Roman tradition or on the development of Christian thought and life had still to be determined. The appreciation of the book by individual readers was well expressed in a letter from C. E. Graves which gave Glover great pleasure. Graves wrote, 'Now let me tell you of the admiration I feel for your splendid book. It is a great and valuable work, and a κτῆμα ἐς ἀεί so far as I am competent to judge. I can judge of the style and the spirit, and I am deeply indebted to you for the book as a whole.'

The Dale Lectures not only established Glover's reputation as a scholar, but also led to increased demands upon him for lectures and addresses on religious history and literature. The Quakers had already discovered him in that capacity. At the close of the nineteenth century, Friends were realizing the truth of Joseph John Gurney's dictum, 'We shall never thrive upon ignorance.' They were increasingly aware of the limitations of traditional Evangelical theology which could not come to terms with new scientific and historical knowledge. As Rendel Harris told them, 'in theology it is a mistake to be born before Darwin'. Those Friends who were alive to these issues, sought to gain and spread a more enlightened understanding of the Scriptures by means of Summer Schools. A layman and a scholar like Glover, whose approach was that of a historian rather than a theologian, was peculiarly well fitted to help them. On the eve of his departure for Canada in 1897, Glover had been invited to take part in a large Summer School at Scarborough. He had given four lectures on the beginnings of Christianity in Britain and had won the interest and approval of no less an authority than Dr Thomas Hodgkin. Glover found the Quaker audience appreciative and congenial.

It was Rendel Harris who drew Glover into the concerns of Friends. In 1903 Rendel Harris left Cambridge to start a new venture at Woodbrooke in Selly Oak, now within the boundaries of the City of Birmingham. The success of the Summer School movement encouraged a group of Friends to try the experiment of opening a centre where such studies might be pursued all the year round. Rendel Harris was asked to become the first Director of Studies, and he declined the honour of a royal invitation to succeed Van Manen as Professor of Ancient Christian Literature at the University of Leiden, and also an invitation to be Yates Professor of New Testament at Mansfield College, Oxford, in order to throw himself into what was to prove a new and original development in adult religious education. Woodbrooke was to combine serious study and freedom of enquiry with a simple sincere devotional life. Those men and women who came as students would come not to read for degrees or diplomas, not to cover an exact and exacting syllabus, but to pursue knowledge both for its own sake and in the interests of their growth in grace and in the power to serve their fellows. Lecturers should lecture on what interested them, provided the subjects were of vital concern. Rendel Harris left his own stamp on the new 'settlement' as it was called. He brought to it his gaiety of spirit, his wit and humour, his zest for discovery and research, his unfailing belief in the capacity of ordinary folk to appreciate the best when it was offered them. All his geese were swans, and in many instances the transformation was actually achieved. Behind his gifts of humour, friendship and learning, were his childlike faith in Jesus and his deep experience of union with God in Christ. Rendel Harris had been much influenced by the teaching of Hannah Whittall Smith, and he had recovered for himself what has been called the lost radiance of the Christian religion. He would never sing the lines, 'And they who fain would serve thee best, are conscious most of wrong within.' No, the Christian life, he held, is a life of victory and joy. Christ's freemen are not to be preoccupied with the sense of wrong within. As George Fox said, they are to look, not at their sin but at the light which shows them their sin.

Glover's recollections of characteristic utterances of Rendel Harris will illustrate these qualities. When Rendel Harris was President of the National Free Church Council in 1907, he organized a Free Church Summer School during August in Cambridge in which Glover took part, repeating some of his Dale Lectures. He records in his diary these sayings of Rendel Harris.

Aug. 4. At meeting in morning J.R.H....First result of criticism of gospels is labels get burnt off. So with us when the Spirit touches us, labels go. We are to go away in a divine carelessness. 'Post equitem sedet atra cura' is a verse you cannot make for a Christian. Jesus has taken anxiety out of his life. Cult of sunshine and open air....Aug. 5. J.R.H. at meeting.... Desiderata in the spiritual life—continuity, depth, stillness. An occasional Christian a poor creature, wonder he is in the classification at all. The New Testament hardly knows him. To be always where you sometimes are and never where you've sometimes been! A shallow Christian is an unspeakable bore. People were never meant to be shallow. As plain become good looking under the influence of the Spirit, so the shallow develop.

It seems necessary to say this much about Rendel Harris and Woodbrooke, to explain the attraction of the place for Glover. It was in this period, 1903–14, that he came closest to the Society of Friends. He first visited Woodbrooke in December 1904. Some entries in his diary reveal the impression made upon him.

Dec. 16. In evening a Bible-class in Lecture Hall on subject of the Holy Spirit, with some right-minded speaking. This is a delightful place. Dec. 17. Much struck during the day by Woodbrooke spirit as instanced in Miss D.W. speaking nicely at devotional service, gaily playing ping-pong after lunch and acting Alice to a splendid Humpty Dumpty and acting it simply and charmingly. This last at party. Capital scene done 'Woodbrooke at work', i.e. talk in library where silence is required. Quotations. I won first prize—box of chocolates, very popular in house. Dec. 19. Ping-pong after lunch and dinner. Devotional meeting after breakfast. So prayer and play go happily hand in hand in this delightful place. One begins to understand the feeling of happiness and freedom which seems to have been in monasteries before they hardened.

This was the first of a series of visits which continued until the first World War. Almost any subject on which Glover cared to talk was welcomed by a Woodbrooke audience. He tried out most of the Dale Lectures at Woodbrooke. Appreciative hearers tempted him to go further afield. The studies in English literature which were later published under the title *Poets and Puritans* were first delivered and some of them—those on Wordsworth and Bunyan, for example—were often repeated for the benefit of Woodbrookers. This association with Friends brought requests for week-end schools in different parts of the country and such requests multiplied from 1908 onwards. As a result of a week-end in Scarborough, Richard Cross introduced Glover to the *Nation* and the editor, H. W. Massingham, was glad to get articles on religious themes from him. These articles were fresh and independent and reflected a layman's outlook and interests. Massingham had long wanted just such a contribution. Glover was becoming more and more attracted to the Friends' approach, especially as interpreted by Rendel Harris. He is intrigued by Kirsopp Lake's suggestion that in John iii. 5 'Except a man be born of water and of the Spirit', the reference to water may be an insertion. Is New Testament criticism lending support to Friends' view of the non-necessity of the sacraments and calling in question the assumption that the sacraments were instituted by Jesus?

From 1908 onwards Glover often attended the Friends' Meeting at 12 Jesus Lane, taking his daughters with him. He not infrequently took part in the vocal ministry. Friends were beginning to think that he belonged to them. In 1911 he gave an address at a representative Young Friends' gathering at Swanwick, and he was invited to give the Swarthmore Lecture at the yearly meeting of the Society which was to be held at Manchester in 1912. This was the first time a non-Friend had been asked to give the Swarthmore Lecture, which is intended to interest the general public in Friends' beliefs and practices and also to provide a background and introduction to the yearly meeting itself. He chose as his subject 'The Nature and Purpose of a Christian Society.' The reception of the lecture by some Friends tended to confirm some misgivings which were already forming in his mind. Attendance at Friends' Meeting in Jesus Lane had suggested the doubt whether Friends made adequate provision for a teaching ministry. Would his children get any clear definite instruction in Christian fundamentals if he took them to Jesus Lane rather than to St Andrew's Street? He was beginning to think Friends too vague in their beliefs. Then he gathered that the Young Friends Movement was becoming intolerant of preaching and tended to exalt silence at the expense of the spoken word. Silence, if of the right sort, can do without preaching. At one time some young Friends were inclined to question whether any communication in a meeting for worship should exceed ten minutes. Even in Woodbrooke such a tendency revealed itself. In October 1912, Glover notes, 'S.H—, deprecating length of my words at devotional made me feel notice to quit, *long expected*, has come.' So the Swarthmore Lecture proved to be the high-water mark of Glover's interest in Friends, which ebbed rapidly from that time on.

Perhaps it was unfortunate that Glover was invited to lecture in Manchester. Leading Friends in Manchester had reacted rather violently from Evangelical orthodoxy, and were convinced that Puritans and Quakers were poles apart. Any reference to human depravity or original sin was likely to be countered by assertions of the divinity in man or of original goodness. Glover's appeal to the historic Church and his emphasis on the doctrine of grace gave offence to some Friends in Manchester. His lecture in proof had been shown to J. W. Graham, the Principal of Dalton Hall, who had criticized it in these terms, 'It is all an appeal to the practice of the historic Church, whereas the Quaker differentia is, for the most part, an appeal against the historic Church, "the apostasy", in fact, to quote George Fox.' The Quaker correspondent of the *Christian World*, who may have been J. W. Graham, in reporting the lecture, repeated this criticism. 'It was', he said, 'a John Bunyan rather than an Edward Burrough type of address.' Graham's letter which had been forwarded to Glover when he was on his way to the U.S.A. with Neville Talbot in March 1912, made him rather despondent about the lecture. Glover, always ultra-sensitive to criticism, wished to drop the lecture altogether. Neville Talbot urged him to go ahead with it, and when he reached Haverford in April, Rufus Jones, who had also seen an advance proof, praised it warmly while not agreeing with all of it. So Glover went through with it. Most unfortunately, by some oversight, no one met him at Manchester and no arrangement had been made for hospitality. He had to find hotel accommodation himself. However it was pleasant to have Dr Thomas Hodgkin in the chair and an attentive audience of about 1000 people. He was glad to have the Manchester expedition over. 'It has been a thing rather burdensome—both the writing and the letters of the critics—and the going and the queer time there, and the uneasy feeling about such a public.'

The lecture sold well, particularly after an appreciative review by T. H. Darlow in the *British Weekly*, but it seems to have sold better outside the Society of Friends than it did within. It would be wrong to suggest that Glover broke with Friends, but in 1912, when he records his three visits to Woodbrooke he adds, 'though with a consciousness of change of attitude to Quakerism which I now find too vague'. Then the war interrupted his association with Woodbrooke, and owing to changed conditions his regular visits were not renewed after the war.

His affection for Rendel Harris continued unabated. Thus on 27 March 1914 he writes, 'We (Rendel and I) had another walk in his garden—it is always refreshing to be about with him again. I can't specify details of what I owe him, but years of friendship, of stimulus and of new ideas, count a lot.' He was, however, becoming dubious of some of Rendel's daring speculations. In August 1912 he was reading the proofs of *Boanerges*, the book in which Rendel Harris discovers more than one pair of twins in the circle of the Apostles. Glover comments, 'His methods seem to me very risky.' Some years later he is reading *Memoranda Sacra*, the earliest collection published of Rendel Harris's devotional addresses, and he finds them rather fanciful. Even the spell of Rendel Harris ceased to bind, and the limitations of the Society of Friends were still more obvious. His considered judgement on Friends is expressed in a letter to Mrs Albert Crosfield, written in May 1921.

My feeling about the Society is that until it makes up its mind on what matters most in fact in religion to-day, it cannot thrive. It will pick up adherents who are indeterminate; but until it decides whether it is really interested in Jesus (as the Friends' Foreign Mission Association is) or not interested (like some other Friends in the North), whether it puts him in the centre or does not naturally allude to him, it cannot grip. The issue is too big for a society of neutrals to count. Again the Birthright Membership may do for Parsis; it does not contribute to the fighting strength of a Christian force engaged against Satan and Satanism; not even half-Birthright Membership [one parent] which I see is being discussed. Again, preaching, viz. the communication of genuine ideas, of experience and of the call to duty, is an essential task of a Christian community—as in all serious human concerns, speech, intercourse and the sharing of thought is vital.

Among Friends the preaching is not taken seriously enough. Some that I have heard has been good and genuine, but lots was improvised and did not go deep enough. We have to-day a youth that is serious and is asking questions; and a silent society that does not attempt to guide and help (and this applies to many beside Friends) will not win allegiance. Men and women want to get the central things thought out into their depths.

During the period 1901–14, Glover was drawn into the orbit of the Student Christian Movement. Under date 24 May 1905 he records, 'Evening, 8.30 p.m. at St Columba's, to hear Tissington Tatlow on the Conishead Conference and agreed to go.' At the time the Student Christian Movement was represented by the Cambridge Inter-Collegiate Christian Union, and drew its support almost exclusively from the members of that Union who were for the most Evangelical Low-Churchmen. C. F. Angus took the initiative in trying to interest some leading Free Churchmen in the S.C.M. He invited Tissington Tatlow to address this particular gathering and Tatlow thus describes his first meeting with Glover.

I remember vividly Glover saying, after I had spoken, 'If I come to your conference, shall I have to meet any C.I.C.C.U. men?' I replied that he probably would, but that there was a great variety of other people as well at the conference and he was not to take the conference as simply typical of C.I.C.C.U. After the meeting was over and he had gone away, I said to Angus, 'Who was that gruff old bear that asked the question about C.I.C.C.U.?' and it was then that I learned for the first time the name of T. R. Glover.

This was the prelude to an intimate and lifelong friendship. The immediate result was that Glover accepted the invitation and attended the Conference at Conishead in July 1905 as a guest, and heard the discussion of the change of name from B.C.C.U. to S.C.M. Here he met John Kelman for the first time, and was impressed by him. He jotted down some sentences from Kelman's address on the intercessory prayers of Jesus. 'Failure in prayer for want of identification with the world's sin and misery.' 'The test of joy is what it has outlived.' 'God doesn't make a solitude in the heart and call it peace.' 'Nothing in this world is so holy as the facts of the case.'

The following autumn Kelman was in Cambridge and Glover went to hear him at St Columba's on three successive nights. Notes from Kelman's addresses figure again in the diaries.

Oct. 24. Went to hear Kelman on the Unknown Self (John i. 26, 'There standeth one among you whom ye know not'). Classification is not knowledge. Jesus remarks on the Jews' inability to classify John. The mystery of life lies in things that look simplest. Nobody is uninteresting for whom you can do a hand's turn. You give yourself more licence by saying you don't count than by any other trick of the devil. God hasn't time to make nobodies. Kelman is in earnest and his words impress one.

The next evening, Glover heard Kelman speak of Jesus. He quoted, 'After Jesus, either his religion or none.' The entry in the diary continues,

Jesus a poet and allowed his imagination full sway, an observer of men and things, with experience. In life only the conqueror can interpret. Christ on God—he said, 'I know him.' He invented the word 'lost' for people who had sinned and thought all was over, and he spoke of their being found. Christ masters all attempts to explain or to do without him. To have command of rest is greater than to have moved the world. Will you keep your will to yourself and give Christ your admiration?

There will clearly be echoes of Kelman in Glover's portrait of Jesus.

The strength of the Scottish contingent at Conishead and particularly the presence of John Kelman, who was then at the height of his power to appeal to students, satisfied Glover that the S.C.M. was not sacrificing intellectual integrity to Evangelical pietism. He is again present as a guest at the Quadrennial Conference at Liverpool in 1908, and as a result he urged Baptist theological students to attend the S.C.M. summer conferences, and along with Sir G. MacAlpine raised a fund to make it easier for them to attend. In 1910 for the first time, he was invited to speak at Baslow. 'My address on "the Bible and modern difficulties" (title chosen for me) was well taken. Tatlow said some liked it as much as anything they had had so far.' It was in the following year that the S.C.M. really discovered Glover as a speaker. This year the conference was held at Swanwick for the first time and John Kelman was once again to be one of the chief speakers for the main student audience. He was called away by his mother's serious illness, and Glover who was present to address the theological group, was asked to take Kelman's place. With many misgivings he agreed and at the end he could say, 'What a week of gladness it has been.' In August he stayed with Tatlow at Ravenscar for a few days and felt himself to be on the inside of the movement. Among other things, he and Tatlow discussed the Quadrennial to be held in Liverpool in January, 1912. At the end of August Glover was at the Young Friends' Conference at Swanwick, and while there he received the following letter from Tatlow.

I think you know about the evening meetings for Liverpool Conference, namely, that they should be an exposition of Christ as the answer to the need of the world, taken on these lines:

1st night. 'The fact of Christ in history'—Dr John Kelman.
2nd night. 'The Glory of Christ's whole life on earth.'—A. G. Fraser.
3rd night. 'The Death of Christ.'
4th night. 'The Resurrection and Absoluteness of Christ.'—Rev. D. S. Cairns.
5th night. 'The Living Creative presence of God in the Church and in the individual soul.'—Canon Cunningham and possibly one other speaker.

The idea is that these subjects should none of them be treated theologically, but that we should have them treated by men who know the theology of their subjects, more or less, and who will therefore handle them in a way that will not raise intellectual difficulties in the minds of their hearers. Now we have been desperately stuck over the question of a speaker on 'The Death of Christ'. A great variety of suggestions have been made. Yesterday Oldham writes this to me:

'After a good deal of thought I am tempted to suggest the name of Glover. Under ordinary circumstances I should not propose him' (I think he means by this that ordinarily he would like a more theological man, because just above he has suggested the possibility of A. B. Macaulay, but he has ruled him out; Macaulay is a theologian of the theologians), 'but I am disposed to think he would do what we want at Liverpool. He would approach the subject from a thoroughly modern standpoint, and this, I think, is necessary, if you are going to do any good to the great majority of thinking people at the Conference. On the other hand, he would certainly approach it reverently and would be in complete sympathy with what we are trying to do. He probably would not reach a dogmatic theory, but I think he would probably get the Conference to see the point of view from which the subject is being approached sufficiently clearly to make those who have a dogmatic theory willing to accept an address that does not go as far as they are prepared to go themselves. I would repeat that in my judgement a very large number of those who will be present, including the men we are most anxious to reach, are not ready for any dogmatic theory. What I think we need to do in the present state of thought is to make living the moral and spiritual presuppositions which must lie behind any dogma. I cannot help thinking that Glover might perhaps do this as well as anybody.'

Now what do you think yourself? It is not a very usual course to take, the course I am now taking, of writing and asking a man what he thinks about himself, but sometimes it works very well, and on the whole I am inclined to think that probably you are as good a judge as anybody, seeing that you know the Movement so well, as to whether you have got something to say which could be well said under the title 'The Death of Christ', in such a series of meetings as we are proposing. This letter, of course, is quite informal, from a friend to a friend. The committee do not know that I am writing to you: they have not even discussed your name yet.

P.S. I have a letter from Miss Saunders who has been up in Edinburgh who talked with Oldham apropos of the proposal of you. She says: 'Mr Glover might be the right man; he certainly held many in Swanwick. He is always fresh, and untheological in wording, and yet he makes one feel that he knows the trend of theological thought. Above all he is certainly an experimental Christian and if he will speak on that subject I think he would be sure to make it real to men.' I make these quotations from Oldham and Miss Saunders because I think they serve, better than anything else, to show what is in the minds of two members of the Committee and what kind of address they are looking for.

Glover indicated his willingness to undertake the address on the Death of Christ, and he found himself committed to a difficult task. He outlined his thought in an address at Woodbrooke and then submitted his sketch to a conference of Liverpool speakers at Swanwick on 10 October. Some 2000 students and dons met at Liverpool from 2 to 6 January 1912 and on the 4th Glover spoke to them from the words 'They laid on him the cross.' 'So it was done and I was glad. People spoke of it kindly and cheered me, as I had not followed the feeling of listeners.' Tatlow confirmed this impression in a letter, 'to tell you how truly glad I was both for the sake of the Conference and for your own sake that the address "came off"....I am sure you must have been both thankful and humble about it.' A note from D. S. Cairns to T. R. Glover's father indicates the kind of impression made by the address.

I can't let another day pass without writing you a brief note to bear testimony to the good done by your son's admirable address on 'the Death of Christ' at the Student Conference a week or so ago. It made a very deep impression on very many, myself among the number, it was so honest and so full of deep and noble feeling. Many of our very best men there have spoken to me about it in this sense. It touched the high water mark of the whole remarkable gathering, and will, I believe, have lasting result for good.'

From now on Glover was regularly on the programme at Swanwick. He is there in 1912, and reviewing the following year he records, 'Still doors keep opening—in the student world. I have been to Glasgow (twice), Leeds, Nottingham, London, Oxford, Aberdeen and Swanwick.' He is in constant demand. His pen is enlisted in the service of the movement as well as his voice. In 1913 he writes a booklet on 'Vocation' and the following year he produced a brief account of the origin and growth of the movement. Arriving at Liverpool on 20 July 1914 from a two-months' tour with Mrs Glover in the U.S.A. and Canada, he goes straight to Swanwick and spends ten days there before going home. Three days later he is staying with the Tatlows at Aldeburgh. When war broke out, his interest in the S.C.M. was at its height.

Throughout the period 1901–14, Glover had become, as he says, 'Observably more evangelical.' This was evident from his renewed attachment to the Baptists. During the latter part of the ministry of Charles Joseph at St Andrew's Street he seemed to be sitting loose to the Baptist denomination and drifting towards Friends. But the appointment of M. E. Aubrey to succeed Joseph in 1913 drew him back to St Andrew's Street, and in 1914 he was elected a deacon. Moreover, he had all along taken a personal interest in Baptist students both in Cambridge and in Swanwick. The leaders of the denomination had never lost sight of him. He had been invited to give a paper to lay-preachers at the Baptist Union meetings in Bristol in 1904, and he chose to speak on enlargement of outlook, commending Wordsworth's advice to let Nature be our teacher. He thought it met with disapprobation. There were some critics and some funny things were blurted out about wasting the time of the meeting. The address was not evangelical enough in the conventional sense. However Principal Henderson of the Baptist College, Bristol, approved and an old gentleman said to Glover's sister, Dorothy, 'They ought to realize that Nature is the garment of God—and touch it.' 'She and I liked that.' Glover attended and enjoyed the meetings of the Baptist Union in Northampton the following year, though he still felt a little sore about the failure to appreciate his contribution at Bristol. But he does not seem to have gone again for some years. In the autumn of 1912, he delivered the Angus Lectures at Regent's Park College, taking as his theme 'The Christian Tradition and its Verification.' This brought him into closer contact with the Baptists, and was a mark of their appreciation of the Dale lecturer.

The Angus Lectures, the fourth substantial book from Glover's pen, is slighter in character than any of its three predecessors. Rendel Harris thought it not so well written as *Virgil*, which he regarded as the best of Glover's works, preferring it to *The Conflict of Religions*. But *The Christian Tradition and its Verification* marks a stage in the development of Glover's thought. John Skinner, the Principal of Westminster College, to whose friendship Glover owed much, claimed half-seriously in December 1911 that he had changed Glover's outlook. 'You are Evangelical now and when we first knew one another you were Wordsworthian and Spinozist.' Actually Glover had never been Spinozist, but contact with Skinner and many other influences had made him noticeably more Evangelical by 1912 than he had been in 1901 or 1904. The emphasis on the use of tradition and the significance of the Christian Church is another striking feature of the Angus Lectures. In this we can see both his recoil from the Quaker lack of interest in the Christian tradition, and also the positive influence of the ecumenical interest which was coming to birth in the S.C.M. He had had misgivings about the entry of Anglo-Catholics into the Student Movement, and he remained suspicious of the High-Church influence. But his meeting with men like Father Kelly of Kelham or E. K. Talbot of Mirfield had convinced him that they were not out to capture the movement, and had also enlarged his sympathies with strands in the Christian tradition other than his own. They helped him to see that to ignore the testimony of the Church is to make up one's mind about Christianity without facing the facts. The experience of the early Church can never be dismissed as irrelevant to our fundamental convictions. The Angus Lectures are also of interest as containing in germ the line of thought which was to be developed in *Jesus in the Experience of Men* and *Christ in the Ancient World*. Perhaps for that reason, the book has not had the appeal of its predecessors. It marks an important stage in Glover's thinking, but the challenge of the war and a year in India were to draw from him fuller expositions of some of the main themes handled in the Angus Lectures.

Chapter VI

THE FIRST WORLD WAR

Moral problems : a year in India : The Jesus of History : other writings : Poets and Puritans : From Pericles to Philip : Jesus in the Experience of Men

The outbreak of the war on 4 August 1914 took Glover as much by surprise as it did most people in England. Perhaps he was even less prepared than many. He and Mrs Glover had spent some weeks in the States and Canada during the Long Vacation. They left Southampton on 3 June and returned to Liverpool on 20 July. The tour had enabled them to revisit Kingston together. They had been too preoccupied with other matters to devote much attention to politics at home, let alone the development of trouble on the continent of Europe. The reference in the diary for 1914 to the Serajevo murders under date 29 June seems to have been added on a later revision. The significance of the murder of the Austrian heir presumptive was certainly not realized at the time. On 31 July Glover notes: 'Things look dark. Everyone perturbed by this horrible prospect of being dragged into other peoples' wars,' but the following day he joined the Tatlows on holiday at Aldeburgh, still not anticipating the rapidity with which the crisis would develop. Tatlow and he read and pondered Sir Edward Grey's speech on 4 August and hoped that Germany might yet be persuaded to respect the neutrality of Belgium. Next morning they learned that Germany had declared war on the previous evening. Britain was now involved. 'The horror of it haunts me—with reflexions on other wars I remember—and thoughts of God's supremacy.'

The early panic which forced the Government to suspend banking facilities for a few days did not affect Glover. He returned to Cambridge on 7 August and settled down to preparing for next term and to ordering family affairs. The education of the two older girls required thought and provision. Mary was in her last year at the Perse School and the question of sitting for scholarships at Cambridge (Girton) or Oxford (Somerville) had to be considered. Anna, it seems, might profit by leaving the

Perse School and having a year or two at a boarding-school. Such matters required discussion and decision. The prospects of next session at the University were uncertain. Actually the number of undergraduates was reduced by one-half or two-thirds in the first year of the war and declined still further in 1915–16. But when term opened, Glover began his Greek History course with nine women and ten men. His duties as Proctor continued, and though diminished numbers lightened the labours of his evening patrol, the war brought its own special problems. As the vacant accommodation of many of the colleges including St John's was taken over for cadets in training, military discipline and proctorial discipline had somehow to be harmonized. In the Michaelmas and Lent terms Glover as lecturer and as Proctor had enough to do.

The outbreak of war came as a challenge and a menace to Liberalism and to Christianity. Can we still be Liberals, can we still be tolerant, can we still be Christian—in other words, can we love our enemies? Everyone who cared about Liberalism and Christianity had to think out his position afresh. An invitation to take part in a series of addresses on Christianity and War, which was promoted by F. C. Burkitt, the first layman to hold a Divinity professorship in Cambridge, in the Michaelmas term, gave Glover the opportunity to formulate his judgement on the main issues. He had been invited partly on the assumption that he could speak for Friends. This he could not do, nor were Friends satisfied with him as representative, and a place was found for Dr Henry Hodgkin to put the Quaker view of war and peace. Glover had great sympathy with the conscientious objectors, and throughout the war exerted his influence to secure fair treatment for them. But he could not accept the pacifist position, and the attitude of some absolutists seemed to him unreasonable. He stood by pacifists because independence of judgement is so precious, and war breeds intolerance. He found most disquieting the atmosphere of the early months of the war, in which the pressure of irresponsible agencies issued in something like compulsory volunteering. Soldiers as men of action he respected and often admired. A brigadier-general who had fought in the Boer War dined at St John's on 27 August. He was good company. The next day Glover met the general's wife, very full of recruiting.

'She gave me an advertisment she had had printed: "Wanted petticoats for young men who have not joined the army or navy." ' The general's wife did not make a favourable impression. Glover found himself averse from hurrah-patriotism, but unable to adopt the Quaker testimony against all war.

His contribution to the lectures on Christianity and War came third and was delivered on 26 November. C. F. Angus, who reported it in the *Cambridge Magazine*, began his article with the sentence: 'After the soldier and the prophet, the historian—that seems to have been the role of the third lecturer...Mr T. R. Glover, of St John's.' The soldier had been Col. H. J. Edwards, whose simple sense of patriotic duty found no incompatibility between war and Christianity. The prophet had been Henry T. Hodgkin who found no way of associating war with Christianity. 'Glover's lecture, which drew a large audience and held their close attention for 75 minutes, was full of interest and stimulus, but, as compared with its predecessors, bewilderingly inconclusive.' He had made up his mind on two points which he could neither harmonize nor abandon. The first was that war was as incompatible as slavery with the new value set on individuals for whom Christ died. Eventually the influence of Christ must end war as it ended slavery. The second was that society and presumably the State which are part of God's ordering of human life may still require and apparently still do require to be defended by war. 'So that sticking to society may mean war, but let it be war with right and repentance, with recognition of a better way, with restraint upon our lips from any hate-producing words which may make peace harder.'

This seemed a lame conclusion, and when a group of pacifists under the leadership of Henry Hodgkin and Leyton Richards met in Cambridge in January 1915 to found the Fellowship of Reconciliation, they did not invite Glover to join with them as they thought him too cautious and too undecided. He could not resolve his perplexity as easily as the pacifists could. On the political issues involved, he followed Sir Edward Grey. He did not flirt with the critics of Sir Edward's foreign policy and he did not doubt that honour and interest obliged Great Britain to oppose German aggression. He was encouraged by finding that Rendel Harris agreed with him on his view of the political issues involved in the war. As early as October 1914 Rendel Harris said there was nothing to be done but to carry the war to a finish, a real finish. Rendel Harris could hold this view along with the conviction that the Christian should refuse to participate in war. Glover was not so clear on the issue of personal duty. When the war began he was too old to enlist. At a later stage, when under conscription he was liable to be called up, he was glad to accept alternative employment, not so much because he had a conscientious objection to serving under military authority, as because he knew himself to be physically and temperamentally unfit for active military service and because he believed the military organization capable of wasting intellectual ability to a ludicrous extent. He had no wish to be enlisted to spend his time peeling potatoes, which, as he believed, had been the fate of some graduates.

As the numbers of students at the University diminished and the claims and satisfactions of academic work declined likewise, Glover welcomed a suggestion from K. J. Saunders that he should go to India for a year and work for the Y.M.C.A. The suggestion soon became a definite invitation, and with the consent and approval of the authorities of both University and College, the invitation was accepted. It was agreed that he should sail for India early in September 1915, and before going should spend a month in Havre, in a camp for soldiers suffering from venereal disease. Though his work in India was not to be exclusively or even primarily among British troops, it was thought desirable that he should have experience of Y.M.C.A. work under some of the most difficult conditions. In a measure his experience as Proctor had prepared him for the problems presented by the V.D. camp in Havre. In a letter to Tatlow, early in 1914, he wrote,

Proctoring has given me a heap of new views into undergraduate life—a closer appreciation of many things—temptation (the imagination is bad enough, but when the young ass talks to a girl and thinks her a lady, and strolls homeward with her— a seat on the common and next thing she perches herself on his lap or comes to tea next day for five hours in his lodgings— different, isn't it? Thank God for the homes we had or something.) Also I am struck with the weakness of character.

Thus prepared, he was not surprised to find good men in the camp, who had yielded to temptation under the strained un-natural conditions of active service in France. He could readily understand how men came to be victims of V.D., and after his visit to Havre, he could speak to soldiers in a way that would appeal to them. But his main work in India was not with soldiers. His lectures and addresses for the most part were of two kinds, 'those that were given to students in the University Colleges of the cities—most of them Hindus and Muslims and Parsees—and those given to companies of Christians, Indian and European, for their refreshment and instruction'.

He sailed from Southampton on 4 September 1915, arriving at Bombay on the 26th of the same month. He began the return voyage from Bombay almost exactly a year later, on 3 September 1916. He landed at Boulogne early on 20 September and crossed to England the same night. The year had been of exceptional interest, 'probably the most interesting I shall ever see' as he wrote at the close of 1916. Throughout the year, news from home had been cheering. Mary had won a scholarship for Classics at Somerville College, Oxford. His brother-in-law Harry Few had come through fighting in France safely. For himself, he had traversed India from north to south, from west to east and back again. He had visited Ceylon and Burma. He had seen men and cities, and enriched his experience in a thousand ways. It was a year of achievement also. He had written out the chapters of *The Jesus of History*, which he had used as lectures in numerous centres, and by the end of the year he had passed the proofs of what was to be his most widely-read book.

If the year in India was interesting and rewarding, it was not an easy one. Glover found, as other visitors have found, con-ditions of travel in India far from restful. 'The journey to Vellore is a little awkward,' wrote a friend, 'you have to change at 2.30 a.m. at Villapuram, but till then you can have a pleasant night's rest.' The ironist! He had a servant to look after him, whose name was Job and who no doubt needed the patience of his Biblical namesake. Job in turn tried the patience of his employer, but on the whole served him well. Travel over long distances and a full programme wherever he stayed proved very tiring. He also had a good deal of trouble with his health, particularly with his teeth, and he needed his last quiet fortnight at Poona, where he was the guest of Dr Nicol Macnicol, and the pleasant voyage home to put him into form again. His enjoyment of the Indian scene was handicapped, as indeed throughout his life his enjoyment of Nature was handicapped, by the fact that he was colour-blind. He saw most things in Nature as more or less the same colour. Consequently he was more interested in form and outline, in change and movement, in light and shade, than in colour-effects. He was interested and observant where birds and flowers were concerned, but it was inevitable that he should be more interested in men, in men's talk, and ideals and achievements than he could be in Nature or pictorial art. Yet he noted the bright colours of the East, the effect of a blue sari on a brown skin, the varied tints on turbans, the rich sheen of brass-pots, a red-spotted horse in Calcutta, though he may have had to confirm his impressions by enquiry. He was never tired of visiting Oriental bazaars, and he could not resist the attractions of the products of the east in silver, brass and lacquer. A parcel and a box were dispatched from Rangoon, with goods mainly of Burmese origin, and another box with things Indian from Colombo. All reached Cambridge without mishap. His adventures in this kind of shopping inspired this sonnet, 'Night in Rangoon'.

> Once, in Rangoon, in sultriest Eastertide,
>   The hot night following day's extravagant heat,
>   We rambled Westward. In the open street
> Tamils, half-naked, slumbered side by side,—
> Sulé towered high behind us in its pride.
>   Strange scene! this night-bazaar where meet
>   The races of the East. Cloths, new and neat,
> And scent and toys and trash, the dealers cried.
>
> There for six pice a little Buddha lay—
>   Pensive, in yellow robe, with gilded head.
>   In India, centuries since, beneath his tree
> He found enlightenment. Japan to-day
>   Makes Buddhas for the Burman. Yet there be
> Who doubt that knowledge of the light must spread!

But for all his interest in the country and its people he did not really surrender to the spell of India. He went out a convinced believer in the missionary enterprise. He returned a confirmed enthusiast. He regretted the aloof critical attitude towards missionaries so often adopted by humanists and anthropologists. Before he went out he reviewed Lowes Dickinson's travel sketches, *Appearances*, and found even that sympathetic humanist at fault.

I have never seen India and China, and I rest on what my friends have told me and what I have read, and I am more conscious of elements which Mr Dickinson seems to me to have missed. My authorities have in many cases been missionaries. This may discredit them (and me) with some readers at once. But I think the missionary, if he is a live man (and I have known quite a number who were intensely alive) comes nearer in than other men to what is going on in the Orient.... His preoccupation is to reach the actual inner mind of the men he lives with— and I am impressed again and again with the interest of the task and the splendid open-hearted way the men grapple with it. It is clear that Mr Dickinson also is in earnest in trying to understand the East in a degree far beyond most of us; that he has real sympathy with the Eastern. So I am the sorrier for the undertone of misunderstanding of my friends in the book.

Lowes Dickinson was attracted by the Chinese, but baffled by the Hindus. He thought he understood the former, and his *Letters from John Chinaman* show that his claim was not ill-founded. Yet Glover was convinced, rightly, that Lowes Dickinson had not the deep insight into Chinese thought and culture, which was possessed by his friend Dr Timothy Richard, his boyhood missionary hero who had spent forty-five years in China. The comparative study of religions and anthropology owe so much to missionaries who have been intensely alive and open-hearted that it ill becomes any of us to sneer at them. Frazer's *Golden Bough* would be a poor book without the observations of John Roscoe and Henri Junod. We should know little of the great religions of the world were it not for the labours of devoted missionaries from William Carey and Robert Morrison onwards. Glover went to India, eagerly anticipating association with men as alive to things Indian as Timothy Richard was to things Chinese.

Contact with popular Hinduism depressed and shocked him. Dr Nicol Macnicol found him at the close of his year as much in revolt as he had been at the start. 'His Puritan soul was repelled by the cities in India which he saw to be "wholly given to idolatry".'[1]

'I took him,' writes Dr Macnicol, 'to some of the temples in Poona and he seemed to be revolted by what he conceived to be the stench of evil of which he was aware there. After his return to England I happened to have to speak along with him in Edinburgh on India and with some dismay I heard him sum up the religion in the words "Hinduism is hell". That is hardly an adequate account of a great religion, but it reveals the sensitiveness of his religious instincts and his deeply implanted Protestantism and Puritanism'.

There was so much in Hinduism that gave offence. Religious prostitution, the use of phallic symbols, the licentious element in myth and in temple sculpture, the little goats waiting to be sacrificed to Kali or Shiva, the many gods and idols, the amazing extremes of ascetic practice, the worship of the cow, the worship of the Ganges—everything seemed to be the embodiment of degrading superstition. Among other things he witnessed the noise and physical violence of exorcism as practised in India. Though in a measure it horrified him, he was glad he had seen it. It threw fresh light on that scene in the synagogue at Capernaum, when in the excited crowd one said to another, 'What is the meaning of this? A new teaching? With authority he gives orders to the unclean spirits and they obey him!'

The painful impression of popular Hinduism limited his appreciation of other aspects of Hindu religion and culture. A thoughtful Hindu student, reading Glover's sympathetic study of Plutarch, the typical religious conservative, in *The Conflict of Religions*, exclaimed, 'I am Plutarch.' In his Dale Lectures Glover might present Christian and pagan with equal goodwill and equal honesty, but when he met the Indian intellectuals who are the counterparts of Plutarch or Plotinus or Porphyry, he found it hard to maintain the goodwill. The lecture on the Christian Church in the Roman Empire which forms chapter IX in *The Jesus of History*, is neither unfair nor offensive to the old

---

[1] 'No man can handle St Paul aright who has not battled with sin and who has not lived with worshippers of idols.' This sentence from his essay on Erasmus may show how contact with Hinduism helped Glover to interpret St Paul later.

pagan faith, but the lecturer exposed the weakness of eclecticism. Unwittingly at Barisal he criticized eclecticism, when as it happened the first three rows of seats had been reserved for the members of a club known as 'The Eclectics'! But when he gave this lecture he suggested that Jesus brought not peace but a sword to the old religion and culture. He was aware of the power of Hindu religious philosophy, not only to defend the old traditional popular faith and practice, but also to absorb and eviscerate a new faith when such demanded recognition. It would be easy to find a place for an oriental Christ among India's mahatmas.

So Glover was distrustful of some of the great leaders of modern Hinduism, who were responsive to some elements in Christ's teaching and story and who yet were very critical of Western culture and of the missionary enterprise which they regarded as an attempt to thrust an alien Western form of Christianity on to Indian folk who already possessed a deeper religious culture than the West ever knew. Glover did not actually meet Gandhi, and his impressions of Gandhi, not unfavourable though not enthusiastic, were all second-hand. He did visit Rabindranath Tagore, and he saw a performance of the poet's charming play *Phalguni* in the poet's own house in Calcutta, and with the poet himself in the leading role. He enjoyed the play, but thought that he detected in it a note of polemic. 'The poet is playing up to Indian sentiment, for all his beauty and mysticism.' The lesson of the play is that 'the new India will be the outcome of the old, and the same as it'. 'It was thus in the third century that Neo-Platonism rallied a dying paganism, interpreted it as a philosophy, invested it with poetry, charm and magic, to combat a conquering faith. Tagore is India's chief bulwark to-day against Christianity.'

Glover found, as Mr Godfrey Philips found, interesting parallels between the Ancient Church in the Roman Empire, and the young Churches in modern India. But we may press parallels too far. Both Gandhi and Tagore were distrustful of Western commercialism, Western restless activity, and Western science, though on this last Gandhi was more distrustful, more apprehensive than Tagore. The latter was more positive in his approach to Western culture, more eager for a marriage of the cultures of East and West. And both might have claimed that in trying to retain, while purifying, some of the more valuable elements in Hindu life and culture, they were in line with the spirit of him who said he came not to destroy but to fulfil.

It is not surprising that Glover found himself out of sympathy with Hindu intellectuals. He was essentially a historian, and it must be admitted that a serious concern with real history, and a true appreciation of historical evidence and perspective have not, up till now, been leading characteristics of the Hindu mind. Subtle argumentation and fluent rhetoric come easier than genuine critical sifting of fact and fancy. During his travel year in India, he was interested to find that C. F. Angus had reached much the same view as he had about the poor thinking of Indians, their want of criticism and want of conclusion, and general indefiniteness of mind. When the rising tide of national self-consciousness found expression in sweeping bitter judgements on the British Raj and on Christian missionaries, Glover felt alienated from the Hindu temperament and outlook. He was asked, on his return, to put on record his impressions of India, that such record might serve as an introduction to India for workers with the Y.M.C.A. and others. But when he submitted his draft, the Y.M.C.A. leaders turned it down, not because the content was not true, but because Glover was out of sympathy with national sentiment in India and because it would seem one-sided and unjust to Hindu readers.

Perhaps the Y.M.C.A. was too cautious, for while Glover was critical of Hinduism, both popular and philosophical, he was not really an unsympathetic observer nor was he blind to the treasures of Hindu mysticism. Ramanuja, Kabir, Tuka Ram, all appealed to him. He could understand the element of Bhakti, i.e. of religious devotion to a personal God which finds expression in the teaching and experience of these great mystics. In *Jesus in the Experience of Men* (p. 40) he says that some of Dr Nicol Macnicol's verse renderings of Tuka might be interpolated among Cowper's poems from Mme Guyon and not be detected without reference to the French. In such a tradition he felt at home. He was charmed by the mystic's use of homely imagery to illustrate our dependence on God and his care for us.

From Tuka Ram he culled these flowers. 'I have had enough of
running: now take me on thy hip: do not make me walk any
more.' 'He fastens us to his waistband and takes us quickly over
the stream—Tuka says, he is a sea of mercy: he satisfies abundantly the desire of all.' 'The mother understands the child's
secret, his joys, his griefs and all his actions. . . . Tuka says, If a man
has entrusted his life to Vitobha, he (Vitobha) knows his condition.' The mystic is a little Indian child, taken on his mother's
hip, or fastened to his father's waistband, or understood as one
whom his mother comforteth. Natural history supplies other
images. Glover was delighted to discover the two divergent
traditions in the school of Ramanuja. Both asserted that God
carries us, but does he carry us as the cat carries her kitten or do
we have to cling to him as the baby monkey clings to his mother?
Glover was never tired of giving addresses particularly to junior
audiences about cats and monkeys. It is not clear which school
of thought he favoured. There is no evidence that he read and
appreciated the *Bhagavad-Gîta* or realized the place it takes in
Hinduism as a living religion. In discussing reform movements,
Glover set a high value on Ram-Mohun Roy and was interested
in both the Brahmo- and the Aryo-Samaj. But Vivekananda,
with his reckless statements and blind defence of everything
Indian, and Mrs Annie Besant, defending idolatry and saying
Yes, Yes to every creed, made no appeal to him. The latter
seemed to him to resemble Madam Bubble (in Part II of *Pilgrim's
Progress*), 'Doth she not speak very smoothly and give you a smile
at the end of a sentence?'

Since Glover's attitude to much in the outlook of Hindus was
plainly unsympathetic, it is perhaps surprising that he received
such an attentive hearing from Indian audiences as in fact he did.
But he was giving them of his best, and if the historical approach
is not the most congenial to the Indian mind, a lecturer who had
something fresh and true to say about Jesus, could count on
a response from Indian hearts.

Much of the material now embodied in the ten chapters of
The Jesus of History had been long in Glover's mind, and had
been used in addresses given over many years. In 1903 or 1904,
the Baptist undergraduates who belonged to the Robert Hall
Society ran a club for street boys in the poorer part of Cambridge.

Discipline was sadly to seek, and an attempt to hold services for the boys on Sunday evenings proved a failure. But on one occasion the boys listened. It was when Glover talked to them about the boyhood of Jesus, and showed them how much could be learnt from the parables and sayings in the gospels about the conditions and surroundings in which Jesus grew to manhood. In what kind of house did Jesus live? A one-room tenement such as is implied in the story of the importunate friend. The householder whose slumbers are so rudely disturbed conducts a conversation with the disturber without going to the door. 'My children are with me in bed; I cannot rise and give thee!' This must have been one of the earliest occasions when Glover outlined the study which now forms chapter II of the book. Some other chapters are based on previous addresses in a similar manner, and of course the sketch of the character and influence of Jesus in *The Conflict of Religions* provided the basic study from which the book grew. But India gave Glover the opportunity to work out his interpretation of the gospel-portrait and narrative in more permanent form. When he reached Calcutta in January 1916, after three months in India, he was able to get the lectures taken down in shorthand and he began revising the typescript in February in Madras. Throughout the remainder of his stay in India he was rewriting these lectures. The Introduction, and the last chapter, 'Jesus in Christian Thought', were the last to take shape, the introduction being drafted at Poona in 14–17 August. Chapters II–VIII were sent off to Tatlow on 18 August. The introduction and chapters IX and X followed on 24 August. Chapter IX, 'The Church in the Roman Empire', had been delivered as a lecture no fewer than twenty-one times. The parallel between the Roman Empire and India seemed so important to Glover.

Tatlow received the manuscript on a day when he was due to travel a long distance northwards. He took it with him to read in the train and realized at once that it was a fresh and interesting approach to the life of Christ. He decided to ask the Archbishop of Canterbury, Randall T. Davidson, to write an introduction, which he consented to do. The brief introduction, which has been omitted from the latest reprint, reached Tatlow on 3 December 1916, with a covering letter in the Archbishop's own hand. His

chaplain, Dr C. K. A. Bell, now Bishop of Chichester, also enclosed a note in the envelope, saying 'the Archbishop is really
delighted with the book and is very pleased at having any part
in its issue'.[1] When the book was published early in 1917, the
Archbishop wrote to Glover, 'I have seldom been more keenly
interested in the reading of a book than I was in reading the
proof-sheets of *The Jesus of History*. For a long time I have wanted
to meet you face to face and to tell you how much I am indebted
to you for a great deal that you have written.' Later in the year
Glover met the Archbishop at Swanwick and at the end of
September he was the guest of the Archbishop and Mrs Davidson
at Lambeth, during a week-end when he was preaching at
Westminster Chapel.

This friendship was valued on both sides, though it exposed
both parties to it to some chaff and criticism. An unfriendly
review in *The Church Times* led to a correspondence, in which
Glover's orthodoxy was impugned. Some of the people who were
most hostile had admittedly never read the book. Tatlow writes,
'I remember talking over the attack on Glover with Archbishop
Davidson, who was himself attacked because he had written the
introduction to *The Jesus of History*.[2] Davidson was not in the
least shaken by the attack; he simply laughed and told me he
thought it was a very good book, taking a new and interesting
line, and that he was very glad to have written the introduction,
which I had asked him to write. On the other hand, some Nonconformist stalwarts thought the book would have been better
without the Archiepiscopal benediction, and one member of the
high table at St John's suggested that the Archbishop was angling
for Glover's adherence to the Church of England—a forlorn
hope indeed! There was of course no *arrière-pensée* in the Archbishop's appreciation of the book or in his friendship with the
author.

Glover's rather spiky Nonconformity was so well known, that
his friends liked to chaff him whenever he came into friendly

[1] *History of the S.C.M.* by Tissington Tatlow, p, 545.
[2] Under date 29 August 1917 Glover notes, '*The Church Times* had a letter last
week attacking the Archbishop for endorsing *The Jesus of History* because of Virgin-
Birth.' Glover makes only a passing reference to the birth-narratives in Matthew
and Luke, and dismisses Jerome's theory that the 'brothers' of Jesus were in
reality only cousins.

touch with Church dignitaries. During his tour of India, Bishop Waller of Madras had perpetrated a limerick:

> That Sphinx-like chameleon Glover,
> His principles none can discover;
> To be Baptist he'll claim
> But we see to his shame,
> That round bishops in gaiters he'll hover.

Glover might have replied with a quotation from Henry Sidgwick which appears in one of his commonplace books. 'Henry Sidgwick said the bishops were the most agreeable individuals of his acquaintance, but collectively they represented everything that he most detested.' Personally Glover's relations with bishops whom he met were as a rule most cordial. On occasion the most friendly bishop might have to act with caution, which Glover mistook for cowardice. Thus, his first visit to Madras, very early in his Indian tour, took place when the Kikuyu controversy was at its height. The Rev. E. Langdale-Smith, of Christ Church, Vepery, Madras invited Glover to preach at the evening service on 3 October 1915, and even announced him as preacher in the local press. But the Bishop felt obliged to refuse permission for reasons set forth in the following letter, addressed to Langdale-Smith.

I am sorry I cannot give leave. Personally I should be very glad to ask Mr Glover not only to preach at Christ Church but also to preach at the Cathedral, but as you know, at the present moment, there is violent agitation being carried on in England against that part of the Archbishop's decision on the Kikuyu controversy in which he stated that it was not contrary to the principles of the Church of England for Bishops to ask the members of other churches who are not in communion with the Church of England to preach in our churches, and I have recently received a pamphlet by Bishop Montgomery in which he makes a strong appeal to the Bishops of those dioceses in which the S.P.G. is working not to take any step in this direction which might cause very serious dissension in the ranks of the S.P.G. at home. Under these circumstances I feel I ought not to throw down the gauntlet and challenge a conflict with the S.P.G. without very serious consideration and also without consultation with the other Bishops of the Province. For this reason I am refusing your request on this occasion though I should wish personally to grant it. Will you kindly show this letter to Mr Glover so that he may know exactly why I have refused and give him my kindest regards?

Episcopal caution was clearly dictated by considerations of Church order and not by any doubts as to Glover's fitness to occupy the pulpit in Christ Church.

The publication of *The Jesus of History* did arouse misgivings in some quarters,'as had the chapter on Jesus in the Dale Lectures. But in general the book was warmly appreciated by readers, clerical and lay, of many different ways of thinking. One of the earliest tributes came from Neville Talbot who wrote, 'I simply revel in *The Jesus of History* and am reading it at this moment a second time.' On 16 June 1917, Glover records that at a Congregation in the Senate-house, 'Sir Clifford Allbutt said he had been reading *The Jesus of History* and was in sympathy. P. C. T. Crick, of Clare, chaplain now in France, asked, was I the author of the book everybody in France was talking about? It was thought the author seemed like a Catholic churchman!' Dr Alan Gray, the organist at Trinity College, and Arthur Gray, the Master of Jesus College, surprised Glover by the warmth of their appreciation. A letter from N. Wedd, of King's, particularly pleased him. Wedd wrote: 'I have just been reading a very beautiful book called *The Jesus of History*. You bring one nearer than anybody I know to the loveliest person in history.'

Such expressions of gratitude were frequent and came from unexpected quarters. But naturally the book did not escape criticism. A belated notice by a Unitarian critic in the *Hibbert Journal* (January 1918), claimed first that the absence of orthodox catchwords from the book showed orthodoxy developing into Unitarianism, and second, that the book makes extravagant claims for Jesus, incompatible with Unitarianism! One Sunday in May 1918, a Girton student came to tea at Glisson Road and reported that Bishop Gore in a University sermon that afternoon had coupled the author of *The Jesus of History*, 'whose orthodoxy is doubtful', with the atheist poet Shelley and the author of *Ecce Homo*, as bad guides for the Church. Old Dr Bonney, the geologist, a great friend of Glover and his family, assured him that the reference to *The Jesus of History* 'was made only in passing, but in a significant connexion—and as implying union of thought with diversity in practice and order'. However, when Glover read Gore's sermon in the *Cambridge Review*, he seemed to think the Girton girl was right. The reference is as follows: 'They [men and women] want to know why the Church has so largely and so long forgotten a great part of its true message— why it was left to a reputed atheist like Shelley, and to men rather off orthodoxy, like the authors of *Ecce Homo* and *The Jesus of History*, to present to us those undoubtedly historical aspects of the teaching of Jesus which appeal most to what is best in the modern world.' Glover may have resented the description of himself as a man rather off orthodoxy, but the reference is clearly appreciative. So far from denouncing Shelley, Seeley and Glover as bad guides, Gore suggested that they were marshalling the Church the way she ought to go, and in fact he frequently advised candidates for the General Ordination Examination to read Glover's book.[1]

The Jesus of History had a large circulation both in this country and in America. Within three years, some 50,000 copies had been sold and, by 1928, double that number had been reached. The substantial royalties enabled Glover to meet the cost of the higher education of his daughters, and the profits accruing to the Student Christian Movement helped to start the S.C.M. Press as a publishing company. At a much later date, when the centre of interest in the study of the Gospels was beginning to shift from history to theology, and from Jesus to the Church—for this, after all, is the real significance of form-criticism—a rather gauche American scholar opined that Glover had written his book as a pot-boiler and not as a serious contribution to the interpretation of the Gospels. Curiously enough, Dr C. C. McCown in his admirable survey of a century of historical study, *The Search for the Real Jesus*, makes no reference to Glover, though he deals with both Seeley and Middleton Murry. Such a disparaging estimate and such neglect are not justified. The high seriousness of Glover's contribution is beyond question. What Dr Macnicol reports of his lectures in India is true of the book. 'It has been claimed that as he reflected during this tour on this subject and

---

[1] Speaking to undergraduates in the Guildhall on 28 January 1923, E. W. Barnes told them to read *The Jesus of History*, 'one of the prophetic writings of our time, and if you have read it, read it again!'

gave his thoughts utterance, his own faith in the Man of whom
he spoke attained a new depth of conviction.' Here I may
interject that the environment contributed to this deepening of
conviction. A great deal lies behind the sentence in *The Jesus of
History*, "Those who know the heathen world intimately will
know best the difference he [Jesus] has made." That Glover's
faith in Jesus deepened in India is certainly true. 'He spoke with
an intimacy and a sincerity that his hearers could not mistake.
They were of many kinds, learned and unlearned, broad and
narrow, but to them all he made their common Master live with
a fresh sense of his reality. As he says in the preface to the book,
his aim was "to deepen our interest in Jesus and our love of him".
That that aim was achieved is surely proved by the eagerness
with which this little book was received and read by multitudes
over the world.'

When a writer announces his aims in such terms, radical critics
may suspect that he will sacrifice scholarship to sentiment. This
suspicion underlies the disparaging estimates already cited. That
Glover's interpretations of particular details are sometimes fanciful and improbable, must be admitted. His characterization of
the element of irony in the teaching of Jesus as humour has not
convinced many. His violent reaction from the thoroughgoing
eschatology of Albert Schweitzer and others led him to under-
estimate the sense of crisis in the ministry of Jesus. But it is the
great merit of the book, that it anticipates and exposes the defects
of the now fashionable form-criticism. Radical critics like the
late Charles Guignebert insist on finding nothing in the teaching
of Jesus which cannot be found in contemporary Judaism. If
Jesus used terms like 'the Kingdom of God' and 'Messiah', he
cannot have meant by them anything that his disciples or his
hearers could not immediately understand. On this approach to
the Gospels which is typical of the modern *Religions-geschichtliche*
school, Glover seems to me to have said *le mot juste*:

It is always bad criticism to give to the words of genius the value
or the connotation they would have on the lips of ordinary
people. To a great mind words are charged with a fulness of
meaning that little people do not reach. The attempt has been
made to recapture more of his thoughts by learning the value
given to some of the terms he uses as they appear in the literature

of the day, and of course it has been helpful. But we have to remember always that the words as used by him come with a new volume of significance derived from his whole personality.

The present phase of criticism with its exaggerated depreciation of the historical value of the Synoptic tradition will pass, and as it passes, the value of Glover's contribution will stand out more clearly. *The Jesus of History* is rightly associated with *Ecce Homo* and with Middleton Murry's *Jesus, Man of Genius*. All three are works of writers whose interests are in history and literature rather than theology. Of the three, *The Jesus of History*, now the most neglected, will be found to be the most illuminating.

The Jesus of History was not the only book of Glover's published during the war. Before he left for India, Methuen had accepted for publication a series of essays on English literature which appeared in the spring of 1915 under the title, *Poets and Puritans*. Later on Glover was inclined to regret the issue of this volume. His friend A. R. Waller, who edited so many English classics for the Cambridge University Press, advised against the publication of these essays. Glover was trespassing on other people's pre-serves, and the specialists in the field he was invading would detect weaknesses. In Cambridge the tendency is to insist that the cobbler shall stick to his last. Glover thought that the book prejudiced his recognition as a pure classical scholar. The book did not sell well, and the title was not an adequate umbrella for the contents. It included essays on Evelyn and Boswell, and 'an acute young critic, who saw some of the proofs has asked, with a hint of irony, whether Evelyn and Boswell were Puritans or Poets'. Nevertheless, as Mr Vernon Rendall points out, these essays are 'plainly the work of a man who has enjoyed his reading'. Glover lays it down in his preface that 'the real business of the critic is to find out what is right with a great work of art—book, song, picture or statue—not what is wrong. Plenty of things may be wrong but it is what is right that really counts.' The essayist in this volume knows his real business and the essays are happy in their appreciations. His inclusion of Boswell and Evelyn shows how Glover is always for wide tolerance.

He points out that the Olney hymns had on their title-page a motto from Virgil, claiming the Arcadians as the only skilled singers. 'Satire calls for wit and Cowper had humour, for hate

and Cowper was incapable of it.' Dealing with Bunyan, Glover
is on his own ground, with a man who will not give up his
religion, whatever is done to him. In prison Bunyan insists, 'I am
for going on'; and Glover adds, '"ἀλλὰ καὶ ἔμπης οὐ λήξω", says
Achilles in a great passage in the *Iliad*. Death is imminent, he is
told, if he does not forbear to fight against Troy; and he knows
it, he rejoins, "and for all that I will not forbear"....' The
difficult task of defending Carlyle's attitude to life is tackled with
as much success as could be expected.

These parerga of Glover's genius have their merits. He con-
veys to the reader his own enjoyment in his reading, and he
keeps ever before us the function of literature as an interpretation
and enrichment of life. Yet these essays were parerga, and they
did not divert Glover from his main interest in the Classics. Nor
was he neglecting the Classics during his tour in India. He must
have taken quite a library with him. He certainly reread
Herodotus and Tacitus, to say nothing of the *Odyssey*, and he
seems to have dipped again into Thucydides and Xenophon,
Aeschylus and Longinus. Each of these authors inspired sonnets,
most of which appeared in the *Westminster Gazette* in the course
of 1916–17. Herodotus he read again in Burma and found him
'delightfuller than ever'. After all, India had been on the fringe
and almost part of the world Herodotus described.

> You come and tell us of so many things—
> Satraps and oracles—Nile and Italy,
> And fairy tales as splendid as there be—
> The Phoenix with his father on his wings—
> Great marvels of Greek art—strange fates of kings—
> Soils, climate, customs and the Southern Sea—
> And how Greek citizens battled to be free,
> And all the breadth of soul that freedom brings.
>
> You loved your story and the things it shows,
> Dear critic, who part doubt and part believe,
> Lean, like the Greek you are, to what man knows,
> Yet hold that in long time and other lands
> God may do stranger things than Greeks conceive—
> You who have met such wonders on all hands.

Glover confidently appealed to Herodotus to counter the foolish
assumption that the presence of miracle discredits the Gospels as
historical authorities.

An ancient writer is not necessarily negligible because he records, and perhaps believes, miracles or marvels or omens which a modern world would never notice. It is bad criticism that has made a popular legend of the unreliable character of Herodotus. As our knowledge of antiquity grows and we become able to correct our early impressions, the credit of Herodotus rises steadily and to-day those who study him most closely have the highest opinion of him.

This judgement was to be defended in detail in the Sather Lectures on Herodotus which Glover delivered in Berkeley, California, some years later.

Naturally as he reread historians and dramatists at this time, he was most interested in their war-time experience. An early schoolboy sonnet on Aeschylus attempted to appraise his difficult style. Composing another at Poona, Glover recalls that the poet fought at Marathon. The sonnet ends:

> No more of words and guesses; facts abide;
> He fought for Athens and in exile died.

Perhaps in rereading Tacitus, Glover found that which most nearly expressed his own feelings about the war.

> At Kodaikanal in the Palni hills,
>> While Europe in self-slaughter rocked and bled,
>> The tale of Tacitus once again I read—
> How brother, wife, and mother Nero kills
> And how his jealousy festers, till he fills
>> Rome with the blood and fame of innocent dead,
>> Then burns the city itself. 'The gods, 'tis said,'
> Adds Tacitus, 'seem indifferent to mens' ills.'
>
> Each day there came fresh word of thousands slain,
>> In quarrels not their own, to keep or take
> A fortress on a frontier. And again
>> Rose the old question—what does heaven make
> Of life and death, of sin and human pain,
>> Of men cut off and womens' hearts that break?

When he was invited to lecture in India on occasions that were social and academic rather than specifically religious, he chose such topics as Euripides, with special reference to the *Troades*, and 'What do we owe to Greece?' He was also glad to talk about Cambridge, particularly glad if, as happened at Madura, he had a jovial Oxford man in the chair! His sojourn in India deepened his affection for Cambridge and he ended his lecture at Madura with the closing verses of a tribute to his own University written during a visit to Oxford in the summer of 1915. Glover's *Alma Mater Cantabrigiensis* cannot compare with the poem in praise of Oxford which clearly inspired it. Oxford critics may legitimately resent the implied criticisms of their own Alma Mater and it should be possible to praise Cambridge without depreciating Oxford. Yet it expresses well Glover's feelings and convictions about Cambridge.

> 'Tis not the Oxonian's somewhat heightened passion
>   That thrills our spirits, when of thee we dream;
> We feel for thee in quite another fashion,
>   Such as might well beseem
>   The children of a rather colder clime,
> Whose slower blood throbs not to fancy or to rhyme.
>
> The place—Heav'n help us! 'tis a cheerless region,
>   Featureless miles of fen and flat and fen;
> And 'Camus footing slow' amid a legion
>   Of sluggish brooks; and then
>   The yellow brick, all that harsh Nature yields
> To build dull rows of streets upon her own dull fields.
>
> Yet take the Northward road, the Romans' planning,
>   Via Devana, some time in October,
> Heav'n lies most strangely open for your scanning,
>   And from the dull and sober
>   East Anglian scene your eyes seek plains of sky
> That wider far and vaster than you dreamed do lie.
>
> Dull is the countryside, yet those slow waters—
>   Gliding in peace beneath the ancient walls,
> Founded for God by great kings and their daughters,
>   Chapels and courts and halls—
>   Keep the grass green; the elms stand unsurpassed
> And lilac flowers each spring more glorious than the last.
>
> Our old grey Alma Mater runs not riot
>   With swift 'great movements,' seeks no dim 'wide views';
> No, but she puts, in earnest mood and quiet,
>   A challenge to be true—
>   True to the fact and loyal in the quest
> Of knowledge; *that* once gained, content she leaves the rest.

Dear grey old Mother! quick to curb our fancies,
How I have chafed against thy cautious mood!
And yet where'er my restless spirit glances,
I feel thee in my blood,
And, checking, thank kind Fortune that my youth
Knew thy controlling hand, thy steady love of truth.

Returning to Cambridge in the autumn of 1916, Glover spent two academic years there until, in the summer of 1918, he was asked to undertake a further spell of work for the Y.M.C.A., training their candidates for service at home and abroad in their institute at Mildmay, London. His responsibilities as lecturer in Ancient History were naturally light during the two remaining years of the war. The numbers attending his lectures were inevitably small, and his work as classical tutor was likewise on a small scale. But in the course of 1917, his first contribution to the study of Greek history, *From Pericles to Philip*, was published. It established his claim to recognition in this field. He could no longer be regarded as a pure Latinist. His old tutor, W. E. Heitland, who was not easily satisfied, welcomed it enthusiastically. In the *Cambridge Review* he described the book as 'full of light all through'. He praised the vital coherency of the chapters, which seemed to him to be 'inter-illuminative'. In 'this stirring and delightful book', he was particularly impressed by 'the masterly and deeply sympathetic handling of Euripides'. This book had been long on the anvil. The manuscript had been submitted to Methuen in 1915, but they had not considered publishing it while Glover was in India. As he read the proofs in 1917, Glover says, 'I have found new links of sympathy with the men of whom I wrote. Their experience is strangely like what ours has been and will be—the strain of a long war, the readjustment of all life to conditions that raise question and doubt, the endeavour to refound society and to find anew a base from which the soul can make all its own again. Much that I wrote has been given for me a new meaning.' Many others found this record of human experience relevant to war-time and post-war conditions. Glover was interested to receive a letter from Lady Courtney in July 1918 soon after the death of her husband, in which she said *From Pericles to Philip* was the last book she and Lord Courtney read together; 'he was so interested in it that he

passed more than one copy on to friends, including one to
Mr Merriman at Cape Town.' A year later Glover met Arnold
Bennett at lunch in the rooms of W. H. Rivers. Bennett said,
'I was told to read your book from Somebody to Somebody else,
if I wanted to understand ancient life. So I got it and read half
of it, but it made my brain reel; you know such a hell of a lot.'
Perhaps Bennett found the chapter on the House of Pasion too
much for him. In spite of his knowledge of law, banking and
shipping in Athens, it was difficult even for Glover to unravel
and clarify all the details of the lawsuits in which the House of
Pasion was involved. But throughout the book, the author's
mastery of detail is most impressive. The book sold well and
reached a third edition by 1920.

The new meanings which Glover found particularly in his
studies of Thucydides, Athens in war-time, and Euripides were
brought home to him by the undermining of justice, humanity
and generosity through war-fever. He had not been quite so
conscious of this in India, as he became on his return home. The
passing of the Conscription Act in the summer of 1916 had
distressed him, and when the Rev. Henry Carter at Emmanuel
Church in Cambridge was in trouble, particularly with some of
the older deacons and wealthier supporters, because of his pacifist
convictions, Glover wrote from India to encourage him.[1] But
in the autumn of 1916 so far as civilian morale and public
opinion were concerned things seemed to be going from bad to
worse. 1917 brought no improvement. Decent business men
thought Henry Carter should be shot, and were quite willing to
bomb German women and children to win the war. A clergyman
in Hull is fined for giving cigarettes to German prisoners of war.[2]

[1] I want to say, Don't be dismayed (you won't be, I know) nor depressed (you
may be), and above all don't let any of this put an edge to your tongue anyway.
If you keep sweet and smiling, if you go on preaching as I heard you do it, right
from the sanctuary itself with the impress of the vision upon you—all will go well.
Some people will talk against you, a little local paper may print its poor little
pressmen's paragraphs, some will say you can't preach because you don't run on—
but men and women will go on finding you a blessing and an inspiration, and you
will help them to face life and trust Christ, when they see and know—by instinct
and by seeing your own stigmata (Gal. vi)—where you have been and with whom
you have been spending your life. As Paul said, The Lord will stand by your side
and put strength in you, ἐνδυναμόω (read your G.T. and use Gk. Concordance).
[2] On this episode Glover wrote a sonnet suggesting a change of vowels from
'u' to 'e' in the name of the city on the Humber!

The prejudice of the Tribunals makes hay of the provision for tender consciences in the Conscription Act. The Cambridge Tribunal is particularly obnoxious. But all over the country hundreds are being sent to prison who ought not to be there, and there was the crowning scandal of Rendel Wyatt and other conscientious objectors being sentenced to death by court-martial in France. Happily the sentence was never carried out.

College Councils are likewise affected. Trinity deprives Bertrand Russell of his Fellowship and St John's treats some of its younger men unfairly. A peace-feeler from Germany in December 1916, of which Glover thought something might have come, is incontinently turned down in the inflamed state of public opinion. Lloyd George and Bonar Law oust Asquith and Sir Edward Grey in the same month. Glover's sympathies are with Asquith. He thinks the new government will be short-lived. It will be the end of Lloyd George. At least it ought to be. 'Had Zimri peace who slew his master?' The poorest elements in the Press seem to have the greatest influence. They make and unmake governments and betray the ideals for which it is supposed the war is fought. The Russian revolution is a warning against the folly of repression. In November and December 1917 Glover seeks relief for his feelings in a series of sonnets somewhat in the vein of Wordsworth's patriotic sonnets.

> One mark there is of all bad government—
>   Fear of the people, fear of thought and light—
>   An instinct to work ever out of sight,
> Lest knowledge prove the nurse of discontent—
> To stifle all free speech, deny all vent
>   To judgement, genius, sense of wrong and right,
>   Till empire base itself alone on might,
> Unhelped of understanding or consent.
>
> In vain the dark endeavour! Soon or late
>   As once in France, in Russia at this time,
> An ignorant people, like a stream in spate,
>   Sweeps all away, deluged with rage and crime.
> England! The choice before thee lies to-day
> Thine own old Freedom or Reaction's sway!
>
>   (5 December 1917)

He was of course swimming against the tide. When the war ended, he did what he could to stem and reverse the tide of public opinion during the coupon election. A letter to *The Times* on 4 December 1918 about the cry, 'Hang the Kaiser', was at least a blow for sanity.

> The growing demand to 'do something' to the ex-Kaiser is distressing to anyone who looks ahead, or who cherishes a feeling for British magnanimity.
> In or about 1836 the British Government reprieved some, but not all, of a group of Boers condemned to death, and the martyrs of Slager's Nek achieved an immortality which they hardly deserved, and which did South Africa no good. General Botha was wiser with De Wet. The man trusted the Germans, made a rebellion, and let loose ruin and death on his friends and countrymen—and was dismissed, stript of all possibility of pose or martyrdom, discredited, and never to be rehabilitated. What a gain to South Africa and to us all!
> How much did the death of Charles I contribute—with the pathetic book published in his name—to the return of Charles II, whether we think it desirable or undesirable?
> Wilhelm II cannot be revived except by ill-advised action on the part of the Allies. I hope they will let him go and live in Spain or Mexico, in such a degree of wealth and comfort as will forever keep him outside the sympathies of his people. This would, I believe, be the wisest policy.
> If, with the Greek dramatist, we believe that the hand of God brings down the mighty and overturns *hybris*, I for one feel that man is better advised not to touch what is done. And since I have alluded to Greek thought, it is an old Homeric virtue not 'to boast over men slain'. I think, too, that in an hour of judgement we English people should recall ideals higher than Greeks knew. We none of us like the fallen man, we never did; he was our enemy; he is fallen, thank God; and let us leave it with God with whom we also must reckon.

It is not surprising perhaps that during this period he was restless and even wondered whether he should do well to return to Canada. He had received an invitation from Kingston in July 1916, and declined it. In April 1918 came an invitation from Toronto. McMaster University had given him an honorary degree of Doctor of Laws a month or two before, and now they offered him the Latin Chair at a salary of $4000, and a pension of

$2400 at 65. He was tempted. He received no encouragement from his closest friends. Larmor was against his going to Toronto, on the grounds that the pay was not enough, and that 'my standing is due in measure to my being in Cambridge; my work, writing, can be done as well here'. When he submitted the problem in a letter to W. B. Selbie, who had succeeded Fairbairn as Principal of Mansfield College, Oxford, the advice to stay in Cambridge was still more forcibly expressed.

I slept—or rather lay awake—over your letter last night and am quite clear that there is nothing in it to shake my conviction that you ought not to leave Cambridge. Canada can offer you no opportunity comparable to the one you have now, and that opportunity will be very much greater and more serious after the war. I don't think anything you have done yet can be compared with what you might do in the new time that is coming. Your influence with young men and women will tell enormously then, and you ought to use it here. Canada is not the same kind of field and the need there is not so great. When I think of what has happened to the young men who ought to have carried on our work I feel that it is up to me and you and men like us to give ourselves, as freely as they did, in the spiritual warfare which is upon us. And without any silly patriotism, I can't but think that to go away from England just now, would be something very like desertion. You have won a great position here among thinking men and women, and you ought not to surrender it just when things are most critical, and when you are most able to pull your weight. Forgive me too if I say that the mere question of a somewhat better pension in prospect is a trifle that ought not to be considered beside the weightier matters involved. There are too many 'oughts' about this—but that is how it shapes itself to me.

The counsel of his friends prevailed.

In the summer of 1918, he was working again for the Y.M.C.A. in London, and found himself in uniform, the grey Y.M.C.A. uniform—a month or two before the war ended. He was the more attracted to this work of training leaders, because he was to be associated with D. S. Cairns whom he had met at Swanwick and for whom he had a profound admiration. Cairns' addresses to students impressed Glover very much as Kelman's had done a few years earlier. Writing to Tissington Tatlow in 1913, he says, 'you have done me a heap of service in hitching me on to your movement—more than I can say; David Cairns has been an immense help to me.' Like Kelman, Cairns was very effective in a mission in Cambridge in the Lent term, 1914. Glover wrote, 'Cairns has done very well here—some six to seven hundred every time and all he says well taken.' During the war, Cairns had thrown himself into the work of the Y.M.C.A., and few men were better qualified than he to draw up the report on the Army and religion. To work in harness with Cairns was a stimulating experience for Glover.

The months he spent at Mildmay Park gave him the opportunity of working out a sequel to *The Jesus of History*, which was later published under the title *Jesus in the Experience of Men*. According to Tatlow, Glover wrote this book in order that people who suspected his orthodoxy might be reassured. Cairns who heard Glover's lectures on such themes as 'The Lamb of God' and 'The Judgement-seat of Christ' says that his struggle with Unitarianism was patent. But Cairns was doubtful about the lectures and the book. He distrusted Glover as a theologian and thought he had best stick to history. Cairns was a frank if friendly critic. He detected the weakness of Glover's verse, 'sometimes very well, but never more than *proxime accessit*'. So when he read the proofs of *Jesus in the Experience of Men*, he did indeed recant his first description of it as 'Moonbeams', and generously recognized its merits ('the book has a definite and noble message and in places rises to real brilliance—really advances things—nobody but you could have written it', he told Glover), but nevertheless 'it wants something done to it to be first-rate—very few books are first-rate; structure is the weakness'. Admittedly, the book is uneven. Glover laboured over it and changed much of the manuscript which Cairns criticized, before the book was published in 1920. But even so, the criticism was still relevant. The review in the *British Weekly* underlined the weaknesses Cairns detected. After some genial praise, the reviewer declared that 'theologically, the author has never grown up and this explains both his strength and his weakness as a Christian teacher'. The chapter on the Lamb of God and on Forgiveness were described as painfully shallow and inadequate. Even admirers felt this to be true. C. E. Raven wrote enthusiastically to say how vastly he had enjoyed the book. He, like the reviewer in the *British Weekly*, disagreed with the chapter on Sacrifice. But of the book as a whole he wrote, 'I say quite frankly that it seems to me a bigger and finer piece of work than *The Jesus of History* and I can't say more.' In intent and scope no doubt it is a bigger and finer piece of work; in achievement it is not so satisfying. What Glover was attempting was beyond any one man's power to attain. But if this essay was inevitably in a sense a failure, it was immensely worth while. It set many to explore the unsearchable riches of Christ, as one grateful reader said.

Chapter VII

CAMBRIDGE, 1919-1923

Proctor : Public Orator : Wilde Lecturer : *Progress in Religion*:
the Prime Minister's Committee : Yale offer : College Councils

In the Lent term 1919 Glover was nominated by St John's as pro-Proctor. He was able to end his commitment to the Y.M.C.A. in February, and he at once resumed his duties 'on the prowl at night on the track of erring youth'. In the following session, 1919–20, he was Senior Proctor. This was his second term of office as he had been Proctor in the year before the war. He had shaped well then and he was nominated with some confidence as the man to handle some of the difficult problems of discipline in the year after the war. There were special difficulties occasioned by the presence of many naval and military officers and many ex-service men who could not easily adjust themselves to the traditional discipline of the University. Glover's appointment was fully justified. His firmness tempered with humour maintained the authority of his office, and he was respected and liked by undergraduates. Very early in his career, he encountered a member of Jesus College coming out of the 'Chimney' and smoking in cap and gown. The man protested against being progged before he had really emerged from college. So Glover gave him thirty yards start, and the youth escaped. Sir Geoffrey Shakespeare relates a similar episode.[1] He met Glover one Sunday morning on Parker's Piece. 'I was without cap and gown.... He was without his bulldogs. He asked me to explain my breach of the regulations. "Can you take cognizance of my offence", I asked, "if you are not on full parade with your bulldogs?" His reply was typical. "The King is King even in his bath. I will give you one hundred yards start."' Needless to say there was no pursuit!

One or two examples of such conduct by the Proctor established his reputation as a sportsman among undergraduates. He was sufficiently popular to intervene effectively on difficult

---

[1] *Let Candles be brought in*, p. 25.

occasions. He was not on duty on 7 March when a Socialist meeting held in the Friends' Meeting House, Jesus Lane, was ragged by undergraduates and naval and military officers, and the speakers were ducked in the Cam. But in October he had to deal with a disturbance at the New Theatre. On Saturday, 25 October, he records, 'Proctored and was 'phoned for to theatre, where trouble. Stink-bombs had been released, smoking was going on, though forbidden: disorder. I sent four home for smoking and six for making trouble.' The following Monday he appeared on the stage, and appealed for a better feeling of comradeship in the following terms:

> The Manager has kindly allowed me a moment to say how much we all regret that the pleasure of all who were here on Saturday was interfered with, as it was.
> I want to say that the Proctors take a serious view of the matter, and will, if the need arises, take strong action. But I prefer to put the matter on a different basis.
> We have all of us, Town and Gown alike, been through five bad years. Those years have brought a certain comradeship, and we want that to continue. We want to come to this place with mutual respect and mutual friendship, and to carry into the enjoyments of peace the comradeship of the years of war.
> Never again, I trust, will there be occasion for a Proctor to be seen across the footlights.

The short speech was loudly applauded and many undergraduates called for an encore.

Incidentally as Proctor, Glover saw more of theatrical life and of actual stage-performances than he had ever seen before. He seldom if ever went to the theatre. He discouraged a proposal from the Fews to take his daughters Mary and Anna to see *Peter Pan*, and when some years later the three older girls went up to London to stay with an aunt, and to combine a shopping expedition with a theatre, he notes that 'Berrycroft ideas as to the last outweigh Bristol up to the present'. But he watched performances at the New Theatre when proctorial duty required his presence, and he made shrewd comments on some of the acts he witnessed. The *Granta* sketch of him as one of 'those amazingly in authority' declares: 'The Senior Proctor is not a member of the Footlights [a University dramatic club]. But I think he'd like to

be. At any rate, he's always about when they have a show on.'
Certainly as Proctor, he did not neglect the theatre, but otherwise he never went except for Greek plays. He did not care for
the cinema either. On board ship he would go to film-shows but,
on shore, the cinema had no attractions for him.

His duties as Proctor also brought him into closer association
with licenced premises than he had experienced hitherto. Knowing him to be a strict teetotaller, his friends had been unusually
intrigued when he had had to serve on a jury, to try an action for
libel brought by a publican against his vicar. Would Glover's
prejudice against drink outweigh his prejudice against the
Church, or vice versa? Actually the truculence of the publican's
counsel ensured Glover's sympathy with the vicar but though he
was foreman of the jury, he could not persuade them to agree on
a verdict. Before he laid down his office as Proctor, it was said
that he knew the front and back doors of every public house in
Cambridge.

Guy Fawkes Day and Armistice Day, 5 and 11 November,
always strained to the utmost the Proctors' powers of discipline
and persuasion. For 1919 Glover records his activities thus:

5 November. Market Place and Petty Cury 8.30 to 10.30 p.m.
Crowds getting up to thousands, surging about doing nothing
but waiting to see what may be done: sent home about 160 undergraduates, taking names of 147; about £7 in fines. I was hustled
by townees swarming round, but rescued by police, foot and
mounted: University men volunteered to help me at a difficult
moment.

On 11 November he was in reserve while a colleague was on
duty, but

about 8.20 the police 'phoned for Senior Proctor on the Market.
Too late! a bonfire in full blaze with snow falling into it (pretty
effect): big ring of undergraduates round it: good temper and
excitement prevailed and folly: huge crowds of townees. Police
and Proctor could do very little. Lavis [one of Glover's bulldogs]
had his face cut by townee weapon. Going round Guildhall in
a flank movement I caught two undergraduates and overheard,
'Damned luck! Damned sound Proctor'. Meanwhile riots outside the theatre and behind the Leys School and outside Newnham. Home after midnight, tired out.

Perhaps the worst rag with which Glover had to deal was that known as the Norman Angell rag on 1 March 1920. The Proctors met in the afternoon, anticipating trouble in connexion with a meeting arranged by the Union of Democratic Control in the lecture hall at St Andrew's Street, at which Norman Angell was to speak. Political feeling still ran high, and naval officers and ex-service men were still as ready as a year ago to resort to violence to express their feelings. The Proctors took certain measures to maintain order, but they proved inadequate. Glover says:

After hall I was abruptly called by the police on the 'phone. So from 8.30 to 12 at that. First, kept sending crowds at door of St Andrew's Street away; then in and pled for free speech and heckling: I had flour bag thrown at me and then 'He's a jolly good fellow' sung. A naval officer fell from outside window and was badly hurt. Crowds of undergraduates outside were got rid of, exit of meeting and worse jams. Norman Angell was rescued by the police. The wall of Merton House was thrown down.

The rag was over about 11.15, and then Glover had to deal with the Welsh Society and with an undergraduate in the police station. 'So to bed about 12.30.' The police had great confidence in Glover's handling of such occasions, and his appointment was highly approved by them.

A more entertaining interlude was provided by the issue of the prospectus of the Emmanuel College Insurance Society against proctorial risk. There were to be two policies, A, covering the risks of ordinary fines except on 5 and 11 November and provided the insured party did not incur more than two fines a term; and B, providing a dinner for four persons and a first-class fare home for any insured party who was sent down. On 17 November 1919 the *Daily Mail* splashed an article about this new society, and by the end of the week the detailed prospectus was printed in a long notice in the local press. The Proctors could not ignore it, and Geoffrey Shakespeare, whose name stood first among the directors was summoned to the presence. He has related the incident in his volume of reminiscences *Let Candles be brought in*.

I received a summons from T. R. Glover, the Senior Proctor, to call upon him [the day after the article appeared in the *Daily Mail*]. 'T.R.' was one of the celebrities of Cambridge: he was leonine in appearance and his conversation was punctuated with picturesque flashes of wit. The interview was rather embarrassing to proctor and progged, for T.R.G. was an old friend of my father [Rev. J. H. Shakespeare, then Secretary of the Baptist Union] and was one of our prominent Baptist laymen. The conversation was something like this: 'How dare you treat the University regulations with contempt?' I assumed an expression of surprised innocence: 'But, Sir, we expressly advise our members to obey the University regulations.' I produced my trump card: 'I am sure Mr Raven [the Dean of Emmanuel] would never have joined our Board, if such an interpretation could be put on our activities.' This was a real brute to answer, because the Proctor could not condemn me without censuring his sub-Proctor. In the end I was fined one pound which I cheerfully paid.

I am not sure that Glover was as surprised by the trump-card as Sir Geoffrey supposes. Anyway he had decided to treat the matter as a joke, and knew it would soon die a natural death.

One unique achievement lent distinction to Glover's tenure of office. On Tuesday, 24 February 1920, he was on duty as Proctor outside the Union, waiting to catch unwary debaters offending against University regulations as they left the debating hall. He was chatting with Captain Fullerton who seemed interested in the system of discipline, and who then and there had the interesting experience of seeing the bulldog, Lavis, stop one of the Princes who was smoking in academic dress as he came out of the Union. It was the Duke of York, later King George VI, who was then in residence along with the Duke of Gloucester. Major Greig, the Princes' equerry, dashed over and said he could not have it, but when Glover insisted, he said, 'All right, go on.' Fullerton thought it democratic and congratulated Glover on his tact. The next day he received a letter from Major Greig. 'I hope you do not think we were uncivil in any way, and the Princes sent me along to say that they are extremely wishful to pay the necessary fine.... If you would rather they came and saw you themselves, this will be done.' However Glover did not send for them: he sent Lavis round with the usual fine notice, in an envelope addressed to Major Greig. Lavis did well out of it, for he saw the Princes who asked him questions for a quarter of an hour and were evidently keenly pleased. They gave him a drink and he asked for their autographs and got them!

Some years later when the Duke of York was receiving an honorary degree, Major Greig told Glover that the King, George V, had been greatly pleased at his proctorizing the Duke. The Duke himself remembered the occasion with pleasure. When C. E. Raven, a Royal Chaplain, was at Sandringham in 1921, the Duke of York referred to the Proctor who had proctorized him by name and sent his remembrances. He also recalled Lavis's visit. At the centenary dinner of the Union in November the same year, the Duke of York referred in a speech to the Proctor episode and talked with Glover about it. King George VI since referred to that cigarette as the most expensive he ever smoked![1]

Glover did not owe his popularity to any slackness. He was vigilant in enforcing discipline, and particularly cautious in sanctioning dances and the attendance of undergraduates at dances. But when he came to the end of his term of office, *The Morning Post* had a paragraph describing him as 'A Great Prog'. Its tribute concluded with the story of a man who was sent down for a serious offence, while Glover was Proctor, with Mr Rushmore of St Catharine's as his colleague, and who was given a public funeral. 'The hearse which took the "body" to the station bore the words, "Messrs Glovemore and Rusher, undertakers".' When trouble, particularly with naval officers, was most serious in November 1919, one of Glover's colleagues at St John's could assure him, 'there isn't a don better liked than you in the University; you don't know how men think about you'. His experience in Canada and his liking for men of action stood him in good stead as Proctor. He enjoyed the office though he found it exacting.

On the last day of 1919, the papers announced the resignation of Sir John Sandys from the office of Public Orator in the University which he had held for forty-three years. Glover at once decided to stand for it. This involved an election and the disagreeable necessity of canvassing votes. When he consulted the Master of St John's, R. F. Scott, who had been elected

[1] Sir Geoffrey Shakespeare, *Let Candles be brought in*, p. 23.

Master on the death of Charles Taylor in 1908, he was assured of the support of his college, and the Master naughtily suggested that if everyone whose toes he had trodden on voted for him, Glover was sure of the election! John E. Marr, the geologist, had said to him on an earlier occasion. 'You disagree with everybody and get on with most people, I notice'. Though Glover was early in the field and his candidature had widespread and influential support, his election was by no means assured. It was customary for the Council to nominate two candidates, and almost at the last moment W. T. Vesey[1] of Caius College stood. Among the few who announced their intention of voting for W. T. Vesey, was Professor William Ridgeway. Ridgeway was a close friend of Glover's, but he was an eccentric fighting Irishman, and he feared that Glover would never do justice to great soldiers and sailors. After the election, Ridgeway realized that his fear was groundless as the following letter shows.

Your letter just received not only heaps coals of fire on my head but makes me realize, still more, if that were possible, your noble, generous and straightforward character. In one respect I differ from you—your very exaggerated statement of anything that I ever tried to do for you. Let me now congratulate you and Mrs Glover most sincerely on your election. My wife has just been in and bids me give you her very best congratulations. She is ever a keen admirer of yours. The irony of the situation was that I supported a candidate to whom I have not spoken for many years against one of my very best friends. Your declaration that by July 1st you will have made me repent what I said respecting your attitude to great soldiers and sailors, gives me unfeigned pleasure.

No one will rejoice more in your success as Public Orator, and in having to make a public recantation than your old and ever attached friend.

                                        WILLIAM RIDGEWAY

More serious misgivings were entertained by those who feared Glover's militant Nonconformity. Conservatives in Cambridge were reluctant to see a Nonconformist in an office which up till now had been held by Churchmen. But others than Conservatives were doubtful whether Glover would present sympathetically Church dignatories for honorary degrees. His friend,

---

[1] Better known as W. T. Lendrum.

Leonard Whibley, hesitated on this ground. When Glover wrote and asked for his support, he replied,

> It *had* occurred to me that you might like to be Orator—but I wondered whether you would find yourself able to speak words of good omen about bishops, colonial and other, deans *et hoc genus omne*. If you are ready to praise such men without excessive irony or approach to satire, you can count me as a supporter. I am serious in my reservation. You will not mind my being thus blunt and frank. Frankness has always characterized our conversation.

A letter from Glover reassured him. Whibley wrote: .

> I took the colonial bishops as a type—you took the reference literally. What was in my mind was that the Orator has to give praise to many whose claim to be mentioned is the *jus dignitatis* which carries the degree. And you, as a Free Churchman, have a temptation to be a little intolerant in your freedom. But I know that you would honestly realize the responsibility of the office. I agree with you about politicians—the Academic mind is critical of their professions, which often have such slight relation to their performances. The Orator's duty is to select what can be said with truth and to be reticent where he cannot praise sincerely.

Of course, some keen Dissenters rallied to his support. Bernard Manning in a charming, characteristic letter said, 'I shall vote for you, as the candidate who represents in a comprehensive way all my politics: the "Good Old Cause"; "The Glorious Revolution"; "What Mr Gladstone said in 1886"; and last but not least that glorious thing, the "Dissenting Interest".' But Glover would never have been elected without solid support from good Anglicans. The Bishop of Ely, Dr F. H. Chase, voted for him, and voted the more willingly because of the prejudice among some Anglicans against Glover as a 'damned Dissenter'. The bishop wrote to Glover after the event, and expressed the hope (1) 'that it will not leave you too little leisure for some more books, and (2) that you will be kind to the many bishops who will be at your mercy! Poor things, how powerless they will be in your hands!' Another of his supporters, A. C. Seward, the Master of Downing, observed, 'How excellent an education the office will be for you; what an opportunity to cultivate the art of saying other things than you would most like to say.' And R. F. Scott wrote, 'Now you can throw the whole poetry of your being into the laudation of bishops. I see that you will soon have your chance.' This was an allusion to the Lambeth Conference of 1920 which was to bring a number of bishops to Cambridge for honorary degrees in the summer.

Glover was elected to the office of Public Orator on 21 January 1920 and he held it till he retired in 1939. He was the forty-sixth in the succession and he enjoyed the position it gave him. In his very first year he had to present for degrees, soldiers and sailors, politicians and bishops. On 19 May 1920 he made his début, Haig and Jellicoe being the principal recipients of degrees. His predecessor and old tutor Sir John Sandys, and Abbé Breuil were also honoured on this occasion. Glover acquitted himself to the satisfaction of Ridgeway who frankly recanted his former doubts.

I listened to you with the greatest pleasure. I could hear you admirably and if I may be permitted to say so your matter seemed excellent and the Latin was felicitous. You did full honour to the great sailor and to the great soldier, and were most happy in your speeches on your old tutor and the Abbé Breuil. The last was perhaps the cleverest of the set. It was a great ordeal and you were right to stick to your script. You will soon be able to drop your script and declaim your orations like your predecessor.

A little later, on 15 June, came the turn of the politicians, Lloyd George, A. J. Balfour and Austen Chamberlain being the most distinguished. Perhaps the speech for the first-named was the most difficult, calling as it did for the fulfilment of the Orator's duty 'to select what can be said with truth and to be reticent where he cannot praise sincerely'. Gilbert Murray congratulated Glover on this particular speech. 'I have read your Lloyd George speech with the attention it deserved, and I think all is well. Truth has been preserved and your immortality has been assured.' Lloyd George himself was pleased, as appears from a scrap of conversation after the ceremony with Sir Donald Maclean who was also among the nineteen recipients of degrees.

Ll.G. (to Sir Donald): Did you understand what the Public Orator said about you?
D.M. Not very well. I don't know the new pronunciation. Did *you* understand what he said about you?
Ll.G. I don't know but the gist was that considering I'm a Welshman, I'm a fairly honest man—but then they always exaggerate!

The translation of the speech, which Lloyd George certainly appreciated, is as follows:

Nature which appointed this island as the dwelling-place of Celts and Saxons, in order that each might help the other, has varied her gifts, bestowing on the Celts, a quick wit, powers of persuasion, eloquence and imagination, and on the Saxons, some other virtues, useful but humbler. You all know how much we owe to this intermixture. You all know how much our guest has done for us, both before the war when he provided land for the poor and comforts for old age, relieving the wealthy of a little of their superfluity, and during the war when he pacified the miners, provided munitions and hastened victory, 'counting nothing done while aught remained to do.' Finally you all know, how he has brought back peace from Paris, not without honour, that equals him with Benjamin Disraeli!

After the soldiers and politicians, the bishops. 1920 was the year of the Lambeth Conference, and Glover had to draw up an address to the Conference from the University and also speeches for the Archbishop of Canterbury and for some of the colonial bishops for whose merits Leonard Whibley was anxious to secure due recognition. The speeches were not delivered in person by the Public Orator, as he sailed for the U.S.A. on 25 June. Canon Charles Raven acted as his deputy and felt obliged to apologize to the archbishop in particular for the sentiments contained in the speeches Glover had written. The following October in presenting the Archbishop of Wales, he gave rein to his Free Church sentiment by describing him as one 'to whom is entrusted the guardianship of a church recently freed from the shackles of the State' (*cui creditur ecclesiae tutela nuper vinculis civilibus liberatae*). Perhaps some expressions in the address to the Lambeth Conference had been more provocative, for there he asserted that the conscience of Christian folk is seldom bound by the decisions of Councils, and still more rarely is the Holy Spirit so bound (*raro enim synodi suffragio constringitur populi Christiani conscientia, rarius quidem Spiritus Sanctus*). But if Glover could not resist entertaining thrusts of this kind, on the whole he treated bishops kindly.

Glover's brevity, his epigrams, his wit and humour were much appreciated. In October 1920 he had to present General Allenby for a degree and Ridgeway complimented him on a very good and vigorous oration, but he added, 'Your real *coup* was the *Lux ex Oriente* for the chemist presented to us by the Oriental Oil Company. This was brilliant.' A year later, presenting the Prince of Wales and Admiral Sims, he could poke fun at America and also voice his teetotal sentiments. Presenting the Prince, Glover said, 'In New York he was regarded by the Americans as almost an American; and a people, taught from earliest infancy to hate kings, has suddenly fallen in love with a prince (*idem Novi Eboraci paene Americanus ab Americanis habebatur; et populus, prima ab infantia reges odisse doctus, subito Principem amavit*).' Introducing Admiral Sims, he eulogized his services in foiling the German submarine campaign, and continued,

We rejoice exceedingly that two peoples, always enamoured of both freedom and the sea, have toiled with one consent in so great an undertaking; we regard this as an omen and anticipate a happier age. We reckon among the good omens the fact that the Admiral agrees with Heraclitus in his preference for a dry soul and also rejoices in a dry America (*populos duos, et libertatis et rei marinae semper amantissimos, hoc tanto in opere uno animo laborasse vehementer gaudemus, immo omen accipimus et aetatem auguramur feliciorem. Nec non inter omina ponimus, quod cum Heraclito consentit navarchus siccam animam esse meliorem et sicca laetatur America*).

Perhaps Glover found his greatest pleasure in the opportunities the office gave him of paying tribute to scholars for whom he had the highest regard and even affection. He was delighted to salute Franz Cumont, the great authority on Mithraism and the religions of the Roman Empire in the first two centuries. 'Perhaps', said Glover, 'it would be superfluous to crown a man who may call Mithras his crown, but crown him we will (*illum forsitan otiosum fuerit coronare qui dicat Mithram esse coronam suam; sed coronabimus*).' J. W. Mackail was another whom he delighted to honour, particularly for his interest in Virgil. Mackail wrote afterwards, 'I have never been called a poet before and probably never shall again.' Above all, the chance of paying a tribute to Gilbert Murray gave Glover great satisfaction. Murray had written beforehand. 'I look forward to your Latin speech. Remember the idiomatic thing is to use plenty of superlatives.' Actually Glover avoided all superlatives, and yet the whole is a superlative, the main feature of the speech being a fine appreciation of Murray's translation of the *Trojan Women.* 'You filled me with confusion,' wrote Gilbert Murray, 'but you emphasized the things I should have wished.' Glover had rightly concentrated attention on the point where the scholar's lifelong interest in the Classics coincided with his long-continued devotion to the cause of international peace.

Among the most happy and most memorable of Glover's compositions as Public Orator were the tribute to Canada when he presented Mr Mackenzie King on 22 November 1926, and the letter of condolence with the University of Oxford on the death of their Chancellor, Earl Grey, in 1933. Harris Rackham of Christ's College attributed Glover's success as Public Orator to the width of his interests. 'That's why you are such a good Orator. You have enough Latin. You know all the bishops and politicians, and give us not academical exercises but real speeches. Did you see that Hewart quoted your speech on Canada?' Lord Hewart, when Lord Chief Justice of England, visited Canada in 1927 and on his return contributed some of his impressions to *The Times*. He began his article:

> In the delightful library of Mr Mackenzie King, the Prime Minister of Canada, I saw not many days ago, at Ottawa, the document which recorded one of his honorary degrees. Therein the Public Orator of the University of Cambridge refers to Canada as 'coloniarum omnium Britannicarum primaria, gentium duarum societate fortis, et bello et pace illustris, frugum magna parens, magna virum, mira montium fluminum lacuum camporum pulchritudine, omnibus et solium et nivium amoenitatibus amabilis'. Was ever a more admirable description so concisely expressed?   (*Translation: see Appendix, p. 226.*)

The letter containing his tribute to Viscount Grey did not attract the same attention, but may be recalled here, since it evoked the admiration of Cyril Bailey, who said he had never seen any more beautiful speech about a statesman in Latin.

Cancellarium vestrum, viri dignissimi, cum mors vobis abstulerit longaevum quidem necdum senectute confectum, scire vos volumus quanto dolore nos cum milibus Britannorum innumeris virum illum desideremus, qui tot per annos intaminatis honoribus inter cives versatus sit, immo qui rempublicam inter scopulos Syrtesque rerum peregrinarum tam diu ipse gubernaverit. Recordari iuvat ambitionem omissam, honores non petitos sed acceptos, vitam totam patriae consecratam, dum luctu et solitudine et paene caecitate afflictus dolores spernit si modo Britanniae laboranti possit subvenire. Nec tantum haec vitae publicae munera tractabat, sed virtutibus eminebat simplicioribus. Avium amator poetaeque nostri otium inter montes lacusque non sine libris malebat consumere, artibus pariter duabus deditus piscandi studiosus legendique, has etiam voluptates purissimas relinquere paratus si vocaret patria, si causa iustitiae propugnatore egeret. Viri, civis, Angli vidimus in illo perfectum exemplar et absolutum ita ut inter aequales nostros praeniteat nemo; absumptum vobiscum lugemus, quem tamen, ut ait Cicero, esse natum, haec civitas, dum erit, laetabitur.

(*Translation: see Appendix, p. 226.*)

For further examples of the many felicities to be found in the Public Orator's speeches and letters, the curious should consult the fine appreciation which Mr R. J. Getty contributed in a long article to the St John's College magazine, the *Eagle*, after Glover's retirement, but here I may add a word on one point of procedure. Sir John Sandys who gave Glover many hints on his conduct as Public Orator, advised him at the close of the oration proper, to step down from the dais, take the distinguished guest by the hand, and recite his titles and honours as he said, 'Duco ad vos the most this that and the other General X or Admiral Y.' Glover on occasion made a profound impression by dropping all titles, as when he closed a speech on relativity simply with, 'Duco ad vos—Einstein.' This was long remembered, but it was not unique as some who remembered it supposed.

Glover's election to succeed Sir John Sandys gave great satisfaction to his friends. It was a substantial recognition of his gifts as a scholar and a man by the University, which up till now had been rather tardy in appreciation. W. B. Selbie, writing to congratulate Glover, said, 'There is balm in Gilead yet and Cambridge is not so bad as your heated fancy sometimes paints it. I hope you will stick to it now.' Outside Cambridge, marks of appreciation continued to accumulate. Honorary degrees were multiplying. His first doctorate, LL.D., had been bestowed on him as far back as 1910 by Queen's University, Kingston. It was fitting that Queen's should be the first to honour him in this way, and it gave great pleasure to him and Mrs Glover. At the close of 1917 McMaster University, Toronto, had conferred a second doctorate upon him. The war prevented his attending in person to receive it. In 1921 he was awarded a similar honour from St Andrew's University. The announcement of this degree brought a jolly letter from D. S. Cairns who wrote: 'Your friends know you have done a sight more for Divinity than 99/100ths of the existing doctorate. They will feel that St Andrew's has done itself honour.' For this degree, Glover was able to go north and spend several days in the delightful city by the sea. He received the degree on 12 July. The return journey from Edinburgh by night train brought an unusual experience. Glover travelled back with A. N. Whitehead and his wife. Whitehead had been honoured at St Andrew's on the same occasion. Glover's record of the journey runs thus: 'Slept fitfully on train, with strange episode of waking and seeing apparition of a man sitting between the Whiteheads. I told them later; they questioned me as to look and shape, and thought it like their son who fell in the war.' It is perhaps not surprising that, after this strange episode, Glover failed to change trains at York and was carried on to King's Cross.

Even more gratifying than honorary degrees was a letter from the Registrar of the University of Oxford 'asking whether I will accept appointment as Wilde lecturer in Natural and Comparative Religion for three years—at £140 a year and eight lectures. This is a great honour.' This invitation came in May 1917. At first he hesitated and thought he would decline it. His friends at St John's overcame his hesitations. E. E. Sikes and E. A. Benians both insisted that it would be a mistake to decline such an invitation. Ridgeway said, 'You aren't qualified, but you easily can be. It would do Cambridge good and you good.'

On reflexion it was obvious that he could not very well refuse. Indeed the invitation had many attractions. His daughter Mary was at Somerville. For the first year of the lectureship he was invited to join the Senior Common Room at Balliol. Apart from that he would enjoy the hospitality of many friends in Oxford. He was sure of a welcome. Had not a distinguished Oxford don hailed him as the only educated man that had come out of Cambridge in his generation? So in the month of May, in the years 1918, 1920, 1921, Glover paid four visits to Oxford, delivering two lectures on each visit. For some reason or other, he omitted 1919. The second set of lectures, delivered in 1920, was based on his book *Jesus in the Experience of Men*, which was in the press at the time. The substance of the first and third courses was embodied in the volume, *Progress in Religion*, which the Student Movement published in 1922.

Glover did not attempt to survey the beliefs and practices of primitive peoples, or to make a comparative study of the great religions of the world. He confined himself to the history of religion in Palestine and in the Greco-Roman world. Progress in religion can be discerned in that history, and the standards of progress are not obscure. After all both Greek and Jew prepared the way for 'a religion that should set the highest value on personality in God and in man and make righteousness, ever more deeply conceived of and understood, supreme'. Progress in this direction is the work in the main of great teachers like Plato and great prophets like Jeremiah. 'The significance of the Jews and of the Greeks in the history of Religion is after all due to the intensity of individuality in their prophets and thinkers.' In this affirmation Glover was consciously tilting at the growingly popular group-theories of religion. Throughout both courses, he interweaves the Greek and Jewish strands. But if he does not make a comparative study of Christianity and Hinduism, he does draw on his experience of religion in India to illustrate different aspects of his theme. Thus he finds a parallel between post-Exilic Judaism and Hinduism.

There is the same writing up of the glories of the past; the same extravagant claim that the foreigner owes all his inventions, his poetry, his philosophy, to borrowed models—the Greek to the Jews in the one case, the Greek and others to the Hindu in the other; there is the same want of criticism, the same indifference to real history, the same absence of seriousness. Side by side with these more outward expressions of natural feeling, we may note further the same exclusiveness in life, in marriage and in food taboos, and the same rigidity in law, while the sicarii and zealots of Roman Palestine have their parallel in the bomb-throwers and Tilaks of British India.[1]

In his closing chapter, where he describes the victory of the Orient over the intellectual genius of the Greek and the practical sense of the Roman, he again discovers a parallel with the traditional faith of India.

The great characteristic feature of Oriental religion as it sweeps over the Roman Empire is...its vagueness....Fog is religion's vital breath at this period. Modern Hinduism, in very much the same mood of fear and reaction, exhibits at once the advantages and the disadvantages of a religion which is anything you like to make it except monotheism, or even monotheism in a sense that makes it meaningless, while it is never anything you can either grasp or criticize. Whatever feature strikes the Western observer as objectionable or of doubtful value, is sure *not* to be Hinduism; even caste, you will be told, is not Hinduism; what actually *is* Hinduism, you are less likely to learn, unless it is virtue and spiritual sensitiveness beyond European standards. Oriental religion as Greek and Roman knew it, was just as odd and heterogeneous and indefinite.[2]

A religion of dissolving views always exasperated Glover. He would often cite the preposterous answer of a don who was asked if he believed in God, and who answered, 'Well I believe in a sort of a kind of something.' Glover once suggested a verse for a Hymn for the last Church of All, in which the Union of all Religions should be consummated. It ran,

> We know Thee not, nor guess Thee,
>   O vague beyond our dreams;
> We praise Thee not, nor bless Thee,
>   Dim source of all that seems;
> Unconscious of our witness,
>   The music of the heart,
> O It beyond all Itness,
>   If aught indeed Thou art.

---

[1] *Progress in Religion*, p. 242.   [2] *Progress in Religion*, p. 323.

In *Progress in Religion,* Glover deprecated the assumption that Christianity can be understood as just one among many mystery-religions. On the contrary, he believed that Christianity was sharply differentiated from all the mystery-religions not only by its rootage in Jewish monotheism and in the Jesus of history, but also by its acceptance of the Greeks' intellectual discipline. Harnack and Hatch were inclined to deplore the marriage of primitive Christianity with Greek thought. Did it not spoil the simplicity of the original Gospel? Glover sided with Wilamowitz-Moellendorf, one of whose sayings he often entered in his commonplace books: 'Das Christentum hat darum die konkurrierenden Religionen des Orients geschlagen, weil es sich am stärksten hellenisiert hatte.' Precisely because Christianity absorbed more of the Greek scientific and philosophic spirit, it overcame the competing religions of the Orient. A hellenized Christianity dispelled fog and refused to take refuge in vagueness. Glover never lost sight of this truth.

Not the least valuable feature of the book as a contribution to the comparative study of religions was the constant reminder that the same words and similar, seemingly identical, rites will have different, perhaps profoundly different meanings in different settings. Anyone who has dipped into the amazing farrago of parallels that makes up the stock-in-trade of the Christ-Myth theorists will know how important this reminder is for any accurate study of religion. In the passage where he notes the close parallel between the hymns of Tuka Ram and Cowper's versions of Mme Guyon, both singing the praises of God's grace, Glover continues:

Distinctions spring up when we ask what it is hoped that divine grace will effect; and we realize that Tuka Ram and Mme Guyon have very different hopes. Mme Guyon looks for salvation from sin, Tuka Ram from rebirth.... Salvation is not a fixed idea; much turns on what it is from which a man seeks to be saved—whether he fears eternal reincarnation or death, physical or eternal, or the pollution and paralysis of his soul by sin.

Just because salvation is not a fixed idea, rites such as baptism and partaking of the Lord's table meant different things to the Christian and the Mithraist. It was well worth while to make this clear.

The invitation to be Wilde lecturer in Oxford and his subsequent election to the office of Public Orator in Cambridge were certainly most encouraging for Glover. He was also gratified by being asked to serve on a Committee appointed by the Prime Minister in November 1919, to enquire into the position to be assigned to the Classics in the educational system of the United Kingdom. The Committee met over a period of two years with the Marquis of Crewe as chairman, and produced its report after its last session on 7 June 1921. Glover had been one of the more regular attenders, as he was present on sixty-six occasions out of eighty-five. At first he found the sessions and the examination of witnesses interesting and throughout 1920 he notes in his commonplace books sayings that intrigued him. Some of these support, others challenge, the views which he held throughout his life on the teaching of the Classics and which he expounded in his presidential address to the Classical Association in 1938. He no doubt applauded R. S. Conway when he said, 'The literary and humane object of classical study must be made more central. Latin must no longer be taught as a kind of Geometry.' Again, 'We cannot afford to have Greek taught mainly as a linguistic discipline.' He liked Alington's reference to 'those who fear that the bones of the majority of the students will be found bleaching on the dreary road which leads through Caesar, Nepos and Ovid'. A. N. Whitehead may have had this in mind when he said, 'Nothing is so dead as dead literature', but did Glover agree with his 'deep distrust of historians'? 'I feel certain', said Whitehead, 'they will always ask the children the things that don't matter.' It was encouraging to learn from knowledgeable heads that 'a good many boys, so clever as to get scholarships in Science or Mathematics at the University would really have done better to be on the humanistic side'. 'The War Office too is moving in the general direction of desiring a general education among men who are going to be officers.' So the Hon. W. Bruce testifies. Again, 'it is not the working-men members of Education Committees of County Councils that are hostile to literary education.' 'The working-man is more of an idealist in education than the manufacturer or the shopkeeper.' So there is hope for the literary and humane object of Classical study in our modern democracy. But what of new methods to commend it? The warning of Walker, High Master of St Paul's School, still stands. 'No funicular railway can be built up Parnassus.' The suggestion of dramatic methods led to an interesting interchange. Could Greek trials be treated in this manner? They are not easy to reproduce in schools. Gilbert Murray recalled the trial in the *Wasps*. 'That was a burlesque', said someone, whereupon Hadow observed, 'All their trials were burlesques.' We might at least expect more from children. J. W. Mackail was of opinion that 'children are talked down to too much in their education', and the chairman remarked later, 'The fact is that there are very few audiences that you need to talk down to on any subject.'

Glover found a good deal of entertainment in the work of the Committee, but he grew weary of it as time went on. The report itself, drafted by an H.M.I., Mr C. Cookson, did not altogether please him. Dull phrases like 'We cannot but confess', and 'We feel it is hardly fair', made it distasteful. And it was difficult to get the style altered. As a quatrain put it:

> It would call for a drastic and resolute man
>   To prevail on Mahomed to change the Koran;
> And it calls for a hero of similar sort
>   To get Cookson to alter his drafted report.

At the final session, on 7 June 1921, when the report was accepted, Glover gave vent to his feelings in Latin verse:

> Rex antiquus erat Solomo qui saepe maritus
>   Dicebat; Finis principio melior.
> Fine frui tandem spes est gratissima fessos,
>   Conjugiis regem, nos ita colloquiis.

The position of Public Orator did not mark the height of Glover's ambition, though it was to be the limit of the University's recognition of him as a scholar. His college lectureship was renewed for five years at a higher salary on 25 February 1921. His fellowship became a life-fellowship when he completed twenty years' service in 1922. In the same year, his University lectureship in Ancient History was renewed for a further period. As the years went on, the University Press became his publisher again, and the Syndics readily accepted almost any book he offered to them. But a professorial chair eluded him. His desire for such a chair was not just ambition. He was getting tired of the grind of a college tutor in Greek and Latin composition. He chafed at the obligation to lecture year after year on the same periods of Greek and Roman history. He would have liked the greater freedom of a professor to choose his own subjects and work on what interested him most.

In September 1916 his old friend and teacher, H. M. Gwatkin had died, thus leaving the Dixie professorship of Church History vacant. No attempt was made to appoint a successor until the conclusion of the war. Glover thought seriously of standing for the chair. Indeed he actually sent in an application, but two or three days before the election he wrote to the Vice-Chancellor withdrawing it. 'So Dixie, ambition of years, is off.' He withdrew his candidature for two main reasons. First, the Dixie Professor is attached to Emmanuel College, and if appointed, he would have had to migrate from St John's to Emmanuel. His friends at St John's were most reluctant to lose him. Larmor, whom he consulted throughout, tilted the scale against the Dixie. J. G. Leathem from whom he often differed on College Council said, 'he would be very sorry if I left St John's'. Leathem also judged that Glover would have a larger influence with lay-students in Ancient History than he could expect to have in Church History. 'He would be glad if I withdrew and I begin to think I will.' Second, when he discussed with Larmor the board of electors to the Dixie professorship, it was apparent that they were not likely to favour a Dissenter. The first layman to be appointed to a professorship in Divinity was F. C. Burkitt, the Norrisian Professor. But as yet no Nonconformist had been considered for such a professorship, and Glover anticipated rejection.

Had he been appointed, Glover would have continued all that was most inspiring in Gwatkin's approach to Church History, as he had been very close to Gwatkin in outlook and understanding. At Mrs Gwatkin's request, he wrote a biographical introduction to a volume of Gwatkin's sermons, *The Sacrifice of Thankfulness*, which appeared a year after his death. A reviewer in the *Church Times* described it as 'a delightful memoir by Mr Glover, a masterly bit of biography in little'. But it is not unlikely that his affinity with Gwatkin would have told against him. The electors probably wanted a change.

The question of applying for the Dixie professorship came up about the time Glover's father died. On 26 March 1919, 'a man came with telegram from Bristol; Father died most peacefully this morning. So the dear old man is gone in peace. I cannot tell my debt to him; of no other man I have seen, would I have wished to be son.' He sorely missed his father's advice when he was considering whether to withdraw his candidature or not. He wondered whether his motives in standing were pure enough—pure enough to satisfy his father's judgement. Was he too concerned about the emoluments of the chair? The sympathy of his friends at St John's influenced him. J. R. Tanner, who, it will be remembered, came from Bristol, wrote a letter about Dr Richard Glover and his influence—'something far more influential upon the mind than eloquence. Even after all these years the influence has not worn itself out for me.' J. G. Leathem and others were equally understanding. This strengthened the reluctance of Glover to leave St John's.

In the spring of 1922, came a tempting proposal from Yale to become Professor of the History of Religions there, at a salary of 8000 dollars a year. The offer was under consideration for some months, and it was on 22 July that Glover finally wrote declining. At first, a good many considerations seemed to favour acceptance. Financially his position in Cambridge did not seem too secure. Income-tax was high in Britain, and his responsibilities for the education of his family would involve large expenditure for some years to come. Could he really afford to go on in Cambridge, unless he got a chair? Ridgeway thought he would stand a good chance of getting the chair of Ancient History when J. S. Reid retired. But as Hazeltine observed, he might possibly be elected Professor and return to Cambridge after a few years at Yale. Hazeltine advised him to go. Larmor at first thought Yale offered better prospects than post-war Cambridge. He would not discourage Glover from going: 'it is the nicest of American places.'

The tendency of changes in the University, proposed by a Government Commission, was to enlarge the central authority of the University at the expense of college sovereignty. Glover disliked and distrusted this tendency. When he delivered an address of welcome to Earl Baldwin as Chancellor in 1930, he said,

'Multa regressus invenies mutata (non ego reformata dixerim, antiquiorum non solitarius amator), "On your return you will find many things changed (I won't say 'reformed' and I am not the only lover of more ancient ways)".' In 1922 he is reading the Commissions' report and he gets 'the idea that University Boards will really appoint our Fellows and Lecturers', and he recalled how secure he was 'in the shelter of St John's, and not dependent on the hateful Classical Board which is worse now with pedants and epigoni, though the influence of Trinity is weaker. I would rather stay here if I am not to be humiliated and to see Colleges degraded.' But the trend of University reform, so called, is ominous, and one might be happier in Yale. He writes to F. J. Foakes Jackson who had migrated to Union Theological Seminary in New York and found himself in his element there; the reply was encouraging. There was no lack of advice but it was conflicting. On one and the same day he received letters from W. B. Selbie and John Kelman. The first denounced the American idea. 'Selbie says he will have nothing more to do with me if I give up work in Cambridge for filthy lucre: God has emphatically put you there.' Kelman on the other hand, was inclined to think that for influence and widespread value of work, the position at Yale would be better than Cambridge. He also spoke well of the Yale staff.

Gradually the scales turned against Yale. Neither Glover nor his wife really felt happy about transferring the family to the U.S.A. The desire to have the children educated in England, which was a prime factor in bringing them home from Queen's University, still held good. Then during this crisis, the 'hateful' Classical Board reappointed him lecturer in Ancient History for a further five years, and the resolution was proposed and seconded by the two members who Larmor had suspected might be opposed to Glover's reappointment. Larmor had changed his mind and now urged Glover to stay. 'He holds out hope of advancement here if I stick to Ancient History.' This was in line with an emphatic judgement of Selbie's, who says, 'My *Virgil* is worth all my others; stick to Classics and leave Theology which you don't know, alone.' So in the end he turned down Yale, with misgiving as he thought he might be condemning himself to shoal-water for life. Curiously enough, after he had sent his letter declining the invitation, he had a letter from C. R. Brown of Yale, regretting that the trust fund on which they were relying to finance the new professorship 'was not available for the purpose'. So the exercise of mind had been unnecessary. Some years later, the invitation from Yale was renewed and again declined.

The hope of advancement in Cambridge did not materialize. In 1921 the retirement of Henry Jackson caused a vacancy in the Regius professorship of Greek. Glover had been among those who prelected but he had not much expected to be appointed. That door had been closed. A few years later, J. S. Reid retired and the Chair of Ancient History, the Classical Chair for which Glover was most suited, fell vacant, but he was passed over in favour of a younger man. Probably the width of his interests, which added to his qualifications as Public Orator, killed his chances of professorial advancement. He could not be persuaded to leave theology alone. In October 1922 the S.C.M. published a volume of his essays on religious themes under the title of *The Pilgrim*, and he was already at work on his study of St Paul, which when it appeared caused Selbie to modify his adverse judgement on Glover as a theologian. As his prospects of University recognition declined, he valued more and more the shelter of St John's.

At the high table and on the College Council, Glover certainly made himself heard. Tissington Tatlow, writing of him in the *Red Triangle* to introduce him to Y.M.C.A. circles said, 'My main impression [of him in private life] is that he is a tremendous talker. He babbles on all the time about everything—life, religion, people, the classics, poetry, history, foreign missions and many other topics.' When the late Master of St John's, E. A. Benians, first joined the high table in 1906, he found Glover there 'a Junior Fellow, accounted rather impulsive by the administration and apt on his side to be very critical of them'. But he was always excellent company. 'He was an admirable talker, quick, witty, ready with the apt quotation and story, humorous and reminiscent, inclined to be personal and not disposed to check his resentments.' He was impulsive and sometimes expressed himself with a brutal directness which gave offence. He lamented these failures when he realized them, and they gave a wrong impression of the man. For as Benians said, he was a very generous man. He would sometimes excuse or explain himself to his friends, by recalling a sentence from William de Morgan, who wrote somewhere, 'The bitterest things are always said—at least such is my experience—by the most tender-hearted people.' He would also cite Dr Johnson's judgement on Levett. 'Levett is a brutal fellow, but the brutality is of his manners, not of his mind.'

Glover was not indeed the ideal conversationalist. He tended to dominate too much. To get the best out of him, you had to stand up to him, as Wynne Wilson would do, who, when he left the high table to become Dean of Bristol, told Glover he would miss him. 'There's no one talks such rot in the Common Room as you do.' According to E. A. Benians, Glover was 'always fond of the younger men; he liked to think that they listened to him and appreciated his humour, as indeed most of us did'. But in the post-war period Glover found it difficult to get alongside the younger generation of scientists. With the scientists of his own and of an earlier generation he got on very well. Professor Liveing, the Nestor of the high table after the death of J. E. B. Mayor, Glover respected and admired. T. G. Bonney was a close friend of him and his family. William Bateson the biologist, J. E. Marr the geologist, W. H. R. Rivers the anthropologist, all appealed to him. When the last-named died on 5 June 1922 at a comparatively early age, Glover wrote, 'So St John's loses a foremost man of science, who has been a great help to us.' Glover was out of sympathy with Rivers' politics as Rivers was out of sympathy with Glover's religion. He once told Glover, that 'when it comes to religion you don't use your intelligence'. Yet the two men appreciated one another and were attached to one another. Glover's closest confidant was of course Larmor, a mathematician, and he appreciated other mathematicians among his contemporaries such as H. F. Baker. But his interest in natural science was limited. During his last year at school he chose a complete edition of Darwin's works as a prize. Muschamp said, 'You will never read them,' and apart from the travel volume on the voyage of the *Beagle*, he never did.

During the war and after, he became increasingly aware of the growing gap between classical and scientific humanism. The young scientists who were coming forward for Fellowships seemed to lack the elements of English culture. The report on the dissertation by one such candidate in 1916 might be summarized thus:

> His style is neither clear nor bright;
> The English tongue he cannot write,
>   Mis-spelling with fatality;
> He lets sense, judgement, learning slip,
> But well might win a Fellowship
>   With such originality.

A year or two after the war, dining in hall with newly appointed Fellows, he finds them an unsolved problem. 'I fancy there is a heavy Philistine element among them.' Their outlook is so limited. Early specialization in natural science had deprived them of the humanizing influence of English literature and the Classics. The menace to the last named had come out in evidence before the Committee on Classics in education. I think Glover must have been shocked by the remark of a headmaster which he records in a commonplace book. 'I don't understand what some of you mean by the value of Greek thought. I never met it.' He had been startled by Rivers, who on one occasion told him that he found nothing of value in Plato's *Republic*. Glover himself did not rate the *Republic* so highly as James Adam had done, but he perceived a tendency in natural scientists to underrate and neglect Plato. So as time went on he found himself less and less in touch with the younger men who adopted the modern 'scientific attitude'.

When E. A. Benians first knew Glover as a colleague, he found him critical of administrators. Later, he says, Glover became more appreciative of their work, though never disposed to seek it himself. 'He took little part in University administration; that was not his bent. He was too independent and perhaps too impatient to co-operate easily in the kind of work, but was for a long time a most effective member of our Council.' Benians adds, 'I sat next to him on the College Council for many years and he was certainly the freshest and boldest mind amongst us. He dominated the scene too much to be popular with every member, but he did good service to the College and was responsible for many of the decisions taken in the years immediately after the war.' Among such decisions must be reckoned the election of G. G. Coulton to a fellowship, a well-timed recognition of a true scholar, which indeed enabled him to do his best work. Glover always supported and sometimes initiated proposals for efficient and economical administration of College affairs, e.g. in the running of the college kitchen. He could be relied upon to favour courageous and generous decisions in the difficult personal problems that arise from time to time in college circles. He found attendance at College Council meetings often boring and sometimes exasperating. The *Manchester Guardian* on one occasion referred to Dr Montague Butler's 'sage guidance of the turbulent and uncouth democracy of which a College Governing body consists'. Irrelevance and indecisiveness rather than turbulence were the features of the proceedings of St John's College Council which most troubled Glover.

In this regard it was not unlike other College Councils. Duckworth who was later to be Master of Jesus College, once told Glover, 'Our meetings are liable to such fluctuations of intention and performance that I cannot allow myself to hope for any decision.' Unfortunately one was almost obliged to sit through sessions in which much was said to little purpose. Larmor pointed out the privilege of the Member of Parliament who can always leave the House when the debate is boring and irrelevant, while the member of a College Council has no such relief. Glover would while away the tedium of council meetings by writing light verse:

> The Master sat at the table's head,
>   Talk surging about him to and fro;
> But never a word the Master said,
>   And much he wondered how it would go,
> And he watched the eddying of debate
> With a growing sense that the thing could wait.

> To and fro the discussion swept—
>   [XY] starting most of the hares;
> Not a man of the twelve to the question kept,
>   Relevant only by unawares;
> Till the Master felt, when it came to his turn
> He might venture perhaps a hint to adjourn.

> Out of the welter a clear voice comes;
>   'Will the Master give the Council a lead?'

The Master blanches; he haws and hums,
  Till he hits on a happy thought indeed;
And he gives the Council the lead they seek
'We could talk it over next Friday week.'

Another member's procrastination prompted the following:

It was on the Last Judgement Day
That [X-X-X-X] rose to say
  He had a feeling many shared—
At least, he felt himself, he owned—
Where many were so ill-prepared
And where the issues were so great,
It might be best for all to wait;
He moved the business be postponed.

Sometimes the triviality of the 'business' caused Glover to break into verse:

The vicar in his letter pleaded
For vestry hat-pegs sorely needed;
  In fact, at the last Confirmation
The Bishop's hat fell off the door,
Was somehow trampled on the floor,
  The Bishop had remarked 'Damnation'.

He felt it very much indeed,
  So trusted to the Council giving
  Some aid to mend a College living
In such a case of special need.
The Bursar on the whole opined,
We might give something if inclined;
The Council like a set of ninnies
Voted the silly ass two guineas.

A revised version let the Bishop and the Council off more easily.

The Bishop—so the vicar fears,
  Or so it sounded to his ears—
Spoke with a hint of indignation.

and,

The Council on such cogent grounds
  Voted the little man five pounds.

Though Glover often lamented the time spent at College Council meetings, yet he liked to be on the governing body of the college, and if he did not exactly turn necessity to glorious gain, he brightened dull proceedings for many weary colleagues.

Chapter VIII

GLOVER AND THE BAPTISTS

The deacon : the controversialist : President of the Baptist Union :
the preacher : the journalist

In 1923, Glover was elected vice-president of the Baptist Union, and in due course in May 1924 was inducted as president at the annual assembly at Cardiff. It will be convenient to review his association with the Baptists both before and after his year of office as president.

Even at the times when he had been most dissatisfied with them and when he had been most drawn in other directions, Glover had never severed his links with the Baptists. He retained his membership at Tyndale in Bristol until he transferred it to St Andrew's Street in Cambridge. A short time before the first World War he had been elected a deacon, and he served the Church at St Andrew's Street during three successive pastorates. The Rev. M. E. Aubrey's characterization of Glover as church member and deacon would be endorsed by his successors.

Unless he is preaching elsewhere, Dr Glover is in his pew twice every Sunday. If he is absent, even if only for one service, he almost invariably gives an explanation to his minister, as of courtesy and right.... His personal attitude towards his minister is much more like that of a Scottish Presbyterian than that of an English Baptist. By far the most distinguished member of the congregation to which he belongs, he is among us as 'he that serveth', ready for the humblest services like handing out hymn-books, showing folks to seats, and taking the collection, or bringing in chairs or counting pennies, and never refusing any service that is asked of him, if it is in his power. He is slow, rather than eager, to take any front place among us, and the last man to wish to be where the minister is usually to be found.

He shirked none of the duties of a deacon. He attended deacons' meetings regularly and took a lively and critical interest in all business. When he was present, discussion had to proceed with a minimum of ventilation! But he was generally very helpful in business matters, having a shrewd judgement and good practical sense, which never allowed money matters to cloud his vision of the spiritual purpose of the Church. He could be relied upon to put first things first. He was always ready to do anything he could, financially or otherwise, to help the Church.

The service he rendered to St Andrew's Street was matched by constant interest in the welfare of other Baptist churches in village and town. He served for many years on the Cambs. Association Committee and also on the Baptist Union Council. Temperamentally he was not at all times an easy person to get on with. He was always suspicious and critical of officials, and though essentially a kind and friendly person, he could be both pugnacious and obstinate to a degree. His close friend, the Rev. Charles Brown of Ferme Park, Hornsey, said of him after a trying session of the Baptist Union Council, 'Reaveley, you have all your father's obstinacy, and not one-hundredth part of his grace!' And on another occasion, Charles Brown said of Glover's father, that he was full of grace and truth, and he added, 'There's some of him in his son, especially truth!' But Glover's prejudices, which made him difficult on committee, were often wholesome. He was a confirmed anti-sentimentalist,[1] and a rather devastating critic of humanitarian schemes or international peace-movements which seemed to him lacking in realism. He greatly admired moral courage and liked people who stood up to him; but he could not always distinguish between plain speaking and a rather crude insensitiveness to other people's feelings.

M. E. Aubrey's tribute to Glover as deacon was written in reply to a critic who thought he belittled the regular ministry and invaded the minister's prerogatives. Actually the son of Dr Richard Glover would yield to no one in his regard for the ministry. But he constantly asserted and frequently exercised the layman's liberty of prophesying. On holidays at Sheringham, he was as regular in attendance at the Primitive Methodist Chapel as he was at St Andrew's Street in term time. The ministrations of local preachers were particularly appreciated. Sheringham was a favourite resort for many leading Free Churchmen in the Easter and summer vacations. The Primitive

---

[1] See *Democracy in the Ancient World*, p. 109: 'The sentimentalist is always above the facts of life, resentful of the ground on which he stands.'

Methodist minister relates how on one Easter morning, a local preacher was occupying the pulpit, a very original old man and much esteemed in the town.

In one seat Glover sat with Rendel Harris, W. B. Selbie, Professor Sims Woodhead and others. The old man began by saying he had asked one of them to preach but they wouldn't, so he had to do it himself. 'Now', he said, 'you mustn't think about the man who is giving you the bread, but about the bread itself.' Rendel Harris was especially pleased and clapped Glover on the knee and said, 'That's the best thing I have heard about preaching—not the man who gives you the bread, but the bread itself!'

The sermons of the ministers under whom he sat were subjected to a discriminating criticism. During the war, he was critical of anything that sounded to him like playing to the patriotic gallery; and after the war preaching that smacked of the social gospel which he had never liked, became more and more distasteful to him. After the General Strike in 1926 I think his sympathies with Labour contracted, and both as a Liberal in politics and an Evangelical in religion he became more and more conservative, more and more on the defensive. In consequence as time went on, he grew rather out of sympathy with the younger members of the congregation at St Andrew's Street, who welcomed preaching which gave them direction on Christian social duty. A sentence or two from a letter to J. C. Carlile in 1936, illustrates his later attitude. The hymns of Isaac Watts, he observes,

were very full of the personal relation between Christ and the man he saves. And that, I think, is not the dominant note in preaching to-day. It may be a sign of old age to look back to the Gospel of my youth and boyhood, but at sixty-six I feel the need of Some One who will care for me and be with me and be interested in my thoughts and temptations and will not exclusively harangue me on public issues.

But Glover never lost his respect for the ministerial vocation, even when he thought his minister was not sticking closely enough to what Wesley called, 'the old coarse gospel'.

Glover's position in the Baptist denomination was never altogether easy. The author of *The Jesus of History* was not universally approved among his own folk. There were many cross-currents of conflicting opinion swirling round him. While many of the younger men hailed him as a true prophet, his orthodoxy was suspect in other quarters, particularly among the disciples of Charles Haddon Spurgeon. On the other hand, his jealous assertion of the position of Baptist and Independents in relation to all proposals for reunion, won him the support of many stalwart Conservatives, though it puzzled some of his more youthful admirers. Some who were dubious about his orthodoxy welcomed him as a protagonist of Independency, and others who found a new approach to the Gospel through *The Jesus of History*, regretted his intransigence in some matters of ecclesiastical politics. But all recognized the contribution which his standing in the academic and religious worlds might give to the Baptist cause. It was obviously right to ask him to accompany the Rev. J. H. Rushbrooke to Bucharest in April 1921 to negotiate with the government of Roumania for the religious liberties of Baptists in that country. The two distinguished delegates saw Take Jonescu[1] himself and secured a more liberal measure of recognition for the Baptists than would otherwise have been possible. The original draft ordinance would have permitted the existence of only isolated village causes, under very strict official supervision. Such little Baptist churches might be served only by resident Roumanian pastors, might have no association with one another, must not receive support from outside the country or maintain connexions with any Baptists outside the country. The pastors might not itinerate or preach in the open air or address joint-gatherings of any kind. They were to be as restricted in regard to propaganda as Baptists are in the U.S.S.R. at the present time. With the exception of the ban on open-air preaching, all the restrictions in the original draft were rescinded as a result of the representations of Glover and his colleague.

In spite of his distinction and his services, Glover could not expect to be elected to high office without a contest. When he was nominated for vice-presidency in January 1923, he anticipated opposition from the secretary of the Union, the Rev. J. H. Shakespeare, and his supporters. J. H. Shakespeare was identified with the policies of which Glover was most distrustful. He

---

[1] The prime minister in Roumania at the time.

was an ecclesiastical statesman, who saw clearly many of the problems which would confront the Free Churches after the war. He saw that the small individual congregations would be unable to maintain a pastor and would have difficulty in surviving. He put all his energy into raising a ministerial sustentation fund and its administration would strengthen the central authority in the denomination and require the appointment of regional superintendents. Glover disliked this development but could not dispute its necessity. It would be difficult to exaggerate the value of J. H. Shakespeare's services to the denomination. In the same spirit and with the same vision, Shakespeare when Moderator of the Free Church Federal Council advocated a United Free Church of England. He perceived that village nonconformity might be crushed out of existence if the little village causes were not prepared to link up with one another. Though his proposals have never been implemented, the existing National Free Church Federal Council owes much to Shakespeare's foresight.

Going still further, he saw that reunion with the Church of England would become a serious issue after the war, and he was not prepared to turn down Anglican proposals out of hand. He recognized that the Church of England could not be expected to surrender episcopacy, and that Free Churchmen would have to consider whether and on what terms they could accept it. Glover on this issue was very suspicious of Shakespeare and his admirers. He thought they were flirting with episcopacy and would sell the pass. Before the Lambeth proposals of 1920, Glover had sought to spike Shakespeare's guns, by submitting a resolution which was carried with some modifications at the Baptist Union Assembly on 29 April 1919 in the following terms:

That, if the price of Ecclesiastical Reunion be the acceptance of Episcopacy, in its historical sense or in some non-historical sense, with the implied necessity of regularizing our ministry by episcopal ordination or re-ordination, the Baptists of this country, wishful to work with all Christians for the Kingdom of God and believing that its coming will not be hastened by compromise on principle, elect to stand by the Priesthood of all believers and God's right to call and consecrate whom He will and how He will.

In 1920 came the Lambeth proposal for reunion on the basis
of the famous quadrilateral—acceptance of the Scriptures, the
Creeds, the Sacraments, and a ministry authorized by the historic
Episcopate.

Glover's position was defined in five letters to the *British
Weekly*, which Heffer's published as a small book with the title,
The Free Churches and Reunion. On 3 January 1921 a representative
conference of Free Churchmen met at Mansfield College, Oxford
to draw up a considered statement of the position of the Free
Churches in relation to the Lambeth appeal. W. B. Selbie was
in the chair, and the Rev. P. Carnegie Simpson of Westminster
College, Cambridge, was joint convener. The latter was most
active in drafting and redrafting the report, and indeed the
document which was published eventually in March owed much
to his skill in drafting. To Glover he seemed rather too dominant,
and at one point Glover naughtily suggested that the report
should start with the phrase, 'It seemed good unto Carnegie
Simpson and to us.' While it seemed to Shakespeare and others
that a new spirit had come into the discussion of the problem of
reunion and they were anxious to make the Free Church reply
as cordial as possible, Glover was not so favourably impressed
by the Lambeth appeal and he set himself to secure a clearer,
more emphatic assertion of Free Church principles, such as the
insistence that the Church is the outcome of the Gospel, and so
the preaching of the Word is of first importance, and that the
Free Churches stand by the priesthood of all believers. He had
serious doubts about the loyalty of both Wesleyans and Presbyterians to Free Church principles as he understood them. In
a Latin letter to John Clifford, which he composed on behalf of
the conference, he wrote: 'We have met to consider whether we
can retain our freedom under episcopal rule though we are
hardly free amid so many Presbyterians and Methodists (*vix
inter tot Presbyteros et Methodistas liberi*).'

Though Glover was thus at variance with Shakespeare over
questions of ecclesiastical policy, he was glad to find they were in
agreement on issues of biblical scholarship. In January 1922 the
Free Church Federal Council held another conference at Mansfield College, this time on the Bible and Criticism. The discussions were discursive but not reactionary, and Glover found

Shakespeare 'very amicable now; he hopes I may be President of the Union'. However, when he was nominated for the vice-presidency in January 1923, Glover thought the influence of the secretary of the Union would be thrown against him. On 18 April he notes, 'In morning had a strong presentiment that I shall not be elected by the Baptist Union—about 12 noon.' The presentiment was groundless, for on Monday, 23 April, he was elected by 798 votes to 544 for his nearest rival, T. S. Penny. The result was welcomed not only by the younger men, but by most of the outstanding leaders. Glover thought, 'They all took the view that it was a denominational pronouncement on the Lambeth issue between J.H.S. and me; also a reply to the Fundamentalists.' The real threat to Glover's election came from the Fundamentalists rather than from J.H.S. T. S. Penny, who met Glover at breakfast the day after his election, 'was quite explicit in saying that he feared my election might injure the denomination. That made me like him better and made me more content that I stood and carried it.' What T. S. Penny feared was not so much a setback to Shakespeare's policy in regard to Lambeth, as a renewal of the Down-grade controversy, and a with-drawal of the more conservative orthodox wing from the Union.

So far as Glover's year of office was concerned, T. S. Penny's fears were unnecessary. Those who feared that Glover's presidential address would be something of a bomb-shell were agreeably disappointed. It was generally admitted that the Baptist Union Assembly at Cardiff in May 1924 was on an unusually high level. This was in large degree due to Glover's initiative. He had chosen as the main theme for the sessions, the central truth, God in Christ. Guided by his experience in the Student Christian Movement, he had invited the main speakers to a two-day conference at Cheshunt College, to prepare themselves for the Assembly. Consequently they had a better knowledge of one another's minds. The speakers understood, supported and supplemented one another and the sessions had a unity seldom attained in previous years. The choice of hymns was another factor making for a deeper impression than sometimes is present in such gatherings. Glover relied in the main on Isaac Watts, Charles Wesley, and Bernard of Clairvaux's 'Jesus, the very thought of Thee'.

But Glover's own address set the tone for the Assembly. While he insisted on the significance of scholarship and science in the history of religion, he did not go out of his way to antagonize the Fundamentalists. His approach was historical and he set out to illustrate the experience of the power of God in Christ at four great turning points in Christian history. He spoke of St Paul, St Augustine, Luther and Wesley. He was in fact describing the only form of apostolic succession which seemed to him genuine and important. His closing sentences did something to reassure the orthodox and conservative. For he confessed, 'As I grow older I want more and more to preach Christ without theory, to tell people the tremendous facts associated with Him—the fact of victory over sin, the changed life, and the most amazing fact of all, Himself.' On the other hand, his opening insistence on the need for culture and science, his assertion that for three of his four great men, the intellect helped to clear the way to Christ, strengthened those who realized the dangers of a narrow Fundamentalism. A correspondent, of Jewish parentage, wrote:

Ever since I became a follower of the Christ of St Paul I have been at a loss to understand the strange spirit of bitter antagonism often exhibited in certain Christian circles towards learning and mental culture as such. To Christians, with the Light of the World shining over them, learning should be the natural food of the mind. . . . And much of such antagonism centred round your name of late; and it fell to my lot to meet with it. So I came up to our B.U. meetings this year. . . with strange forebodings. . . . And you, sir, have done my mind as well as my soul much good. To me the B.U. meetings at Cardiff 1924 have been a great turning point in my life as a follower of Jesus Christ. I think that in the modern world the Christian ministry must be learned as well as devout if its work is to be effective in the best sense.

Unusual responsibilities of a practical kind came upon the president in Glover's year of office. In the course of 1923, J. H. Shakespeare fell ill, and at the first session of the Assembly his resignation was announced and accepted. Finding a successor was no easy matter, and a good deal depended on the judgement and guidance of the president. He had to support the acting-secretary, the Rev. J. C. Carlile, who was not hoping or wishing to succeed J. H. Shakespeare. Eventually, the Council unanimously invited the Rev. M. E. Aubrey to be secretary. Glover was involved in some delicate negotiations, in which his judgement as president of the Baptist Union was in conflict with his judgement as a deacon at St Andrew's Street. At first he told Aubrey that he must not think of it, but later he had not a little to do in persuading him that he ought to accept the appointment. Not the least valuable of Glover's services as president was the settlement of the secretariat.

Little more need be said about Glover's attitude towards reunion and the Lambeth proposals. Conversations between Anglicans and Free Churchmen were still going on, and Glover himself was one of the Baptists who accepted Sir Henry Lunn's invitation to a conference on reunion at Mürren. This was a private conference and non-committal. In the more official conferences Glover took no part, and they proved abortive so far as any practical result was concerned. The Baptist reply to Lambeth drafted by the Council came out on 17 April 1926, when the conversations had reached a stalemate. It was endorsed by the Assembly at Leeds on 4 May. The reply was a friendly but firm rejection of the Lambeth quadrilateral as a basis of reunion. Glover had been in America when the matter was considered by the Council and he was not present at Leeds; but he heartily approved of the Baptist reply. Soon after the reply appeared and had been the subject of a leader in *The Times* A. E. Housman met him. He said, 'Did you write the Baptist reply to Lambeth?' Glover replied, 'No,' Housman then said 'I thought it was very well written'; and added with a smile, 'I am against the Church of England condescending to negotiate with Roman Catholics or Baptists.'

About the same time, Glover received a very thoughtful letter from Canon Quick, who suggested that the real difference between the Anglicans and Free Churchmen was that the Anglicans wanted nothing less than organic reunion, while the Baptists advocated a loose Federation as the next step, if not as the only tolerable form of reunion. He pointed out that to insist on episcopacy and episcopal ordination as a condition of full reunion might be reasonable and indeed necessary while neither necessary nor reasonable for a loose Federation. He added that Anglicans regarded Federation not as half-way to reunion proper, but as a mistaken substitute for it. He felt that Anglicans and Baptists were arguing at cross-purposes, because the first thought of reunion and the second of federation. Glover replied that reunion such as Quick and the Anglicans hoped for was not at present possible because the disagreements go too far down. The only immediate possibility was some form of federation which should be regarded as a half-way house and nothing more.

Criticism of Glover from the conservative-orthodox side was moderated but not finally silenced by the favourable impression of the Cardiff meetings. In the summer of 1928, Glover attended a World Baptist Conference in Toronto. Among Baptists in Canada, there had long been an extreme fundamentalist wing, a Baptist Bible Union, under the leadership of a Dr T. T. Shields, who edited a weekly 'Gospel Witness'. For a time Dr Shields had been a member of the governing body of McMaster University, a Baptist foundation, and Glover had followed with interest the attempt of Dr Shields to prevent the appointment of the Rev. L. H. Marshall, of Queen's Road, Coventry, to a chair at Mc-Master, in 1925. The attacks on Professor Marshall were renewed in 1926, but the Baptist Convention of Ontario and Quebec stood by the University and its Professor. When Glover arrived in Toronto on 22 June 1928, he was made the subject of a violent attack. Dr Shields announced that he would give three lectures upon 'Three Rotten Apples', namely L. H. Marshall, Shailer Mathews and 'the English pippin', i.e. T. R. Glover. However, by this time, Dr Shields had more or less discredited himself, and in any case Glover swept all before him by his address at a Bunyan celebration, at which nearly 10,000 were present. Though his speech was cut down and bisected by a hymn and a cheer-leader in American style, yet it 'carried the palm of the speeches at Toronto. The pressmen hardly knew what to make of it.' One such reporter wrote, 'To be honest, I was so entranced by the man, who, by the way, was one of the three rotten apples referred to by Dr Shields, that I could not take notes.' The reporter of the *Toronto Star* did contrive to take a few notes.

Dr Glover is almost I should say the 'white-haired boy' of this great gathering. Boy, indeed, in many ways he still remains. There plays about his eloquent mouth a certain whimsicality, half pout and half smile, which pervades all his utterances and fascinates all his hearers. His humour is perpetual and refreshing. Famous scholar though he is, he is yet not afraid of the word 'converted', a word almost now stricken from the terminology of educated religious people.

The criticisms of Dr Shields who looked askance at such Evangelical stalwarts as F. B. Meyer, Munro Gibson and Professor James Orr, did Glover no harm, but he ran into troubled water with the more extreme wing at home in 1932. In 1931 the Baptist Union Council initiated a discipleship campaign, and in preparation for it they proposed to issue a study text-book on Fundamentals. As the primary aim was to appeal to lay folk and young people, Glover was invited to draw up these outlines, since his approach was not that of a technical theologian and even bare outlines from his pen would be stimulating and original. Glover accepted the invitation, and as usual, when he was disposed to do a thing, he did it very rapidly. He arranged his matter under the following headings and in this order. He began with Sin, and followed with Punishment, Repentance, Conversion, Salvation, Atonement, Justification, and Sanctification. He was clearly following a Puritan Evangelical tradition in his arrangement and he was hoping to put a fresh living interest into old time-worn conceptions. The outlines were in proof by July 1931, and they were submitted to some theologians for comment, among others to Canon Raven, who wrote to Aubrey, the secretary of the Baptist Union:

I strongly approve of the general position that lies behind the positive and constructive suggestions of the syllabus. Old-fashioned and timid folks will be led on to a fresh and reasonable understanding of the terms familiar to them. His desire to help the reactionary, explains, I suppose, the sequence of the studies. For myself, I cannot ever start with sin; this is Protestant theology, not the Christian religion. Jesus begins with 'Our Father'. Nevertheless, if your readers are to be won from the old 'scheme of salvation', it may be well to do as Glover has done and take its sequence.

Actually, Glover was not concerned so much with old-fashioned and timid folks as with young people to whom the great words of Protestant theology had ceased to convey any real meaning. He wanted to help them to find in the Scriptures and in experience, interpreted in a wider literature, meanings and values that were not adequately represented in a traditional 'scheme of salvation' which had ceased to appeal to them. Canon Raven in a further comment suggested that the treatment of what 'life in Christ' involves was not adequate.

The question of Christ's relationship to God—call it the problem of his power to forgive or the doctrine of the Incarnation—cannot be shirked and these outlines shirk it. This is, of course, the basic weakness of Glover's position; he has never... worked out a Christology. And it is futile to think that you can have a doctrine of Atonement while your Christology is 'in the air'.

It is true, of course, that Glover, as he had said in his presidential address at Cardiff, was concerned to preach the fact of Christ and not theories about Him. He may have committed himself to a separation of fact and theory which is too facile.[1] But it is important to recall what he really meant. The return to the Jesus of history was an attempt to relive the experience which gave rise to Christologies, and by which Christologies must be tested. If in a sense he never advanced beyond the Jesus of history and his Christology remained 'in the air', he was enabling his readers to approach the key problem of theology, which as Raven said is 'that of the nature of Christ', with a fresh understanding of the facts which create the problem. The weaknesses which Raven and other theologians detected in Glover's outlines might be assets in a booklet designed for laymen. So Aubrey thought. In forwarding Raven's letter to Glover, he wrote:

Frankly, I think that from the point of view of the trained theologian who wants a logical order, you often start at the wrong end, and the lacunae in the series dealing with Fundamentals are rather appalling. At the same time, as I have said to Raven, the fact remains that laymen who do not think much of what we preach about, have a feeling that you are dead on the spot, so that the wrong end for us may be the right end for them and we shall all thank God if between us we are able to reach a wider area than any of us could reach alone.

---

[1] A correspondent writes: 'He could never make up his mind about the Atonement and some irreverent younger ministers used to say that when he got out of his depth he would say, "Let's sing a hymn".'

The publication of the pamphlet disturbed and alarmed those who clung to the old view of the Atonement, which held that Christ bore the punishment of our sins in our stead and that this was necessary to satisfy the claims of divine law and justice. In his book on St Paul, Glover had emphasized the truth that the Apostle speaks of Christ dying to reconcile us to God, but never of Christ dying to reconcile God to us. He argued that Christ's death was to change our attitude to God, not God's attitude to us. In his outlines he suggested that the substitutionary view of the Atonement was derived from ideas of sacrifice and Roman law which were not accepted in the New Testament. But his references were tentative rather than provocative. However, the Rev. Tydeman Chilvers, pastor at Spurgeon's Tabernacle, and the Rev. Thomas Greenwood felt that this was a lacuna in Glover's fundamentals which left out the heart of the Gospel. In February 1932 Greenwood wrote a letter to the members of the Discipleship Campaign Committee, protesting against the issue of such a pamphlet by the Baptist Union Publication Department. He challenged the section on the Atonement as an attack on the doctrine which had been the most prominent theme in the preaching of Spurgeon, Moody, Wesley and Whitfield. Greenwood claimed that he was not commencing a controversy, but replying to an attack. His detailed criticism was temperate in tone and well reasoned. He concluded, 'Dr Glover has told me that he is not pleased with the book; if he should wish to withdraw it I respectfully ask you to give your assent; and, if he does not move in the matter, to ac yourselves.'

Glover's first reaction was that he would withdraw nothing. The responsibility must rest with the Campaign Committee and the Baptist Union Council. Between the writing of Greenwood's letter and the meeting of the Council on 7 March, some three weeks elapsed, and the discussion in the *Baptist Times* and the *Sword and Trowel* (the Spurgeon-wing's monthly) became heated. The officers of the Union and some of the older statesmen began to fear that they were in for a second down-grade controversy, before the earlier breach was fully healed. Glover himself feared some compromise or surrender by the Council, and at one point threatened to leave the Union if the pamphlet were disowned. His best friends in the Council told him not to worry and not to threaten. He could rely on them to see that his pamphlet was properly defended. But when the crisis was most acute, even the Rev. Charles Brown, a staunch supporter, urged him to withdraw the pamphlet himself, as the only dignified way out of the impasse. However, when the Council met on 7 March a happier solution was found. Greenwood moved his resolution that the booklet should be withdrawn. Glover did offer to withdraw it rather than hurt the feelings of his brethren, but the majority clearly felt that it would not be the wisest thing to do. Before a vote was taken the chairman had an opportunity during an adjournment, of consulting Greenwood and Dr Percy W. Evans, the principal of Spurgeon's College, and as a result made the following statement:

The Committee of the Discipleship Campaign and Dr Glover learned with surprise and regret that the pamphlet had been understood by some as an attack on the views held by many who were in the Union; that nothing was further from their thought; and that, if Mr Greenwood withdrew his motion, he would move from the Chair that another pamphlet, setting out other views of doctrine, should be issued, and that the pamphlet should be distributed as 'Fundamentals' had been.

Mr Greenwood and Mr Soper, in view of the resolution, withdrew their motion, and Mr Ellis from the Chair moved the foregoing resolution, which Dr Glover seconded. Dr Glover said he was very conscious that his representation of Christ's sacrifice was inadequate and incomplete. He knew no representation of that great fact which could be regarded as adequate and complete. To him, Christ was everything. He was Saviour, Friend and Lord. For many years he had been trying to understand Christ's teaching and the meaning of His death. He was more sure than ever that Christ was all in all; he could sing the Evangelical hymns that delighted his friends. He believed them; he did not use their form of speech or their metaphors. He was seeking to reach another constituency, and followed other methods. Of course he had no objection to another pamphlet setting out other views. The more they considered the mystery of the Cross, the more they would see how impossible it was to fathom its meaning, but they could unite in saying, 'He loved me and gave Himself for me'. The thankfulness and relief of tension which resulted from such a conclusion may easily be realized. The chairman wrote to Glover, 'I want to say how touched I was at your gracious speech and by your seconding my motion. Aubrey was jubilant. He told Glover, 'Your stock was never higher than it is to-day. Laus Deo. You couldn't have done better. Both your silence and your speech told heavily.'

But before the end of the week Glover was in trouble again. *The Times* had been publishing a series of articles reviewing the last fifty years, and on 26 February, Glover was invited to write such an article on 'The Free Churches these last fifty years'. He was pleased to do it and he dashed it off in no time. He spoke among other things of the waning of Spurgeon's influence, and of the value of the contribution of Fairbairn and Mansfield College. As ill-luck would have it, the article appeared in *The Times* on 11 March, Friday, and it was made the more offensive to admirers of Spurgeon by an editorial headline, 'Defeat of Spurgeon'. The fat was in the fire again. It was a brilliant article. A card from Sir Donald Maclean ran, 'Why did you write that article in *The Times*? It caught me in my dressing-gown and I had to finish it. You completely disorganized my time-table for the whole day. You have no business to write such fascinating stuff and ruin a day for busy men!' Rendel Harris wrote, 'I was wading through *The Times*...when I came across thy double-columned sword with two edges. It was simply lovely, though I still do not think you have done Spurgeon justice.' Glover's difficulty in doing justice to Spurgeon was a matter of heredity, inasmuch as he always supposed his father to have been one of the ministers whom Spurgeon suspected and refused to name, when challenged to do so by the Council. Any criticism of his father ranked with Glover as an almost unforgivable sin. Aubrey was naturally distressed. He had to send a letter to *The Times* dissociating the Union officially from Glover's judgement on Spurgeon. To Glover he wrote, 'For the love of Mike go slow for a bit!'

The storm blew over, and fortunately did not permanently estrange Glover from such loyal Spurgeonites as Principal Evans. He was among the speakers at the Assembly in 1933 and he continued to be in demand as a preacher.

Though he was by no means a finished speaker, Glover will be remembered as a great preacher as long as any who heard him survive. 'An orator with an atrocious elocution', he commanded attention by the challenge of his thoughts. He seemed to be wrestling with his subject and inviting you to wrestle with him. He and his congregation were thinking things out together. For this his 'easy conversational pulpit style of a somewhat staccato kind' was the proper mode of address. He did not always make himself heard, especially in his early days as a preacher. This was due in part to faults in elocution, which he never entirely overcame, and in part to the seriousness with which he was thinking things out as he spoke. He usually spoke from notes, brief notes in little pocket-books, and not more than two pages to a sermon as a rule. In preaching he seldom if ever used a written-out sermon.

Dr J. Fort Newton, while waiting for a passage to the U.S.A. in August 1918, records this impression of Glover as a preacher in his diary for 12 August.

Whether I get a steamer or not does not matter, so long as Dr Glover preaches at Westminster Chapel....At times his manner suggests a professor in a class-room but he is a truly great preacher—simple, direct, earnest with no thought other than to make clear his vision of Jesus in the lives of men.[1] Rarely have I heard sermons so packed with forthright thinking and fruitful insight....Perhaps the outstanding impression is a fresh vivid sense of reality, as of one who is looking straight at the truth he is talking about. He 'speaks things' as Cromwell would say. Vital faith and fearless thinking are found with a conviction of the genuineness of the man and his knowledge of Jesus in his own experience. He dodges no issue, no fact, no difficulty, and his knowledge of the social intellectual and spiritual world in which Jesus lived and in which the Church began her morning march is extraordinary. He has a curious power of taking us back into those times.

Two years earlier, a writer in *The Christian* characterized his preaching in somewhat similar terms.

To say that Dr Glover is a great preacher, is to be met immediately by the assertion—voiced most loudly by himself—that he

[1] At the time Glover was using in his sermons much of the material which later appeared in *Jesus in the Experience of Men*.

is not a preacher at all. But while he has not chosen the ministry as his life-work, and while his preaching suggests the lecture-room and the students' conference rather than the pulpit, he preaches none the less, and preaches all the time. And his greatness as a preacher lies in the freshness of wonder with which he faces Christ, in his perennial sense of the amazing gladness and largeness of the Gospel. He speaks as one thrilled. The wonder is expressed in the simplest, most colloquial, and practical of language: but the thrill is there none the less, in all its self-communicating and propagating power. 'Why, he only just talked', is the comment of the hearer who expected an eloquent discourse; but somehow the talk had a dynamic quality, and a trick of leaving a glow in the soul to which, perhaps, it had been long a stranger. For it was the talk of a man who does not know what it is to view the Gospel with dull, conventional eyes. The rest may sigh for the early dews of morning, the first radiant freshness of Christian experience; for him each day's contact with Christ is a new discovery, a wondrous exploration of un-guessed worlds. For his soul it is always morning, with Jesus standing on the shore.

G. H. Sedgwick,[1] who heard Glover preach 'three very good sermons' in Ottawa in 1936, wrote to a friend, 'He speaks English and much more unusual, he *prays* English—modern, alive. One could get along without ritual if all were like that.' His language in prayer as in sermons was simple, direct, not stilted or conventional. Someone who heard him often reports that 'he had a curious mannerism in public prayer. He never began with any mode of address to God, but launched off as if he were conversing.' J. Fort Newton relates how he was present in Westminster Chapel on 4 August 1918, the fourth anniversary of the declaration of war.

Memories of that great decision, thoughts of its meaning, its cost in blood and sorrow, filled all our minds; and instead of the morning prayer Dr Glover spoke to us out of a full heart in the gentle words which men use when they speak of such matters. What is the meaning of this 'long-lived storm of great events?' he asked. What difference has it made? He reminded us that the Old Testament is the record of the reactions in the life of a nation to the terrible deeds of God.... Who will read for us the new and living Word of God, written in the facts and events of the day?...

[1] The Hon. G. H. Sedgwick, chairman of the Tariff Board, Ottawa.

Then he asked us all to join in the Lord's Prayer as alone adequate to upbear the thoughts and yearnings of the hour. Never have I heard that brief grand prayer so surcharged with feeling, lifting a troubled people into the fellowship and consolation of God.

Glover spoke to large audiences in big buildings like Westminster Chapel and the City Temple, but he was equally ready to speak in little village meeting-houses and in college chapels, and in some ways his manner of speech and thought was most effective with the smaller audience. Compulsory attendance at college chapel was very generally discontinued after the first world-war, and rather more was made of addresses, especially at evening services, than before. Deans possessed and used their liberty in inviting speakers and Glover was often called on. One Lent he gave three addresses at Magdalene College, and on the second occasion A. E. Housman, who was dining as a guest that night, learned that Glover was speaking and came early to hear him. He also on occasion occupied the pulpit at St Edward's Church, where F. D. Maurice had at one time officiated. Glover's attitude towards preaching and public worship was a little like that of Maurice. He felt as Maurice felt unworthy to deliver the message and yet not only obliged but also glad to deliver it. Somewhere he compares the preacher to St Sebastian, a martyr exposed to the arrows of his critics. But still more searching is the self-criticism of one who feels himself standing before the judgement-seat of Christ.

Both the preparation for a service and the delivery of a sermon were exacting experiences for him. He usually felt exhausted and depressed after preaching twice on a Sunday, and as Dil Calvin records, would beg his friends to say a kind word, any Sunday after preaching. He held that a sermon should be like a poem, as Milton conceived it—simple, sensuous, and passionate. By 'sensuous' he meant an appeal to the imagination which might stir the affections, and his sermons abounded in vivid concrete illustrations, drawn from his knowledge of history and his wide experience of life. It was said of Glover that he had many sermons but only one theme. Whatever the text, beginning from that scripture, he preached unto men, Jesus. Like Augustine, he had no satisfaction in any sermon from which the name of Christ was absent. He never felt that he was cut out for a preacher. He was sure he had done right to remain a layman, and his preaching was the more effective because it was non-professional. Incidentally, Glover did not decline fees for preaching at places like Westminster Chapel, but he was very willing to preach in little country-places without reward, and when he preached for a particular cause such as the Missionary Society, he usually added the fee to the collection. Because his living did not depend on it, his witness in the pulpit made the deeper impression. In an age when as he said in *Jesus in the Experience of Men* 'anyone who is definite disturbs our modern scientific poise', Glover was ready to make public confession of his faith, and he made no secret of his passionate loyalty to Jesus Christ. The preaching of the Cross is still foolishness, and he knew it, but he was willing to be a fool for Christ's sake.

For five or six years in the decade after the first World War, Glover was actively engaged as a religious journalist. In September 1922, Henry T. Cadbury, who was devoting himself to making the *Daily News* an effective Liberal influence on public opinion, invited Glover to contribute a series of eight Saturday articles to the paper on religious themes. This was an experiment which proved successful, and Glover was asked to write regularly for a year. The articles (whose length and quality may be judged by the tribute to his father included in our opening chapter, pp. 3-5) attracted many readers. There was nothing quite like them in any other daily paper. Even from the point of view of circulation, this new feature of the *Daily News* was worth while. But Henry T. Cadbury and a remarkable young member of the editorial staff, Hugh Jones, were interested in Glover's work for its own sake. In May 1923 Hugh Jones wrote, 'I have again discussed with Mr Cadbury the continuation of your articles next year. We have no doubt as to the wisdom of going on, if you can see your way to do so: it is a valuable piece of work which we are glad to be associated with you in doing.' The arrangement was renewed and continued until 1928.

So long as Hugh Jones was at the headquarters of the *Daily News*, Glover felt sure of sympathetic understanding and support. But in January 1927 Hugh Jones died at the age of forty-three. He had worked himself up from very humble beginnings.

'As a lad he had sold papers in the street for a living: but he was an unspoilt self-made man.' He had been so impressed with the kindness with which he had been treated as a young patient in hospital in Manchester that he swore if ever he grew up he would do something for hospitals. He fulfilled his vow, when on the staff of the *Daily News* he by his initiative and labours brought it about that wireless was provided for the London hospitals, for Borstal institutions, for lighthouses and lightships through the *Daily News* fund. Glover to his astonishment learned from Hugh Jones that there were no fewer than 200 hospitals in London. Hugh Jones appreciated Glover and Glover admired and trusted him. Glover spoke at his funeral service on 4 February 1927. He related how on visiting a friend in hospital in the previous September, he spoke to him of Hugh Jones and his friend said, 'I wish you would tell him how much the wireless means to us here. They put out our lights at eight o'clock and then for two hours we have the interest and entertainment of the wireless.' Glover continued,

You take these 200 hospitals full of people, broken and beaten many of them. Life must have seemed empty to a great many of them, but a great spirit seized the opportunity of giving life, animation, interest and variety to them. That was typical of him....During four years I was constantly in touch with him. He heartened one up for one's work and gave one fresh faith in the kindness and goodness and decency of mankind.

Glover did not feel as happy with Hugh Jones' successor, Tom Clarke. The new managing editor preferred shorter, more topical articles. The *Daily News*, which had to compete with the Harmsworth Press, was tending to become more popular, putting more into headlines and less into columns. On 31 October 1927 Glover saw Tom Clarke, who then had articles in stock that would last till February. Glover would write them off in batches and naturally they did not refer to happenings about the date of publication. Clarke complained that they were not topical enough and too long, more suited to a book than to a daily paper. Subsequently a selection of these articles was published under the title *Saturday Papers* and made an excellent book. As a result of Tom Clarke's attitude, Glover felt more and more uneasy. When Henry T. Cadbury wrote in the following March and pressed the same suggestion about topical articles, Glover wrote that he did not think that worth while. 'If the articles are not to touch the permanent, they are not to be done.' In August 1928 the series ended. Though this was his main experiment in journalism, Glover wrote and continued to write reviews and articles for many papers. But he did not undertake another contract for regular contributions to any journal.

In June 1926 looking back over twenty-five years since his return from Canada to Cambridge, he declares it has been good because he had been able to see so much of his parents in their closing years, and because he had secured for his children the education in school and University that he desired for them. He also feels that the work for the Baptist Union has been worth while, and he adds, it has been 'rather disappointing academically. I have over-estimated myself or wasted my gifts.' His final disappointment had come on 26 February 1925 when he failed to be appointed Professor of Ancient History in succession to J. S. Reid. As Larmor had anticipated, the electors preferred a younger man, F. E. Adcock of King's. For some years Glover marks the anniversary as a black day, the death of his hopes of further academic distinction in Cambridge. But on 26 February 1932, he notes, 'Seven years to-day Adcock was elected Professor; he has done better than I should have done, and I could not now face finish in two years, so I reach a sort of contentment.' He had neither over-estimated himself nor wasted his gifts, except in so far as his venture in journalism meant that he was writing too much. But he was spending his gifts in directions which did not improve his chances of a classical professorship.

In the autumn of 1923, he had delivered in Berkeley, California, the Sather Lectures on Herodotus. They had been published in 1924, but had not attracted much attention in England. This was his main contribution to classical studies since *From Pericles to Philip*, unless his charming renderings of R. L. Stevenson's *Child's Garden of Verse* into Latin lyric form were to be counted to him for righteousness as a classical scholar. He had been spending more time on St Paul. On 12 June 1925 he received the first copy of his book, *Paul of Tarsus*. A second edition was called for in October. It secured warm approval from W. B. Selbie. 'It is great stuff and most timely just now and ought to do a great deal of good. I am inclined to withdraw all I ever said about your sticking to Classics.' This would not help him to a classical professorship. A review in *The Times Literary Supplement* was even less helpful. 'It said I am "well known as perhaps the most stimulating writer on Christian origins in this country". Then it adds "he is a popularizer with abundant learning in the background". Nothing can palliate that word among scholars and that is where I am wrecked. "This book is written in his American lecture style, which is not his best literary form." Oh dear!' Adcock told him a tale of Oscar Browning which he felt applied to his own case. 'There are three things Cambridge never forgives a man for—being known outside, knowing anything outside his own subject, being able to express himself lucidly in speech and writing; and of all three, said O.B., I am guilty.' However, Glover did not waste his gifts by writing on St Paul. Selbie was not alone in his appreciation.

Another direction in which Glover had spent some of his energy in 1923 and 1924, was the preparation of *Cambridgeshire Syllabus of Religious Teaching in Schools*. In this he was associated with Alexander Nairne, Regius Professor of Theology, and Sir A. T. Quiller-Couch, King Edward VII Professor of English Literature. As his two colleagues were both at Jesus College, the business was mostly transacted after hall in Q's rooms. Typical entries in Glover's diaries run thus: '7 May 1923. Dined in Jesus with Nairne (Tommy Watt on religion; Nairne on hymns). Up both of us with Q and drafted a syllabus for 1st year on gospels, etc. for Elementary school.' '12 May. Did a syllabus which I took to Jesus College and had delightful chats first with Nairne and then with the splendid Q who took me into garden.' The next day, Sunday, 'Dined in Jesus with Q and after commonroom his rooms with him and Nairne over syllabus; Nairne got a bit tempery and left me feeling uncomfortable, despite peace restored. This sederunt 9.15 p.m. to 11.15 p.m.' Glover conceived a great admiration for Q and the two got on well together, in spite of the fact that they differed *in toto* on the subject of alcohol. But they had in common a vigorous Liberalism, a love of literature, and a love of the West country, though Glover seldom went further west than Bristol. Q told Glover that he regarded himself as the blank page between the two Testaments, but he left Glover to guess with which Testament he identified Nairne and with which he identified Glover.

Glover's main contribution was made to the earlier years of the syllabus, Nairne making the first draft for 14–16 years. There were some difficulties over a proposal, brought forward in full committee by Anderson Scott of Westminster College, for a series of lessons on 'the character of the Church'. Nairne supported the proposal, and complained of Glover bullying them when he opposed it. Q had to make peace, and a compromise was arrived at. The Cambridge triumvirate also produced in 1924 the *Children's Bible* for use with the Syllabus, and the *Little Children's Bible*. Not the least merit of the Syllabus and the Bibles was the subordination of the Old Testament to the Gospel. In the *Little Children's Bible*, the material from the Old Testament is ranged under the heading 'Stories that Jesus would learn from his mother'. I think this is one of Glover's suggestions. The influence of *The Jesus of History* can at any rate be detected in the *Cambridgeshire Syllabus*. A couple of sentences from the preface to the *Little Children's Bible* reveal the strength of the prejudice engendered by bibliolatry in some quarters. 'To prevent misunderstanding—for there have been criticisms of the Syllabus and of the *Children's Bible*—it should be explained that it is in no sense intended that this small selection shall be a substitute for the whole Bible. On the contrary, it is hoped that the possession in a convenient form, of those parts of Scripture most attractive to children may lead to a lifelong love of the Christian story and the Word of God.' If this kind of criticism is now silent, the proved worth of the Syllabus and the Children's Bibles is responsible.

The *Cambridgeshire Syllabus* has been adopted by many authorities and has set a standard which is reflected in many admirable syllabuses produced since the Education Act of 1944. Certainly Glover was not wasting his gifts in promoting this real service to national education, but like his work for the Baptist Union, and his religious journalism, it did not strengthen his academic prospects. In part because he was disappointed academically in Cambridge, he welcomed every opportunity of extended visits to the U.S.A. and Canada.

Chapter IX

A CITIZEN OF THE WORLD

The Atlantic voyager : sojourn in California : revisits Canada :
the Oxford Group Movement : renewed Yale offer : *The World
of the New Testament* : visits to Toronto

Glover made twenty trips across the Atlantic, no fewer than
fifteen of them in the period between the wars. Between 1919
and 1929 his visits were made in response to invitations to lecture
at various university centres in the U.S.A. He gave Lowell
Lectures at Harvard in 1922, the Sather Lectures at Berkeley,
California in 1923, lectures on the Sharp Foundation at the
Rice Institute, Houston, Texas in 1925. He visited Oberlin,
Ohio and Chicago in 1926 and he was at Yale in 1928. More
often than not he went or returned via Canada, travelling by the
Canadian Pacific line. During the first decade, he usually fitted
in visits to Canada, particularly to Kingston and Toronto. In
the later half of this period, 1930–8, Canada was his main
objective. He was fulfilling engagements to preach in the summer months more often than not at Yorkminster Baptist Church,
Toronto, and in Ottawa. His last trip and his fortieth voyage
took place in 1938.

Glover enjoyed life on board ship. He liked making new
acquaintances and drawing them out. He was equally pleased to
find old friends, particularly Cambridge friends like F. M. Corn-
ford or S. C. Roberts, crossing the Atlantic with him. But he
noted with peculiar interest the way life on a liner throws
strangers together and fosters something like the cosmopolitan
temper of the Greek world after Alexander. He says of that
world that in it the thinker had to start as an individual, face to
face with the universe.

The universe is the most splendid of societies, but. . .it is a dull
club, a poor home.... It is like a university without colleges.
The best a man could do was to pick up with whom he could,
as one does on ship-board; and as on ship-board, the antipathies
are dulled. You sit next a foreigner, but it is not for long, and by
and by the courtesies of the table open your minds. So in that

world there was no longer any sense in race-feuds and very little in any feuds at all.... Of course you can have quarrels on the *Mauretania*, or in Alexandria, but they are not the same—they are sour not fierce; and on the other hand the friendships are not the same.... Courtesy, kindness, the good turn received and repaid—they were nothing, the mere decencies of ship-board; but being nothing, they came to be something—the expression, half conscious, of a new sense of common humanity.[1]

Glover made the most of his opportunities on board ship. He seldom paced his measured mile or two on deck without compelling someone to do a Glover. His table at meal-times would be enlivened by argument and anecdote. He liked to get acquainted with the officers and sailors, particularly with the engineers. Among the passengers he would seek out practical men, men of affairs, for he was most interested in men of action and their doings. That was part of the attraction of life in the Dominion of Canada for him. Empire-building is a fascinating study, 'if you can get at the heart of the men who build Empires and watch them at work—fur-traders, diamond-seekers, sailors, farmers, and pro-consuls'. Characteristically he was enthusiastic about M. A. Grainger's *Woodsmen of the West*, 'one of the most delightful books ever written about the New World'. The book was first published in 1908, and in 1932 Glover wrote to *The Times*, urging that it should be reprinted.

The book describes a scene, a life, an industry that have passed or are so transformed as to belong to history. The camps with their primitive machinery and their primitive characters (specially the latter) live in Mr Grainger's pages. The sea, the inlets, the steamers, the 'hotels'—it is all alive. The book is full of conversation, well handled; he knows how to 'squeeze the sponge' and give you as few can, the full flavour of talk without its drag. Old Andy and Carter are characters indeed; and I think again and again of Andy's question why is it that 'education takes the natural savvy out of a man'? It did not take it out of Mr Grainger.... Books like his make the Empire more real.

It was not only in books that Glover delighted to meet characters such as Andy and Carter. He welcomed the opportunities that travel gave him of meeting them in the flesh. On

[1] Cf. *Progress in Religion*, p. 200, and *Christ in the Ancient World*, p. 18.

Atlantic liners he often had the chance to show his interest in
sailors, by taking the chair at the concerts normally given in aid
of seamen's charities. In the delightful memoir prefixed to *The
Springs of Hellas*, S. C. Roberts has described one of these
occasions.

> Amongst the passengers were some notable artistes. There was
> an eminent violinist from Roumania, a magnificent negress with
> a contralto voice of great depth and power, an 'eccentric' dancer
> from the Palladium, and the champion tight-rope walker of the
> world. Most of their names have escaped me, but there was on
> board another couple whose names it is less easy to forget—
> Naughton and Gold. With all this talent . . . it was inevitable that
> there should be a ship's concert; it was equally inevitable that
> Glover should be asked to take the chair. He made, of course, an
> appropriate little speech on behalf of seamen's charities; what
> was more interesting to me was his enjoyment of Naughton and
> Gold. Wearing ordinary evening dress ('We work in dinner-
> jackets,' they told me) they did an unpretentious little act as two
> British workmen at which Glover rocked with laughter. I was
> pleased to think that he had seen a really good music-hall turn.

As S. C. Roberts discovered, Glover crossing the Atlantic or on
the other side of the Atlantic was less on the defensive than he
was apt to be in Cambridge. He felt liberated and exhilarated
by the ocean itself and by the new world, and he was ready to
welcome all sorts of new contacts and experiences. A colleague
at St John's once said of him, 'Glover as a hedonist is a failure'.
He was less of a failure on the high seas than at the high table.

The more outstanding of his visits to the U.S.A. were the term
he spent at Berkeley, California, in the autumn of 1923, his visit
to Texas in 1925, and the visit to Yale in 1928. For the first of
these visits, he had to get leave of absence from his duties in
Cambridge, as he was to be away for the whole of the Michaelmas term. He sailed from Liverpool on 29 June and arrived
back on 5 January 1924. He was at Queen's, Kingston, in July
and proceeded in leisurely fashion across Canada, calling on his
old head master, R. L. Leighton, in Vancouver. He reached
Berkeley, California, on 18 August and took up his quarters in
the Faculty Club. His main contribution to the work of the term
was to be the Sather Lectures on Herodotus, which he had
already prepared in typescript. The book was to be printed by

the University of California Press and to be published as soon as possible after delivery. He was invited to give the Earl Lectures at Berkeley, and for this course he used the ten chapters of the book on St Paul on which he had been at work in 1921 and 1922 and which was published in 1925. As he journeyed home from California in December, the Earl Lectures in shortened form were repeated at Hartford, Connecticut and at Cambridge, Massachusetts. In addition to his main courses he lectured on Roman history at Berkeley. He was not frequently preaching on Sundays, and so had the opportunity of attending the First Baptist Church, Berkeley, where Dr E. A. Hanley ministered.

He had not been more than a month in residence, when he witnessed the great fire of 17 September. The entries in his diaries are vivid enough.

Monday 17. The hot north wind—curiously hot against the face blowing hard from Sacramento Valley, and tables and things strewn with fine dust and tiny ash....3 p.m. Fierce hot wind blowing smoke thick over campus....North Berkeley and hill side afire and blazing—awful afternoon—wind slowly dropped, and by five it was clear the campus would be saved; it's said 1000–1400 houses burnt; students working hard to rescue things and fight fire.[1]

Tuesday 18. Cable from Hugh Jones for 300 words on the fire for *Daily News*. With military pass, I went all over the area, dotted with chimneys, all else gone to dust and nails. Cabled my 300 words by 5 p.m....Eighty-three professors or members of staff have had their homes burnt; many freshmen lost all and their jobs.

Later the damage was estimated at £2,200,000. His cable to the *Daily News* expands these memoranda.

Berkeley lies between hills and San Francisco Bay, a university town of 60,000 with 9000 students. Up the hillside wind roads where the gardens are full of palms and flowers, and there are Swiss cottages and Italian villas—a charming suburb.

On Sunday night the north wind began to blow, bringing heat from Sacramento Valley and a smell of burning. Monday was sunny, with a fierce hot gale and people said the woods behind the hill were afire.

[1] A later estimate reduced the figure of houses burnt to 600.

By the afternoon a thick, hot smoke blew across the University campus, creeping through a gap. The fire was racing down upon Berkeley. The hillside was all burning houses. Meanwhile, the fire crept southward along the ridge, and threatened us both ways. The classes stopped in the University, and students swarmed uphill to fight the fires, and the campus filled with refugees, with the little they saved. By four o'clock it was quieter. At five the smoke from houses blazing towards the level rose perpendicularly. The University was saved, and the southern part of the town. By six the fire was under control in the town, and bodies of men went off to fight it on the heights. To-day I went through the burnt area. From above it looked like the chess-board map in *Alice through the Looking-glass*. It was scored with hard asphalted streets, and the brick chimneys stood gaunt like obelisks on bare sites amid ashes and rails—all that was left of 600 houses. Fourteen students' clubhouses were burnt and professors' libraries and gardens, palms and oaks destroyed, yet the people seem wonderfully cheerful, facing their loss undaunted.

The Sather Lectures are a detailed development and justification on the judgement on Herodotus included in the opening chapter of *The Jesus of History*. That judgement itself had been confirmed on his rereading of Herodotus during his tour in India. 'It is bad criticism that has made a popular legend of the unreliable character of Herodotus. As our knowledge of antiquity grows and we become able to correct our early impressions, the credit of Herodotus rises steadily and to-day those who study him most closely have the highest opinion of him.'[1] In his second lecture in the University of California, he took up the issue again, and dealt faithfully with a witticism of Mark Twain, which naturally secured the notice of reporters. The *San Francisco Examiner* summarized the argument effectively.

Dr T. R. Glover of Cambridge University has revived and brought to life Herodotus, best loved of the Greek story tellers, in this year's Sather lectures.... The subject of the latest lecture was 'The Story and the Book' following the initial address on 'The Man and the Place'. Mark Twain's 'quotation' from Herodotus, 'Very few things happen at the right time and the rest do not happen at all; the conscientious historian will correct these defects', Dr Glover says he does not himself recall in

[1] *The Jesus of History*, p. 8.

Herodotus. He believes it to be wanting in the best European texts and doubts if any manuscript earlier than 1890 attributes it to the historian.

But while Juvenal's jibes and Plutarch's impatience show that Mark Twain's humor has some support in ancient prejudice toward the father of history, nevertheless anyone, says Dr Glover, who will read Herodotus till he knows him with real intimacy, will not readily put up with the suggestion that he is other than the most candid and truthful man.

If the course on Herodotus was well received, the Earl Lectures on St Paul were even more popular, attracting an audience of eight or nine hundred. The emoluments of these lectureships were substantial and must have meant a considerable addition to Glover's income for the year.

The climate of California and the congenial company he found at the Faculty Club made Glover's stay at Berkeley memorable and delightful. He was among a lively set of colleagues whose idiosyncracies inspired many sonnets and limericks. He fills one of his small commonplace books with sayings and stories. R. T. Holbrook, the author of two or three works on Dante, particularly attracted him. It was Holbrook who complained that 'the path of fame is so encumbered with celebrities, one can't get by'. From this source Glover culled this specimen of a child's wit: Parent to daughter: 'What are you doing, Ethel?' 'I'm writing a letter to Georgie de Forest.' 'But you don't know how to write.' 'Well, Georgie doesn't know how to read.' The same raconteur fed Glover's sardonic humour where women were concerned by relating the story of the lawyer who received a letter in these terms, '5000 dollars down or I will carry off your wife', and who replied, 'I have not the 5000 dollars, but I am very much interested in your proposition.' It was, however, from R. H. Lowie the anthropologist that Glover learned something more about 'the complex and august character of one's mother-in-law'. It appears that among the Assiniboine Red Indians there is a taboo on speaking with one's mother-in-law. Discussing this with a chief, Lowie observed that white people do it. The chief remarked, 'White people will do anything.' Leonard Bacon, Professor of English Literature, reported the sentence of a student in examination. 'Browning had a firm belief in God, but he had it well under control.' It was in Chicago on an earlier occasion that Raymond Robins told Glover that 'Christian Science reminds one of a guinea pig; it isn't a guinea and it isn't a pig.'

Apart from the conversation of his colleagues, Glover's wide-ranging observation derived entertainment from many trivialities. He was amused by a notice in a Berkeley coffee house: 'Don't crab at our coffee; you'll be old and weak yourself some day.' This entry in the complaint book of the Faculty Club also attracted his attention. O'Neill wrote: 'I found a nail in my spinnach to-day.' Lapsley added: 'I found two "n"s in O'Neill's spinach to-day.' There is no doubt Glover thoroughly enjoyed his time at Berkeley and his visit was appreciated by the University. He was told when he came to leave, that they would like him to stay and that his visit had helped better feeling for Englishmen and had lifted religion a bit in the regard of the campus.

He paid brief visits to Canada and the U.S.A. in 1925, 1926 and 1927, but his most protracted stay was in 1928. He left England in June 1928 and did not return till the close of January 1929. This was a most eventful trip. In the first instance he went to attend the Baptist Convention in Toronto. At the end of June he went to Montclair, New Jersey, where he was preaching in the non-episcopal churches for the two summer months, July and August. Returning to Kingston in September, he was taken ill and had to undergo a serious operation. In November he was sufficiently recovered to go to Yale and fulfil engagements there. While there he came into close contact with Buchman and the Group Movement and was urged to throw in his lot with it. His visit to Yale led to a renewed invitation to a chair in the university. He was thus again faced with difficult personal decisions.

At Montclair, in July and August, the heat was very trying, and even with churches holding united services for the summer months, congregations were not large. Glover had no other engagements except the two services on Sundays, and he was in danger of finding time hanging heavy on his hands. Good friends took him joy-rides, and Foakes-Jackson was close at hand in another suburb of New York, which gave him the opportunity to exchange Cambridge reminiscences and current gossip. But at first he felt 'a great want of definite employment'. 'My father said I would lose the power to take a holiday.' Alison, a cousin of Fred Glover, once told him he should learn 'to potter like Fred, the prince of potterers'. He notes in his diary for 6 July 1928: 'I miss the necessity of producing those *Daily News* articles, which came to be the regular outlet of my thoughts.' However, before the end of the month, he had found a job of some interest. He accepted T. E. Page's invitation to edit and translate Tertullian's *Apology* for the Loeb Library. Both text and translation present difficulties, but by 24 July he is well launched on this enterprise. Two-thirds of the way through he wonders whether it was worth doing. 'Not so impressed as I was thirty years ago.... He does not seem to me so great as he once did—awfully clever, keen, dedicated, but stamped with traditions he never had from Christ. Yet the book is a real picture of life.' On 21 August Glover notes: 'Back to Tertullian's *Apology* and finished it by 1 p.m.—an incredible happiness (like getting engaged to be married) to be done with it.' Rather to Glover's regret the *De Spectaculis* was associated with the *Apology* in the Loeb edition. He went through with that, and his work satisfied his rather exacting editor.

He fulfilled his last preaching engagement on 2 September, the general impression of his visit being adequately conveyed by Foakes-Jackson in a four-line verse. As Presbyterians, Methodists, Congregationalists and Baptists had united to form his audiences, Foakes-Jackson wrote:

> O Montclair! where all sects do congregate
> Anxious to hear my T.R.G. orate,
> Their views may differ; yet they all agree
> That if we have a prophet, it is he.

On the eve of his departure from Montclair to Kingston, he confided in a friend that he was troubled by some disagreeable symptoms. The friend strongly advised him to get medical advice on his arrival in Kingston. On 8 September Phillip Macdonnell, who was on the medical staff at Queen's University and whom he knew and trusted, examined him and pronounced it to be prostatic trouble that would require an operation. After consulting the surgeon, Mr Etherington, Glover went into the General Hospital, Kingston. A day or two were spent in settling in and in writing necessary letters.

On Wednesday, 12 September, the operation was performed. Though two nights before he had stumbled on Jeremiah xxx. 17, 'For I will restore health unto thee and I will heal thee of thy wounds, saith the Lord', yet he anticipated the worst when he was wheeled into the operating theatre at 9.30 a.m. He was however calm and collected: 'Very tranquil in feeling I should not return and not afraid on that score, whatever the reason.' He found himself in his bed when he regained consciousness at 11.0 a.m. The chief cause of trouble was a small tumour, and the operation was entirely successful. He had to stay in hospital for a month, and then for a week he was guest patient in Mr Etherington's house. It was fortunate that Glover was in Kingston when this trouble came upon him. He was surrounded by friends, and they rallied round him magnificently. Between 9 September and 12 October he must have had nearly fifty visitors. Some like W. F. Nickle, James Cappon and Hiram Calvin paid several visits. Among the more frequent visitors was Nathaniel Micklem, who cheered him with talk of Woodbrooke and Mansfield. The best medical and nursing skill in Kingston was given him. In honour of his nurses, he wrote a set of sapphics of which the closing phrase was once confidently attributed to Horace.[1] His room in the hospital looked out on the Great Lake, and the patient was never tired of watching it. Nature and history conspired to make the scenery a fascination as this sonnet indicates:

> I have seen Katrine and seen Windermere
> Lakes of the mountains, famed in poesy;

[1] Dil Calvin's reference to this is of interest. 'On the same page with the formal Latin dedication of his *Challenge of the Greek* to Queen's University, there is a fragment in praise of "The Friendly City" (Kingston). [The fragment runs,

> Ego mente laeta
> Regium nomen referamque laudes
> Urbis amicae.]

A Cambridge don assured me that the fragment was undoubtedly from Horace, but that he could not name the poem in which it occurred.' Later Glover wrote that it was 'Not from anybody more ancient than T.R.G. in Kingston General Hospital. It was the tail end of my sapphic ode to my nurses.'

Yet there is larger beauty; and to me
The broad face of Ontario is more dear.
Here the Saint Lawrence leaves it; far and near
Are wooded isles: but yonder it breaks free
And touches heaven. Far as the eye can see
It takes the mind to grasp it, broad and clear.
Here the great dreamers dreamed yet greater dreams,
La Salle and Frontenac; here the Loyalists came,
Exiles for freedom; and the quiet lake
Keeps their old memories, while its vastness seems—
Great as the range the human soul may claim—
Claims for an outlook still more wide to make.

In such surroundings and with such care, Glover made a good
recovery. Etherington told him that the mortality in this operation was at that time about 20 per cent, and admitted that he
felt some risk in operating, as Glover was so far from home.
Besides what would Baptists do to him if anything went wrong?
No wonder Glover appreciated a remark of W. F. Nickle. Referring to one of his visitors, Glover said, 'Her face is a benediction,'
whereupon W. F. Nickle remarked, 'What you want is a
doxology.' 'And so I think I do.'

By the beginning of November he was able to proceed to New
Haven, Connecticut. In the previous May he had accepted an
invitation to lecture on the New Testament in the Divinity
School at Yale during the semester, October 1928 to January
1929. He was already a month overdue, owing to his illness.
K. S. Latourette writes of his visit:

I remember most happily and vividly his months here at Yale.
He had had an emergency operation for the prostate in Canada
only a few weeks before his duties at Yale began. That meant
that he was only convalescent when he arrived and the first
month of his stay with us was correspondingly difficult, especially
to one of his temperament. For the first few days he lived in one
of the dormitories, but for one in his state of health that proved
trying. He was given hospitality in one of the charming houses
of the city by the Oxford Group. During that year, the Oxford
Group had its headquarters in New Haven in a home which
had been lent them by one of its members. Dr Glover found
the home physically very pleasant and until late in his sojourn
with us had happy relations with members of the Group.

Glover met Frank Buchman during his year in India and he had
run across him subsequently on two or three occasions. He had
been interested and inspired by some of the work initiated in
the older universities by Buchman, but he had had no prolonged
or intimate association with the Group until he came to Yale.
He much appreciated the kind hospitality of Ray Purdy and his
wife in whose home he was staying, but the more he saw of the
movement, the more he began to wonder about it. 'Does it
sidetrack Christ for a sort of mystical Theism? Is it setting down
to direct inspiration what ordinary sense would suggest?' A little
later he wondered whether direct inspiration did not arbitrarily
override common sense. At the end of a month's stay he gave
Purdy a cheque for $75 as his contribution for the month, 'but
he tore it up, as his "guidance" was and is that I am to be guest.
I don't know what my guidance is, but I thought it sense to
give it.'

Naturally enough Purdy was attracted by Glover and was
eager to secure his help in the movement. Before the month was
out Purdy was planning Glover's future. He suggested a year of
travel in the service of the movement, and then twenty years in
an evangelical pulpit. Glover drily observed, 'My "guidance"
does not yet confirm it.' He was persuaded to go to a house-party
at Northampton, Mass., at the turn of the year to which he
contributed some very helpful addresses, but the result was that
he began to be conscious of considerable questioning in his own
mind as to their methods. He confessed that he found it a great
relief to be back in New Haven on 3 January. But both Purdy
and Buchman were sure that he ought to throw everything up
and join them in personal work for Christ, as they understood it.
They urged him to take part in two other house-parties. They
pressed him to delay his return and sail later on the *Mauretania*
for the sake of the house-parties. 'They don't seem even to try
to understand my obligations to Yale and my need to be rested
by the time I reach St John's again.' On 10 January the clash
came.

    Buchman and Purdy, insisting on two house-parties and
change of my plans, dismissed considerations of obligations to
Yale and to St John's, of health and need to rest. I was refusing
to be used for Christ; I needed Christian Science or something

for my health. Purdy argued that I let fear have too large a part in life, and he could play on my fear of draughts and other things. There was much talk of 'guidance' but it was clear that mine was to be subjected to theirs. But I knew my own obligations and stood by them.

The next day brought two telegrams from Buchman and Purdy which produced a wicked comment from Mrs Toennies—'they pursued it with smiles and soap'. But Glover stood firm. He had grown increasingly clear that he was not in the movement, despite the hospitality which he recognized had done so much for him.

His more mature judgement was contained in a letter to J. C. Carlile in 1932, advising him to be cautious in his references to the Group Movement in the *Baptist Times*. He wrote:

I have known Buchman since 1914 or 1915, and been friendly with him, though we are a good deal parted by now. I lived as guest with a group of his followers at Yale, Nov. 1928 to Jan. 1929—after consultation with the Dean and President of Yale. It was after my operation and in many ways they looked after me well and kindly. But with many good features Buchmanism won't do. Look here—PRO: great activity in getting conversions; great affection inside the group; real gains from Satan who become active evangelizing forces (I know some of these men, and they are real and genuine). CON: the open confession is sometimes supremely silly, sometimes foolish and thoroughly unwise and never very certainly desirable. (I can give instances that would surprise you). A great deal of assurance running into arrogance—they know. Then their 'spiritual surgery'—they are urged to probe into you, to lay bare your secret sins and very young persons try it. Buchman has 'hunches' (vulgar word and American; the group call it 'guidance') as to men's sins... some of his friends admit that he concentrates too much on erotic sins... the 'guidance' is often impulse or fancy and sometimes on extremely trivial things—a most awkward and dangerous belief for untrained minds—dear souls as some of them undeniably are. The fact is that there is an awful want of *thought* in it all—no Theology, no Christology, a concentration on an unexamined experience of Grace (often real enough); and as for guidance I told some of them I thought it too like the Quakers' 'Inner Light', an *ignis fatuus* that may have no relation to God. It is all a deal too easy thinking.... Some of the converts are capital fellows and some of the adherents. Others are naught.

Some fall away. In all it wants great care before we commit our Baptists and their paper to it. There's something unsound in it.

Whether the development of the movement into the Moral Rearmament Campaign would have appealed to Glover it is difficult to say, but he might have modified some of his criticisms in view of this development. In this later phase there is more concern for right personal relationships in industry and politics and less concentration on problems of sex ethics.

At the time when Buchman and Purdy pressed him to throw in his lot with the Group Movement, Glover had received a renewed invitation to become a professor at Yale. Above and beyond his existing commitments this too weighed the scales against Buchman's proposal. Yale was very attractive, and the discovery of a fellow Baptist in Professor Latourette added to its attractions. Professor Latourette recalls how Glover 'preached in the church of which I am a member, and attended it from time to time. I remember his statement with the characteristic twinkle in his eye, that he enjoyed coming because the service was "so very vulgar".' Apart from the prospect of finding good friends in Yale, to be asked to succeed B. W. Bacon in the New Testament chair was a very great honour, not lightly to be declined. He could not of course decide until he had returned to Cambridge and had had time to consult his family and his friends. A premature announcement in the *Christian Century*, reproduced in the *Christian World* on 15 February, to the effect that the invitation to succeed Bacon had been accepted, proved a great embarrassment.

Conflicting judgements and appeals now came unsought. Mrs Glover was not enthusiastic for it, but Mary thought it might be a new lease of life for her father. She hoped her aunts would not dissuade him. When he first broached the Yale question to his older sister she shut down on it at once. 'She said, I ought to stay at home more. Why has my lot been among so many decisive women?' His younger sister was perhaps less decisive, but her judgement was also against acceptance. At college, while his friends did not want to lose him, none said Don't go. But his Baptist friends were distressed. Charles Brown wrote, 'Why, oh why, are you leaving us? Honestly I think the Baptist

Churches in this country could scarcely suffer so great a loss. You have been our pride and joy with all your stubbornness and sometimes hastiness of temper. I am profoundly grieved. The loss will be irreparable.' J. C. Carlile, F. C. Spurr and Henry Townsend wrote in the same sense. Meanwhile letters of congratulation and welcome began to arrive from the other side of the Atlantic. Actually no decision had been reached. The financial position had to be clarified, and the possibility of combining part-time duty in Cambridge with a similar appointment in Yale had to be considered. This suggestion was dubiously practicable, and in spite of the generous offer from Yale and the prospect of a longer tenure of a professorial chair in the U.S.A., Glover in the end declined. On 13 April he records: 'At last reached decision and cabled: "Reluctantly conclude family, Baptists, finances, Cambridge, health indicate definitive refusal of most congenial proposal".'

He wrote and told Charles Brown of his decision, and received this reply:

I much appreciate your kindness in sending me the welcome news of your decision to refuse Yale. Surely you have decided wisely. You could never have lived that divided life. We should have felt that you were half in America and it would have demanded more and more of you.... Your half-going ending perhaps in a whole going would have been a serious loss to us. I don't agree with you everywhere. But I rejoice in you, though I have to confess that I sometimes think you somewhat deficient in the Catholicity which characterized Richard Glover.... I court fellowship with all members of Christ. Don't persist in thinking discussions on Christian unity waste of time, Reaveley, they are according to the mind of Christ.

A year later he talked the whole matter over with Rendel Harris whose judgement confirmed the decision and helped to banish any lingering doubts. 'The dear old man tells me to hold on to the oratorship, the biggest place a Dissenter has had here in Cambridge, and to hold out against enemies. I must not try to ride two horses at once. I am not a circus-rider, and can't do U.S.A. and here.' So Cambridge was to be his home till the end of his days, and on the whole he was growingly content that it should be so.

He paid one more extended visit to Canada and the U.S.A., involving absence from Cambridge for the Michaelmas term in 1930. He was away from the end of June till the end of December. As he also paid a brief visit to the States in the Easter vacation that year, he was away from Cambridge for no fewer than thirty-three Sundays. The main feature of the longer tour was an undertaking to traverse the Dominion from ocean to ocean, lecturing mainly on classical themes, for the National Council of Education. Similar tours had been undertaken by Michael Sadler and Henry Newbolt. The proposal was made to Glover as far back as 1926, but he could not accept it and carry it out before 1930. His later trips were all undertaken to fulfil preaching engagements in the summer vacations.

During his short visit to the States in the Easter vacation of 1930, Glover delivered a course of six lectures on the World of the New Testament at Lafayette College, Pennsylvania. A year later, they appeared in book-form with that title. It was a companion or sequel to the book, *Christ in the Ancient World* which had appeared two years before. In the earlier book, Glover outlined the changes in the thought, life and faith of the ancient world, which resulted from the influence of Christ. Perhaps the great interest of the later book was its justification of Glover's endorsement of Sainte-Beuve's judgement on Virgil. 'La venue même du Christ n'a rien qui étonne, quand on a lu Virgile,' says Sainte-Beuve. Glover commented in a footnote,

This phrase was criticized in the *Spectator* as 'a silly and audacious epigram, which...will hardly be accepted by real students of Virgil and of the Gospels.' After an interval of years I still deliberately accept it.... The early history of the Church illustrates the truth of this conclusion. To minds touched with the same sense of life's problems which pervades the poetry of Virgil, the Gospel brought the rest and peace which they could not find elsewhere.[1]

That Christ came in the fullness of time is a thesis which may be interpreted in many ways. In Sir Edward Creasey's *Fifteen Decisive Battles of the World*, the significance of Alexander's conquests is held to lie in the creation of a Greek-speaking world, ready for Christ's coming. The establishment of the Empire

[1] *Virgil*, p. 332 and note.

under Augustus completed the unification and pacification of that Greco-Roman world. Dean Colet, lecturing on the letter to the Romans, could illustrate from Horace and Juvenal, from Suetonius and Tacitus, the moral deterioration of Roman society, and justify the sombre picture of 'a world decaying for lack of God and social morality' presented to us in the first chapter of St Paul's letter to the Romans. Both comments on the fullness of time are justified.

But Glover in *The World of the New Testament*, took a different line. He was concerned to show how much that was good in ancient culture was, as it were, looking for Christ. St Paul's cento of passages from the psalms in Romans iii goes too far. There were seekers after God in the world of the New Testament. There were men who practised kindness. Christ came to stop the moral rot in the ancient world. He came also to preserve and fulfil the legacies of Greece and Rome. It was a world that needed saving, because of its failure of nerve, its lack of moral power. 'A great deal of the morality of this period is admirable; but somehow or other there is lacking the dynamic which will set men free from what is not so admirable.'[1] But it was also a world worth saving, because it was

a civilized world with a great education and a splendid past, a world with a literature, a philosophy, a history, an art, a spiritual ancestry, familiar and beloved for centuries....This is the world that the early church had to win, and the grandeur of its task and the greatness of its victory give us the measure of its power. 'I came not to destroy but to develop' is a sentence that has proved true.[2]

So Glover offered his readers 'a study of a thought-out society at its best'.

The World of the New Testament is one of the most attractive of Glover's smaller books. It is also of interest because in its dedication it commemorates one of the closest and most valued of Glover's friendships. It is dedicated to Dil and Eleanor Calvin. Dil Calvin's father, Hiram Calvin, was one of the trustees of Queen's University, Kingston, who welcomed Glover when he became Professor of Latin. The son had attended Glover's

---

[1] *World of N.T.*, p. 186.   [2] *Ibid.* p. 17.

classes, and became along with his wife, Eleanor, Glover's most intimate friend and correspondent. Glover sought every opportunity of visiting the Calvins in their home in 12 Bryce Avenue, Toronto, and from 1925 onwards he wrote constantly to them from England. There were few homes in which he felt more at ease, and for this, the forethought of his hostess was largely responsible. Glover used to wake early. Even before he grew older, he slept little after 6.0 a.m. and he would give way to blank depression while waiting for breakfast. Mrs Calvin, way back in the 1920's, began the practice of providing him with a thermos flask of coffee and some bread and butter when he went to bed. As the cup from which he drank his morning coffee was decorated with a pheasant, he came to call 12 Bryce Avenue, 'The Sign of the Pheasant', and the book, *A Corner of Empire*, which he wrote jointly with Dil Calvin is dedicated to his hostess at 'The Sign of the Pheasant'. This relief to early wakefulness became almost a necessity for Glover, and he would solicit the same provision from other hostesses, and he used to say, 'At the Judgement day these harassed hostesses will point at you, Eleanor, and denounce you as the author of their extra labour!' Many many times, hearing the family astir, he would call to his host to come to his room and ask, *how* do you sleep till half-past seven? The bed would be littered with books and papers, for he did not waste time.

On his journeys Glover always took several books with him. They often seemed to be the chief contents of his luggage. Some he would unload on his friends—the Calvins reckoned that at 'The Sign of the Pheasant' they amassed some 150 books presented or left behind by T.R.G.—but he usually acquired more as he travelled. In his diary for 1928, he has a list of twenty-nine books brought by him to the U.S.A. of which he gave eight away. By purchase or gift, he acquired at least nine others in their place. Novels, works of history and books of travel bulk large in the list, but also of course a Bible and a concordance and one or two classical authors. Horace was his constant companion.

In 1919, I had to cross the Atlantic, and just before I sailed, I picked up on David's bookstall in the Cambridge marketplace the neatest little Horace you ever bought for sixpence. It had belonged to the Harvard scholar, Charles Eliot Norton. It was the luckiest purchase. Since then I have crossed the Atlantic again and again and never without that little volume. At the end of each book of the Odes is a list of the ships in which I have read it, of trains and islands and mountain places in Canada and in the States and of old scenes in England too where I have passed my time with Horace.

Books were one unfailing or almost unfailing resource for Glover on ship-board, though he did once confess to S. C. Roberts, on a day when seas ran high and concentration of attention was difficult, 'You know there are times when books fail to satisfy me—and then I really wish my parents had taught me to play cards or something.'

Naturally, Glover liked not only to read books but also to discuss them. As the Calvins discovered, he had an extraordinary ability to draw out his close friends and give them a feeling that they too knew something about English literature—Browning or Wordsworth it might be—though they knew they were actually far behind him.

On his visits to Toronto and in his correspondence, Glover's characteristic predilections and prejudices found free expression. The Calvins could discount his prejudices, against Welshmen for example or against dogs, and rag him on these and other matters. He could let himself go without fear of being taken seriously. He could make fun of his own limitations. He often spoke of his own 'perpetual anticipation of disaster', which even extended to catching trains. 'My religion says it is wicked to be less than twenty minutes at the station before the train goes. You may have noticed this?' Jesting about the biography which he half-seriously proposed Dil Calvin should write, he wonders if patience is one of his outstanding virtues or only a minor excellence. 'If you are to write my life, you will need to think this out.' In the Calvin's home he could easily relax. After his address on Bunyan at the tremendous Baptist rally in 1928, he made his way back to 12 Bryce Avenue and collapsed into a chair, with 'I say! its good to be back among sinful people. Can I have some food?'

Among his predilections, Glover's delight in apposite quotation and allusion charmed his friends. Dil Calvin recalled how,

in the autumn of 1928, after his serious operation, Glover came
to stay with them in Toronto. 'He was still shaky and at the
foot of the stairs, I took him firmly under an arm and said, "Let
us begin and carry up this corpse." "Singing together", added
Glover, and roared with laughter.' Misquotations and little
twists in familiar sayings also delighted him. He liked the
American version of a well-known Latin tag, 'De mortuis nil
nisi bunkum'. He also notes another variant, 'De mortuis nil
desperandum'. He jotted down several of such little twists in
the sayings of Linley Sambourne of *Punch*, as recorded by
F. Anstey. For example, 'There was such a silence that you
could have picked up a pin in it'. 'He was left literally without
a rag to stand on.' 'There it is, like a white elephant round his
neck.' 'You mustn't take me too seriatim.' 'I can tell you, I've
had to keep my nose to the gridiron.' 'You'll be running your
head into a mare's nest.' Glover's daughter Elizabeth provided
him with many treasured examples of the same order. She
might be 'torn between two stools', and 'the chronological
moment' might find her 'grinning like the Cheddar cat'.
Americanisms also interested Glover, though he was impatient
with American pronunciation. He liked Oscar Wilde's saying,
'We have really everything in common with America nowadays,
except of course language.' He notes such phrases as 'to talk
turkey', 'it went over big', 'when it comes to a show-down',
and the observation of Wilbert White, 'We're long on organization and short on things to organize.'

    Glover's ever-growing affection for Canada in general and for
Queen's, Kingston, and 12 Bryce Avenue, Toronto, in particular
is of course apparent through all his correspondence and contacts
with the Calvins. In 1933 and 1934 he did not cross the Atlantic,
and at the close of 1934 he writes: 'How I want to see the Sign
of the Pheasant and its proprietors after two years' absence! It
is long since there was such an interval. Next year—oh, I hope
so.' The old Queen's days and the men he knew there are often
in his thoughts, and he's always sorry to leave Canada. The
climatic contrast between Canada and East Anglia enhances
the attraction of the Dominion. Glover was always hankering
after a land where January and February are unknown, or at
least where January and February do not bring the damps and

cramps of Cambridge—wet, chilly and depressing. Writing one September evening he says, 'It was cool, so knowing the passion for ventilation that devastates English houses, I fled to college.' Canada has the advantages of central heating, of which Glover thoroughly approved. One chilly April day as he entered 12 Bryce Avenue, he said, 'I say, it's good to come into a house that's warm everywhere.' Then there was the fascination of the scenery. On Garden Island where the Calvins had a summer residence, Glover would sit on the shore looking across the St Lawrence, here two miles wide, to Kingston. He commented on the vast sweep of water, leading into the great lakes and so running up for a thousand miles into the continent, and flowing out over a thousand miles into the Atlantic. Then he added, 'I know some men in Cambridge who ought to sit here and look and think—it would enlarge their minds.' When he wrote the preface to his collection of essays, entitled *The Challenge of the Greek*, he realized that a good deal of autobiography had gone into its pages. 'Here are the things that have made the life— the great Classics, the *great lake and river by which I lived, the Dominion*; interwoven are the memories of friends and colleagues, outlooks, fancies, impressions and impulses of deeper birth.' The Classics and Canada had combined to enlarge his mind.

Much as he enjoyed his visits to the States and his contacts with Americans, particularly with American scholars, Canada remained his first love. After all, Canada was and is British. Compared with the U.S.A. it is law-abiding. 'In 1927, there were 327 murders in the city of Detroit and not one in Windsor, Ontario. On the Windsor race-track the gambler swung his hand to a revolver in his hip-pocket. "For God's sake, Jim, don't!" cried a friend, "remember you are in Canada."' Glover turned into Latin the saying of Sir John Macdonald uttered in his last election campaign and cut on the base of his monument in Kingston which was his home: 'A British subject I was born, a British subject I will die.' 'Civis sum natus moriarque Britannicus idem'—the thought Sir John's, the immortal form, T.R.G.'s.

In 1926 he had an opportunity of showing his affection for Queen's University by contributing to an endowment fund which

Dil Calvin was actively promoting. His covering note reveals his mind.

I learn that an endeavour is being made to secure a proper endowment for Queen's University. I look back with gratitude to years of happiness there. I realize constantly how much I owe to my colleagues and to my pupils—the upper and nether millstones, if you like; and I am happy to think that the old bonds still unite us. I hope that you will allow that I am a Queen's man and will accept £20 toward the endowment scheme, a small contribution to a big fund but an expression of the real affection that all Queen's men have for Queen's.

A little later Glover presented to Queen's a marble head of 'the young Augustus'. In 1935 the necessity of finding a new principal for Queen's elicited from Glover a letter on the qualifications of a principal in response to Dil Calvin's statement that 'Fyfe (now Aberdeen) is for J— M— to be Principal of Queen's.'

Now about Queen's. You may remember I was interested in the J— idea, before ever Fyfe came on that excursion....J— is a real business man, has experience of Oxford and Queen's—*two* universities of quite different types—understands the points of both, is the antithesis of the 'UNIVERSITY OF TORONTO + CHICAGO PH.D.' type, and therefore is *not* omniscient (and not to be omniscient is a big factor in a Principal); and he has the experience of the war in Europe and business in Montreal and Toronto; a pretty big range—and he carries his experience well, and knows men and knows his own limitations. On the other hand, I think he probably *won't* do it (I mean will refuse), and I can understand why. Education is a deal more complicated business than in good old Geordie's [G. M. Grant's] golden days, when we went on Edinburgh lines and aimed at educating citizens, 'breaking up their dogmatism and putting them at a universal point of view' (John Watson); to-day a university to hold its head in the air must be a super-glorified ultra-trade school, run on an Americanized adaptation of German lines, its business to create specialists who have no literature and no philosophy, to research on remote physical problems, and to advance Bio-Chemistry, Psychology, vitamins and Gestalt-theories. Literature yields to encyclopaedic amassing of facts about authors and theories of influence. History condescends to the minutest detail and misses the movement in the minutiae—

do you think a necklace is made of beads or string? Well, the
modern historian is all for beads and forgets the string. J— may
well feel that he is out of it among these *Fach*-men (look up *Fach*
in your German dictionary). They are arrogant and not very
intelligent. To stand up against them you want somebody who
did Greats at Oxford, and has had experience (say) of a pro-
vincial university in Britain or Ireland. Failing J—, I would
say, come over here and try again, or you will infallibly get
a Toronto-cum-Chicago half-bake, or somebody *hypnotized* by
that type. Not that Canada has no really educated people, but
the Trustees will be bullied—'everybody's doing it'—into getting the Ph.D. Chicago; and the real people will feel they ought
not to attempt the Principalship without the Chicago hallmark.
At least that is how I fear it may be. J— would safeguard us;
but he is nervous too, and has not the cheek to tell them that *he*
knows what real education is.

Early in 1934 Glover suggested to Dil Calvin that they might
produce a joint volume on things Canadian, 'not a complete
handbook, history or cyclopaedia, but a book to make readers
think "Canada must be pretty interesting".' 'Canadian Days'
was the title first suggested, and Glover was proposing to include
in it almost anything he had written about any part of Canada.
But in the course of two years' correspondence, he agreed with his
collaborator that the projected Canadian Days would be too
diffuse. So in the end the authors concentrated on Kingston
and adopted the title, *A Corner of Empire*. 'We must say in our
preface that it *is* a corner (and we will expatiate in our corner)
but it is a corner of the Empire (and we will bring out how it
concerns the Empire and has done so, since first the white man
built his ford in 1673).' After outlining the content of the book as
now conceived, Glover added, 'My dear Dil, if this isn't going
to be a book—yes, sir, a real human British Empire no-hole-nor-
corner BOOK—find me one or dream one.' The book was completed and published in 1937, the preface being dated Dominion
Day (1 July) 1937. The honours and the labour are fairly
distributed between the two authors. Glover was responsible
for the opening sketch of historic Kingston. In the closing
chapter, he was able to pay a generous, if discriminating tribute,
to 'Geordie'—to G. M. Grant, the principal under whom he
served and who did so much to establish Queen's. Glover took

great pleasure in this book. He had toyed with the idea of writing a history of Canada. This he found he could not do, but it was a great satisfaction to have paid his tribute to Kingston and to Queen's, to have recalled 'memories of friendship and happiness, "rememberable things" that nature speaks, in the beauty of a great lake and a great river, open water and open sky'.

Chapter X

CAMBRIDGE, 1932-1943

Glover as Phil-hellene : friendships and the home circle :
closing years

During the ten or twelve years before his retirement in 1939 from
his positions as Public Orator in the University and as college
lecturer Glover's predominant interest lay in the field of Greek
studies. In this period his most noteworthy books were *Greek
Byways* published in 1932, and *The Ancient World* first published
in 1935, and now included in the Pelican series. He did not, of
course, drop his other concerns, and it may be well to say something of these other activities before attempting to assess his
contribution to our appreciation of the legacy of Greece.

The pulpit still claimed a good deal of his time, especially on
his visits to Canada in the vacations. Many of his sermons provided themes for articles in the *Baptist Times*, which now became
his chief outlet for religious journalism. An invitation to deliver
the Donnellan Lectures at Trinity College, Dublin, in 1932 led
him to crystallize some results of his further study of the gospels.
He spoke on the use of particular words in the Synoptic records
of the teaching of Jesus. A year later he recast these lectures
under the title, 'Reading the gospels again'. The revised course
was given at Bangor in 1933, and was subsequently repeated at
Woodbrooke. But these lectures never appeared in print.
Nothing comparable with *The World of the New Testament* or with
Saturday Papers came from Glover's pen during these years. After
his retirement, Cambridge University Press published for him
in 1941 a slim little volume, *The Disciple*—a fitting successor to
The Pilgrim. It was to be his last work in this kind. It may not
be out of place to record here that his effective association with
the Student Christian Movement ceased when Tissington Tatlow retired from the secretaryship in 1928. There was no dramatic breaking of his links with the movement, and though he was
out of sympathy with some trends of thought among students,
such as their interest in the social gospel and in Christian reunion,

this did not occasion his withdrawal from active participation in the movement. He had had a longer run as a speaker at Swanwick than most of his contemporaries. His frequent visits to the U.S.A. and Canada meant that normally he was out of England at the time of the Summer Conferences. When Tatlow left, his chief personal link with the S.C.M. was severed. Moreover, the publication of the *Saturday Papers* in 1927 ended his connexion with the S.C.M. Press. From that time on Glover looked to the Cambridge University Press, and the books he was to write in the 1930's obviously were more fittingly published by the University Press than by the S.C.M.

The increasing attention which he gave to Greek History did not impair his interest in Latin literature and things Roman. His witty Latin orations continued to enliven degree days. In 1931 he gave four broadcast talks on Virgil. Early in 1932 he was invited to give the Lewis Fry Lectures at the University of Bristol. He chose Horace as his subject, and the two lectures, delivered in December 1932, appeared in print next year. In addition to this charming appreciation of Horace, Glover wrote the chapter on the literature of the Augustan age for the tenth volume of the *Cambridge Ancient History*. F. E. Adcock, the editor, in a letter to Glover said, 'May I add that several of our young men have been exceedingly pleased with your chapter? I almost felt envious as I heard their praises.' A. Nairne too was enthusiastic. He sent 'an outcry of delight and gratitude...Virgil just perfectly done.' The little book on Horace and this chapter in the *Cambridge Ancient History* were almost his last contribution to Latin letters. The later volumes of essays with the title, *The Challenge of the Greek* and *Springs of Hellas*, contain the one, an appreciation of Virgil written for his bimillenary in 1930, and the other, studies of Quintilian and Cicero, but as the titles indicate, the Greeks are the centre of interest.

Three Hellenic cruises, in the spring of 1928, in September 1929 and in August-September 1933, gave Glover great pleasure. He not only enjoyed repeated visits to Athens and Constantinople, to Rhodes, to Cnossos and to Syracuse, but he was also stimulated by the company he found on board ship—for the most part a congenial company. On the first trip, on the *Lotus* from Marseilles, he found himself with H. A. L. Fisher, A. E. J.

Rawlinson and others. His cousin, Lewis Glover, was a member of the party, and T.R. was glad to be his patient when, as was apt to happen on these cruises, dubious food brought on diarrhoea. In 1929 on the *Théophile Gautier*, which too sailed from Marseilles, he was particularly glad to find himself with Sir Donald Maclean, who had long been his friend and with whom he was most closely in sympathy in politics. They belonged to the same school of Liberalism. Ramsay Muir was another Liberal with whom Glover had much in common. J. T. Sheppard, now Provost of King's College, and R. W. Livingstone, of Corpus Christi, Oxford, helped to make this voyage memorable for Glover. J. T. Sheppard shared a table with him on his third cruise, on the *Kraljica Marija* ('British-built and good if elderly') which sailed from Venice.

Sheppard's company was particularly welcome, since his bantering levity was the kind of stimulus to which Glover most readily responded. He notes in his diary, 'J.T.S. is a great resource; he says J.S. Reid, reporting long ago on his Fellowship thesis said, "Unfortunately, he has a certain lightness of touch which might be corrected by a year at a German University".' Fortunately the correction either was never applied or never succeeded. So on this third cruise, Sheppard could remark, 'I want to say once for all—whatever is said at this table, Glover, is said with affection and admiration for you, to pull your leg.' Glover had the greatest admiration for Sheppard as an interpreter of the Classics. He thus describes Sheppard's lectures in his diaries; 'On the *Théophile Gautier*, on 6 September 1929, after dinner, J. T. Sheppard's much-looked-for lecture on Trojan scenes in *Iliad*: readings in a loose-hung verse translation of his own from early books: vivid glance, voice, gesture;—quips at editors: *ipsissime*; and a very great success; he really put it across.' In 1933, the lecture on the *Odyssey* was equally successful. Under date 4 September of that year, we read that

Sheppard gave his long-desired lecture on *Odyssey*, and a capital thing it was—portrait of Ulysses as seen by this, that and the other: Athene, daughter of the mind of Zeus and her relation with Hagia Sophia: religion—Zeus on the troubles that mortals add for themselves to the mixed lot the gods give: explanation of the conduct of the suitors: a long Nausicaa passage recited in his own rendering—the bit Samuel Butler said showed the author was a woman, but J.T.S. suggested the possibility that Homer was a married man! Audience was sympathetic and it went happily, and Schuster moved thanks for 'Cambridge Scholarship and Cambridge Taste'.

A week later Sheppard followed this up with a 'magnificent lecture (nothing less) on Aeschylus, *Agamemnon*; warmly praised by all'. The audience included Her Royal Highness, Princess Marie Louise, who sat in front, doing embroidery. Glover had earlier been presented to Her Royal Highness, at her wish. She had been impressed by his address on Luther's 'Begin first with the wounds of Christ', which he had given on the first Sunday service of the cruise. On the same voyage, Glover also met 'Her Royal Highness, Infanta Beatrice of Spain (daughter of the Duke of Edinburgh) an exile, but a bright lively woman who learnt to love books and first editions from Stephen Gaselee.'

The company on this third and last cruise seems to have been unusually distinguished and varied. Dr Arthur Gornall records some impressions of his contacts with Glover on this voyage.

In 1933 I met him on one of the cruises organized by the Hellenic Travellers' Club. We visited the Dalmatian Coast, Greece, Turkey and some islands, and our distinguished company included two Princesses, lots of noble Lords and Ladies, including the present Marquess of Salisbury, and 'small fry' like myself. Of all the lectures to which we listened on deck in the evenings, the one by Dr T. R. Glover was the most outstanding in my memory—it was on 'The Forest and Greek Life'. I knew none of the ship's company before the cruise, but I did know that Dr Glover had attended the Bristol Grammar School, where I was a scholar under Sir Cyril Norwood for several years—I, therefore, very soon contacted him and made myself known to him. He seemed to delight afterwards in introducing me to friends by saying, 'We were at the same school you know,' and then after a suitable pause, 'but not at the same time.' The difference actually was thirty years!

Unfortunately we had a serious outbreak of sickness, colic and diarrhoea which attacked about 150 of the 270 passengers one night, and when I met Dr Glover for the fourth time at the nearest convenience, at about 3 or 4 in the morning, he said to me with a very straight face, 'Doctor, I wish you would sign my death certificate.' I told him I hoped that this would not be necessary. He said, 'I would rather a Grammar School boy did it than anyone else,' and not until then did he break into his usual and inimitable smile. I am glad to say that we recovered quickly and enjoyed the rest of our cruise.

The lecture on 'The Greek and the Forest' was included in the essays in the volume *The Challenge of the Greek*. On the earlier cruises, Glover lectured on 'The Vitality of Greece', 'The Greek on the Sea', and 'Diet in History'. These all appeared in *Greek Byways*.

This volume of essays contains some of Glover's most original and most exact scholarship. The Dutch historian, G. Renier, has deplored the scarcity of such studies in this country.

Excursions into the by-ways of the past offer possibilities of recreation to the serious historian who does not wish to play patience or solitaire when he needs a rest from his main task. The French are brilliant and often sound at this kind of work, because they do not despise it, but most English historians are as loath to enter into By-path Meadows as Christian's companion Hopeful.

Greek Byways does something to remove this reproach. Though the book did not escape some adverse criticism, it was on the whole warmly appreciated and enhanced Glover's reputation among classical scholars. That Foakes-Jackson, to whom Glover dedicated the book in singularly felicitous terms, was enthusiastic in its praise, is not surprising, yet his judgement was not more than just. He wrote,

To feel that I have your friendship so warmly and graciously expressed is much, but to find that the book itself is one of your best is even more. The learning you display fills me with envy, but the ease with which you deal with it appeals to me still more. After all, literary skill plus wide learning is necessary to make antiquity interesting.

Classical scholars who regretted Glover's excursions into Church history and who were out of sympathy with his religious interests, welcomed *Greek Byways*. 'The real T.R.G. coming out at last,' they said. A. E. Housman in his 'bitter-sweet' way allowed some commendation of *Greek Byways* to escape him. Ernest Harrison of Trinity, the Registrary of the University, whose interests in

the classics were different from Glover's, thought the book
'damned good' and extremely well written. American scholars,
E. K. Rand, James Loeb, and Paul Shorey, were equally
appreciative.

If the book appealed to scholars and experts, it appealed no
less to that elusive person, the general reader. The wide range of
topics included in the volume make difficult an adequate characterization. Two features of the book as a whole may be thrown
into relief. First, the essays show Glover's close acquaintance
with and discriminating use of Hellenistic authors. He cast his
net more widely than most of his fellows. In *Democracy in the
Ancient World* he wrote, 'Little as classical scholars of the stricter
profession will go to Hellenistic authors it remains that...the
Hellenistic world with all its exhaustion and its disappointments,
is more significant and more fruitful than is commonly admitted.'
How fruitful the reading of such authors may be, *Greek Byways*
amply demonstrates. In the second place, many of these essays
are concerned with the social-economic side of history. Glover
was always interested in men's activities and daily work, in the
conditions under which they lived. The conditions and methods
of agriculture and industry, of trade and commerce were subjects of constant enquiry. With the first three essays in *Greek
Byways*—'The Greek on the Sea', 'Diet in History' and 'Metal-
lurgy and Democracy'—must be associated the essays on
'The Greek and the Forest', 'The Greek Farmer', 'Emporia',
and 'Feeding the Athenians', which appeared in a later volume.
These studies are not so much ventures into By-path Meadows
in search of recreation, as enquiries in preparation for a social-
economic history of Greece which Glover would have liked to
write. He had the great advantage of neither despising economic
factors nor exaggerating their importance. As he wrote in 'The
Greek and the Forest', 'Flood, drought, deposit of silt and
debris, fires and the destruction of humus—such factors mean
declining return from agriculture, lessened or lost crops and
increase in the cost of living. There are of course political and
other factors to be considered; no single group of causes can be
supposed responsible for everything; but those named are not to
be lost from the reckoning.' Fortunately Glover never fell under
the spell of Karl Marx. He could see class-conflict in its true

perspective and escape the obsession which ruins Marxists as historians. He was more alive to the problem posed by Malthus— the pressure of population on the means of subsistence—and he was particularly interested in the colonial enterprises by which the Greeks sought to solve it.

If *Greek Byways* exhibits Glover's capacity for detailed study of subsidiary themes, *The Ancient World* shows his gift for interpreting the main features of a familiar story in an illuminating and original manner and for setting them in their true perspective. The University Press suggested to him the project of writing a text-book on ancient history for schools. He was always eager to capture the interest of sixth-formers. Let him try his hand at it in a school history of Greece and Rome. The result did not correspond exactly to the original intention. *The Ancient World* is much more than a school history. It is a little masterpiece. Larmor wrote of it a few months after its publication in 1935, 'I have been thinking of you while I have read *The Ancient World* at least twice over. The reason that education is so rotten is that the said book is "not suited for any examination". You are the only scholar in the ancient literary sense that is left, unless you count the Professor of Latin.' Glover had not succeeded in producing a text-book to prepare sixth-form boys for the Higher School Certificate. He had done something much better. He had brought out in a fascinating manner the abiding interest of the story of the Greco-Roman world.

The Greeks are, of course, the heroes of the story. We start from Troy and end in Constantinople. To a list of dates taken from the *Cambridge Ancient History*, Glover adds three later dates and the choice is significant. They are 1453, the Fall of Constantinople to the Turks; 1834, the recovery of independence by the Greeks, and 1934, the re-dedication of the Theseum in Athens as a Christian Church. The outcome of the story which seems to Glover of supreme interest is to be found in events which re-establish Greek freedom and associate the spirit of Greece with Christianity. Throughout the story, the Greeks hold the centre of the stage. Other peoples come in as the Greeks discover them and as they contribute to Greek culture. Glover looks at them through Greek eyes. Naturally the Roman story cannot be entirely subordinated to that of Greece, yet Hellenism is the triumph of captive Greece over her Roman captor. And the story of the Roman Empire culminates in the marriage of Greek culture with Christian faith. This note is sounded early in the book. For on p. 69 we are told, 'to the end the Greeks were quite certain that no one could match the Greeks in thinking; anything to be first rate had to be Greek somehow; and they were right. A great German thinker said a very suggestive and probably a true thing, when he said that "the thoughts of Jesus were never properly expressed till they found Greek words".' This was a favourite quotation with Glover, as was also the assertion that Christianity triumphed over the mystery-religions because it was most fully Hellenized.

All Glover's cherished ideas, even his prejudices, find expression in this book, and he uses his wide experience and observation to illuminate his theme. He begins with geographical and climatic factors, of which residence in Canada had made him more fully aware. Mountain ranges, rivers and roads play no small part in the life of peoples. But his experience in Canada and the U.S.A. comes out in detail. When he writes of the burning of Carthage he recalls his experience at Berkeley. 'Polybius stood by Scipio, the conqueror, as it burned—and you need to see a city burning to understand what it is like, with wooden houses and wooden roofs ablaze, the masses of smoke and glowing ash in the air, the heat and the horror of the galloping flames, and the sense of man's helplessness.' Canada taught Glover what Gaul may have meant to Julius Caesar in liberation of mind.

One feels, as one looks at Caesar's later work in the government of the whole Empire, when it became his, that he has learnt to handle great issues with a freedom which he could never have learnt in Roman streets. No Roman governor or general had ever been away from Rome for so long a consecutive period. 'The great open spaces' change a man's thoughts; and a new world sends him back a new man to the old world.

Glover had made this point at greater length in his book, *Democracy in the Ancient World* (p. 223), where he wrote:

It is perhaps overlooked that Caesar came to the government of the Roman world from nine years of Gaul. It is, I am afraid, true that years of life in a colony affect the outlook and character even of the modern Englishman, unless he is quite sealed against new impressions and observations—which no one would assert of Caesar. Men may laugh at colonial talk of the great open spaces where a man is a man—at Joseph Chamberlain's 'illimitable veldt'—but no one who has felt such things will laugh at them; for the newness, the sense of opportunity, the very vastness are spiritual quickening.

The great open spaces did not however blind Glover to 'the charm that goes with the little'. He reminds his readers that 'Troy town covered roughly as much as New Street Railway Station in Birmingham, perhaps a little less.... Troy has meant more in history and so far has done more for human happiness.' This comparison had earlier prompted a sonnet.

> Right in the heart of Birmingham there lies
>   The New Street Railway Station. There, they say,
>   The ancient Troy might well be stowed away
> Her walls and streets and palaces. To our eyes
> Troy seems a village. Numbers, bulk and size
>   Make up the glories of our modern day,
>   And to the ruins of the past we pay
> The half contemptuous tribute of surprise.
> Yet Birmingham has no such tale as Troy
>   To set the heart of the world's youth afire;
> All else is hers, but not the pulse of joy,
>   Not deathless heroism, not Homer's lyre;
> Troy holds mankind; and Birmingham in vain
> With Hector matches Joseph Chamberlain!

That Glover's prejudices slip out only enhances the entertainment one derives from the book. You would hardly expect his prejudice against Anglicanism to figure in an account of ancient Greece, but we read: 'It must never be forgotten that Greek religion had no creed and no dogma, nothing standardized, and if plenty of priests, *no episcopate.*' His views about women and their proper functions find incidental expression in his account of early Roman society where the wool was spun and woven by the women. 'Women altogether seem to have been more really useful in these early times than progress now permits them to be.'

In the very generous and discriminating tribute to Glover, which Harold Laski contributed to the *New Statesman and Nation*

some six months after Glover's death, he nearly but not quite
seized on the essential core of Glover's political judgements as
these are revealed in his historical writings. Glover he suspected
to have been an intelligent conservative, who thought the average
man spiritually important but politically incompetent.

I would not say he took a low view of human nature, but
I doubt whether he expected very much from it. But I think he
had a power of hero-worship which made him feel the greatness
of the really great man overwhelmingly. One catches that note
in his sentences, for example, whenever figures of the stature of
St Paul come upon the scene. At such moments, his writing
takes on a kind of extra quality; there is, pretty obviously, an
emphasis of excitement which puts a new emotion into the
learning he conjures up for his reader. One almost feels that he
takes the misunderstanding of a great man by his age as a
personal insult. He can never have forgiven Brutus and his fellow-
conspirators. Who were they to challenge a mighty dream?

Any one who reads chapter XIV of *The Ancient World* will realize
how true or how nearly true this is. The emphasis of excitement
is obvious in the portrait of Caesar. The condemnation of the
action of Brutus and his fellow-conspirators as 'the most foolish
thing done in antiquity' is emphatic and unmistakable. In hero-
worship Glover was not ashamed to be Carlyle's disciple. Yet
he did not surrender to Carlyle's tendency to glorify brute force
and success. Glover did not follow Shaw in his adulation of
Mussolini and Stalin, nor would he have followed Hazlitt in his
homage to Napoleon. Brutus is not condemned for challenging
a mighty dream. Caesar understood the realities and needs of
the situation as Brutus and Cassius did not. Caesar, as Glover
claims, had imagination, but he was no dreamer. Caesar is
great, not because he was a military genius and could play
power-politics successfully, but because he had vision, understanding, magnanimity. Glover's standards of greatness were
more exacting than Carlyle's.

When Laski suggests that in condemning Brutus, Glover was
condemning the average man as incapable of sound political
judgement, and when he continues 'the average man is, for
[Glover], pretty average.... The part of wisdom is for him to
know his betters when they step upon the stage of history;

politics and the deeper issues are for the elect who are beyond his ken', I think he fails to appreciate Glover's actual political outlook. He was not the Conservative of Laski's imagination, unless a Liberal of the old school is no more than an intelligent Conservative. In 1928 Glover was asked to contest West Bristol in the Liberal interest. He declined because he felt it to be incompatible with his calling both as preacher and scholar.[1] But he believed in our parliamentary democracy and never wished the average man to leave deeper issues to his betters. Glover never toyed with oligarchy or dictatorship. On the other hand he did not idealize democracy or flatter democrats. He can sympathize with Theognis, the aristocrat, as well as with Hesiod, the peasant. 'It is possible to sympathize with both. "A man's a man for a' that", sang Robert Burns; but the democrats of Greece, like those of France in 1793, forgot that aristocrats were men; they may have had provocation.' But provocation is not justification, and democrats can betray humanity. Respect for the average man does not mean blind confidence in him. The clue to Glover's attitude is to be found in what he says of Jesus in the chapter on the Christian Church in the Roman Empire.

He stands alone among the great figures of the past in his belief in man.... He stands nearer to common men and is in deeper sympathy with them, and rates their power to absorb and understand and handle the profoundest ideas higher than any administrator, reformer or archbishop has ever dared to put it. But this he did, without the reformer's vague dreams; he knew what was in man, and expected men to crucify him.

Glover was well aware how difficult it is to make democracy safe for the world.

Beyond *Greek Byways* and *The Ancient World*, the chapter on Polybius in the *Cambridge Ancient History*, vol. VIII, was another outstanding contribution to Greek studies, belonging to the years before his retirement. Public recognition of his gifts as an

---

[1] He was advised by some of his best friends that it would injure his unique position and influence. 'Your work', wrote his old Bristol friend Edward Robinson, 'has cleared and is clearing the vision of men, and strengthening and sustaining their characters; I speak from experience.' Heitland also suggested to Glover's cousin Fred, his doubt whether Parliament is exactly what would put T.R.G.'s gifts to the best use. 'His energy is ever fretting at the solemn limitations of academic life.'

interpreter of the Greek mind came when he was asked to broadcast a national lecture on 19 December 1934. He spoke for forty
minutes on the challenge of the Greeks, and the lecture was the
subject of a leader in *The Times* the following day. Further
academic recognition came in the form of honorary degrees.
Glasgow gave him an LL.D. in 1930, and in 1936 Dublin
honoured him with a D.Litt. along with Sir John Lavery,
Thomas Bodkin and H. W. Nevinson. Glover enjoyed his company as well as the honour of the degree. He was never elected
a Fellow of the British Academy, perhaps because, as Foakes-
Jackson said, 'you can't make learning dreary'. He was however
invited by the Academy to give the Hertz Lecture on 'The
Mind of St Paul', which he delivered on 9 July 1941. He was
President of the Classical Association in 1938 and his address on
'Purpose in Classical Studies' contains his last considered plea
for the retention of the Classics in education and his reflexions
on the interpretation of the Classics which is essential if that
retention is to be justified. His presidential address and the
broadcast lecture were included in the volume of essays to which
the latter gives the title, *The Challenge of the Greek*. The lecture
on St Paul is included in the posthumous volume, *The Springs of
Hellas*. In those two volumes, we possess the aftermath of the
main harvest of Glover's work as a Classical scholar.

It was fitting that *The Springs of Hellas* should conclude with
the essay on 'The Mind of St Paul'. Whatever its merits as an
interpretation of St Paul, this, the last of his published writings,
reflects admirably the mind of its author. This reading of the
mind of St Paul is Glover's last testament of faith. What he set
out to do is clear from a letter he wrote to Richard in March
1941.

Did I tell you I have to give a formal lecture to the British
Academy next July on 'The Mind of St Paul'? I have been
busying myself with it. I mean to stress the idea that, in interpreting a creative man, we have to get a perspective in his ideas,
get the big thing big, the central thing central; note the *accent*,
of course, for that is a bit of him. (Foakes Jackson had some old
relative bred a Catholic who used to say that J. H. Newman was
a Calvinist all his life; the born and bred Catholics, I gather,
have never liked what we used to call the perverts.) Well, back
to Paul. Three problems of unity and division—(1) the cleft

between Jew and Gentile, was it in God's design or not? (2) the division of mankind, world and all, from God, to be reconciled in Christ; (3) fundamental, the division in Paul's own nature (and yours and mine). See Romans vii. Charles Raven says, rearrange the last two; but I think not: it is all right to say as in the beginning of Ephesians, etc., that Christ will reconcile all things—it is like talking about 'humanity' and other abstracts: but will He reunite the discordant elements in *my* make-up, and (quite a different problem from 'peace on earth') put peace in my soul, peace with myself and peace with God? If He can do *that*, then I can believe a bit in no. 2 in that list. But any real reader of the Gospel will tell you that 'humanity' is an easier problem than 'thy neighbour' or 'thy brother': these last come too near home; and you will notice our Lord leaves abstracts to the half-baked, the people who look at men through a telescope and never come to grips with the detail.

This distrust of abstractions, this insistence on coming to grips with the actual and this preoccupation with the problem of personal salvation are all characteristic of Glover's approach to literature and life. They are essential features of his faith in Christ.

To turn to more personal matters, Glover was very dependent on friendship. One who relies on walking and talking as his main recreation must have companions. Apart from that Glover was warm-hearted and really interested in persons. His sensitiveness craved sympathy and understanding. I think he realized with Rendel Harris that we do not deserve our friends; we enjoy them. He certainly appreciated his friends and he had many. It is true that sometimes he allowed his friendships to lapse or cool off because of a serious difference of judgement or even because of some trivial misunderstanding. Particularly in the ten years before the second World War, he became increasingly impatient with and distrustful of pacifists, and this led to the lapsing of some friendships. Pacifism seemed to him to be politically unrealistic and sometimes religiously uncharitable. Fundamental Christianity was being identified too simply with pacifism. Glover's misgivings found vigorous expression in a correspondence on 'Pacifism in the Pulpit' in the columns of the *Baptist Times* in 1935. When C. J. Cadoux proposed to translate one of the Beatitudes, in the form 'Blessed are the Pacifists', claiming that this was the exact translation of the Greek *eirenopoioi,* Glover countered with the suggestion that on the same principle Barnabas and Paul must have said to the men of Lystra, 'We are homoeopaths like you'. But it was not often that his friendships were allowed to cool off for such differences of opinion.

He retained many lifelong friendships and he found new friends among younger men, particularly among his pupils, whose doings and achievements he followed with keen interest. If any of them found their way to Canada, Glover was delighted. C. C. Love who was a student of his, went to Canada in 1933 and became classical master at Bishop's College School, Lennoxville, Quebec. Just because Love was in Canada, Glover wrote to him frequently at first and replied to any letters from Love without fail. Two or three of these letters bring back his abiding interest in Canada and his ability to enter into the position of an Englishman in the Dominion. The correspondence opens with a letter on 14 September 1933.

Brave boy! And all good wishes to you! I have been at Lennoxville, and it is a lovely region, much pictured in the famous old W. H. Bartlett book of about 1840, before there was a North West for an artist to draw. You will be homesick, I am sure; take that for granted; and perhaps you will wish for a speedy return—I did, and (Deo gratias!) didn't have it; and now for long since I count my five years out there among the best in my life. I hope a man like you *won't* come back, but will find a life of happiness in building up the Dominion. Remember even in your depressed moments (if they come—or am I picturing you as too like myself?) that you will count more there than here, and that your presence and work and character are building something more real than you quite guess, being a moderately modest man. I am quite serious about that, and always rather sorry when such a man as —— comes back who counted so much.

Let me know how you get on. My own son sails on Saturday, returning to Harvard, as a post-graduate student. All good wishes my dear lad.

Another letter supplemented Glover's wishes for a pleasant first term. 'October is good in Canada and you are in a pleasant part. Probably someone has a car and will hurtle you to lakes and rivers. Write me a line after a bit and tell me how you get on.

I live in hope of recrossing the ocean!' Glover followed this with a letter timed to reach Love before Christmas 1933.

A line to wish you a happy Xmas and New Year. I think, as I write, of someone else, a man of your own age from Oxford, now at Harvard, and rather remote from Glisson Road. I hope you will both have a happy day, even if you are across the sea and away from home. I am quite sure you are both doing the right thing—though I wish he were back at Saskatoon or some good college of the Dominion.

You will be realizing perhaps for the first time what a real winter is like, and how wonderful sun on snow can be in a dry crisp air. You may see (I won't say I wish it; it is too cruel to the trees) an ice-storm that turns every tree and bush to glass—a sort of fairy forest, with the sun shining on it. Look out for snowbirds, too. Have you come to Drummond's book of poems called *The Habitat*? It gives you your country, or rather the river and gulf end of it, with some real feeling for the French who surround you. After all it was—the river at any rate—their country first, and they count (as I now see) more in the Empire than you might think.

I wish, but the chance seems to grow dimmer, that I might be there in Septr and early Octr. We might manage to meet. Meanwhile, every good wish, and I'm glad you're there—Ripae ulterioris amore.

As it happened, the two correspondents were apt to miss one another in the Long Vacation, since Glover would be going to Canada and Love coming to England.

In 1936 Glover's Christmas letter enclosed a new photograph of St John's College gate.

The enclosed view was taken lately by a friend of mine. I got some copies, thinking I might have some friends in Canada who would be glad to see it. Perhaps you know the scene and may be glad to recall it—as I recall *your* scene after nearly 40 years (36 to be exact + a few months)—and how the man in college slammed into my room in the dead of night to rag a friend and found a stranger, and how, when he said 'I beg your pardon', the stranger yelled out 'So I should think,' and the man was gone never to be identified, and the stranger wished he had said something else.

What about that dream of marriage you were cherishing, when last you wrote? And not to dally with love in the abstract, what about C.C.? And how does his 'thinning' blood stand the climate—and the boys?

Do you know Trinity College School at Port Hope? My son Richard is there, since Septr, when I saw him there in jolly rooms, with his Ph.D at Harvard achieved.

All good wishes for this and every Xmas.

At the close of 1938 Glover sends a budget of College news.

A happy new year to you and the lady, and may you love Canada and your work more and more. Your boys will hardly, I suppose, range so far as Port Hope, Ont. but if they do and you go with them speak to a man called Richard Glover, and tell him you also suffered under his parent's admonitions in your youth. He, like you, has taken a wife, an American, who I hope may become a good British subject in time.

St John's is building a new court between my back windows and Bridge St. They have piled a huge mound of earth up in front of those windows, happily stopping before all light was shut off. I have begged the Senior Bursar to have snapdragons on it next summer; at present it is a snow-clad Alp. Do you toboggan? I am too old.

Sikes has left off teaching, and gone for a second January to southern France. Getty—was he up with you?—is teaching instead of him, a very able and likeable man. We have swarms of young Science Fellows; and our charming Celtic scholar, once Classical, K. H. Jackson, is going to Glasgow University. I am glad he has a good billet, for this progressive place seems to be on the verge of deciding that Celtic language and literature are not needed, as against the many branches of anatomy, chemistry and worse things.

How I hate snow in this furnace-less country! And we are having days of it. What would befall the shop-keepers, when no one who could help it would go out and look at their goods, I don't know.

I cease to teach next June. I was telling A. B. Cook this, and put it in a phrase of *In Memoriam*, that I am to be 'Cast as rubbish to the void', and he instantly rejoined with a wicked echo of the next line, 'I hope you've made your pile complete.' The College is going to let me stay in my present rooms, C Second Court, familiar to you, I think, for I have been in them since 1907. Come and see them and me, whenever you revisit this country. But I know from experience that one of the most obvious drawbacks of marriage is that you have to take two tickets instead of one, without necessarily having your income automatically doubled. I hope you find compensations for this domestic immobility—Hunstanton, as it were, instead of Italy. You go probably to the Gulf or NS in summer, and pretty good too. All good wishes, my dear man and unknown lady.

For all the disrespectful things he said or quoted about women, Glover was a firm believer in marriage and the family. Klausner has described the Greco-Roman world of the first century A.D. as decaying for lack of God and social morality. Home-life decayed along with the decay of religion. Glover wrote in *Progress in Religion*, 'Scepticism is not a working basis of life; a man cannot maintain a family on scepticism. Faith and hope are the foundations of the family, and they are laid by love, unconscious of its great spiritual venture in laying them.' He had learned this as a boy in his father's house in Bristol: he realized it afresh as husband and father in his own home in Cambridge. He notes somewhere that 'the ideal family is generally one with the exact number of children that the speaker may have'. For Glover, the ideal family had six children, four girls and two boys who came in this order, Mary, Anna, Elizabeth, Richard, Janet and Robert. In view of this ideal, Glover suggested that votes for women should be confined to the mothers of six children. Experience of parenthood confirmed Glover's belief in original sin and he would sometimes describe his function as a father, as an outpost of civilization in the midst of barbarians.

Though his theology was not shipwrecked on the rock of the good baby, what fatherhood really meant to him comes out in two references in *The Jesus of History*, which emphasize the charm of children as children, apart from any questions of original sin or original righteousness. In one of these passages he wrote, 'How Jesus likes children!—for their simplicity, their intuition, their teachableness, we say. But was it not perhaps for far simpler and more natural reasons—just because they were children and little and delightful? We forget his little brothers and sisters or we eliminate them for theological purposes.' The second passage is directly concerned with fatherhood.

What is the innermost thing in a father's relation to his children? Is not one of the most real features of parenthood, enjoyment of the child? Do not men and women frankly enjoy the grappling of the little mind with big things? Is there not a charm, as one of the Christian Fathers says, about the half-words that a child uses as he learns to talk and wrestles with a grown-up vocabulary? About the extraordinary pictures he will draw of ships and cows, the quaint stories he will invent, the odd ways in which his gratitude and his affection express themselves? Is it a real fatherhood where such things do not appeal?

Certainly such things appealed to Glover. He tried to record phonetically Mary's earliest attempts at speech. Richard's drawings of beasts and birds were carefully preserved, but they were extraordinary for their firmness of line and their fidelity to nature. Richard displayed a precocious talent, particularly in drawing birds. His picture of 'the unprofaterbel servant' burying his talent under a tree—a neat little sketch of a British workman digging, with a serviette beside him, waiting to be buried—was perhaps extraordinary in the sense his father had in mind. Sayings of the children were treasured, particularly some of Anna's shrewd utterances. When some visitor comparing the formidable height and depth of the bath with Anna's diminutive person asked her whether she was not afraid to climb into the bath, Anna replied, 'What is the good of it? Being afraid won't help you into the bath.' Anna's literalism was sometimes entertaining, as when her mother took her to buy a pair of sandshoes in Sheringham and the shopman said the price was one and ten, she asked, 'Why doesn't he say eleven?' This literalism enabled her to counter some of her father's civilizing admonitions. In a vain endeavour to eat the white before touching the yolk, Anna developed a method of eating an egg which distributed the contents over a wide area, and on one occasion her exasperated father said to her mother, 'Look at that child! she's all over egg', whereupon Anna lifting the hem of her frock, retorted, 'There's none on my knees.' This entry in her father's diary for 1906 shows Anna's response to his religious instruction. '22 July 1906. Heard Anna's prayers. "Thy shall be done", she said—so we discussed God's will and its application to the nursery. But if you have a fight, I said and she chimed in, That would be Thy won't be done.' Anna was not the only member of the family to exhibit an independence and originality of judgement. Elizabeth's penetrating remarks and odd turns of speech, to say nothing of her gift of mimicry, were a constant delight to her father, for in her own phrase, she did not 'hide her light under a talent!' Watching over the opening minds of his children Glover protested against what he called 'one of the most damnable heresies of to-day, the assumption that all children are idiots'. 'I have six and not one answers to that description. Sensible people are sometimes almost as sensible and intelligent as children.'

Naturally the children were impressed by their father's interests and preoccupations. Richard seems to have been under the weight of his father's anxiety about finances. He wished that his father had been a milliner and his mother a millineress! He thinks up plans to strengthen the family budget. One day during the war in 1917, Richard brings home some stray ears of corn, which he proposes to sow next year, to raise crop, reap and make bread—bread to be sold and a goat bought, in which case we can churn our own milk! Another scheme put forward by the boy was that he should write a number of books, and erect a bookstall, like David's, outside 67 Glisson Road, and pay the proceeds of the sale into the family exchequer. His mother discouraged an outside bookstall.

If Richard wanted to follow in his father's steps as a writer, Anna and Robert would emulate the preacher. Mrs Few reported a service at which Anna preached to an audience of two, her sister Mary and her grandmother. The most striking passage in the sermon ran thus: 'And when Jesus came back from being dead, he walked upon his feet towards the multitude. If he asked for some bread, would you give him a stone? or if he asked for some fish would you give him a circle?' (Mrs Few wrote, 'Here Mary quickly gave me a smile.') He would say, 'Go to Satans.' The reading was announced as from chapter one thousand and four, and it also was concerned with 'The fire that is never squenced, which is hell.' At the conclusion both children bowed their heads and reverently repeated the Lord's prayer. Robert at a tender age preached up in church in the nursery. Describing the heads of his discourse, he said, 'The first was about Jesus who lived above the sky and then about God; but I said nothing about the Holy Ghost.' The child was following his father's model more closely than he knew, for his father's main theme was Jesus who lived in Galilee and who lives still above the sky, and then God. His father was criticized as a preacher because he said little or nothing about the Holy Ghost. But this omission reflected Glover's acceptance of a dictum of R. S. Franks, at one time Principal of Western College, Bristol: 'The doctrine of the Holy Spirit is chaos and never has been anything else. There has been no new work done on the Holy Spirit since the New Testament.'

It was natural that the children often tried their father's limited stock of patience with results that led Janet to say on one occasion, 'Now, father, you needn't go and get the "sterics".' And in some respects Glover's ideas of parental discipline may have been old-fashioned, but the children were encouraged to ask questions and to think for themselves. Glover once said of the home in which he was nurtured, 'In our home there was no nonsense about the children having the right to think for themselves. It was their duty to do so.' He carried on this tradition in his own home in Glisson Road. 'All men are afraid of books who have not handled them from infancy', wrote Oliver Wendell Holmes. Glover's children had no fear of books. They were brought up in a home where religion, life and literature were taken seriously, though not solemnly and uncritically. All six received a university education either at Oxford or Cambridge, to the joy and pride of their father. Glover was singularly fortunate in his marriage and his home, and he knew it. He might pretend that he thought marriage had a deleterious effect on masculine originality. Did he not record in a commonplace book, President Taft's saying: 'Men are different, husbands are all alike,' and did he not cap this with the verse,

> Because he was different from other men,
> In mind and manners and frame,
> She married the man and then she began
> To try to make him the same?

But Glover was a manifest disproof of any such thesis. Though his was a restless spirit and he was a constant traveller, his home was his sure anchorage, a constant source of a deep and abiding happiness.

Naturally, Glover followed with the closest interest the career of his son Richard, first as an advanced student at Harvard, where he took his doctor's degree with a thesis on a historical subject, and then as a member of the staff of Trinity College School, Port Hope, Ontario. In the summer of 1938 Richard married Miss C. White of Holyoke, Massachusetts, whom he had met during his year at Harvard. Mrs Glover, along with Mary and Anna, represented the family at the wedding. Glover himself did not go, having a horror of conventional occasions, and believing that he could spend the passage-money with more advantage to Richard and his wife. He wrote to his son,

Mary opined that I *ought* to come to the wedding, but was willing to absolve me, if I paid you my passage-money, to help furnish some kind of dwelling for the future Mrs Richard. The Cambridge story about A.B. the great mathematical infant who succeeded C.D. as professor (F.R.S. at an early age) is that it was not till *after* he had married the Hungarian widow that he realized he would need a house to put her in. You may have thought of that, for you are not a mathematical genius, or she may have hinted it.

Nearer the date of the wedding, he writes:

People either cry or make ancient jokes at weddings; and when they murmur good wishes and all that sort of thing, they rarely find fresh words for them, or dare to say how much they care for you or all that they hope for you. But they mean well—remember that when, after the ceremony, bufferdom burbles dimly at you. I shan't be present exactly in person or I might murmur things of a conventional sort. Well, you know that the domestic circle is like other circles—they are all the same; and parents are terribly alike. If you want to *hear* what we think, try to catch what Mr White says to his daughter.... My dear boy, I can't tell you all I wish the pair of you, but I do wish it.

Later in the year Glover was over in Canada and was able to meet his daughter-in-law. On his return home, early in October, he wrote to her.

I wonder how you have found life since September 9 when you and Richard waved farewell to me at the taxi window. Do you like the Canada which means so much to me? Do you find yourself insensibly every day more British? Do you catch yourself humming 'God Save the King'? Do you begin to relish cabbage cooked in water, with no more flavour than the water?

Do you cease to hanker after 'English Breakfast Tea' and 'Orange Pekoe' and the other dilutions of America?

Of course there are other questions more intimate—all about Richard—whether you find him well trained, or merely raw material—whether his individuality successfully resists a wife's endeavours to make him the exact counterpart of all other men, especially her own male relatives—whether his parents seem to have missed something in ideal or achievement. Do not blame them too severely. As Browning says, 'What hand and brain went ever paired?' This does not exactly mean that the mother supplied the brain and the father the hand. A son is not always the facsimile of his mother. Waiving for the moment more intricate questions, let me put it as a hope rather than an interrogation—that you are very happy at Port Hope and that you find in Richard, if not quite what you anticipated, compensations which on the whole you prefer: that the actual Richard, if different from the imagined, is a good substitute for the dream-figure.

He goes on to refer to Richard's devotion to bird-watching and to surmise that his wife must be content with the view of the lake from the windows of their home and 'such visions of your husband as a telescope gives of one among the marshes or on the shore'.

Unexpectedly the letter contains a brief reference to the international situation. A casual allusion to the Czechs causes him to add: 'I can't tell you the relief of last Friday's promise of peace. The Labour politicians may yap at Neville Chamberlain's heels, but everybody human is grateful that war is averted.' For the moment before the promise proved illusory, Glover could rejoice in the prospect which opened out for his son and daughter-in-law.

His happiness in his home and in his family did not save him from moods of depression and frustration which were perhaps more frequent in the later period of his academic life. He felt himself to be at the height of his powers in the early 'twenties and he never quite got over his disappointment at not being elected to the Chair of Ancient History. As he wrote of Tertullian, 'hopes are often harder to renounce than realities'. But he took to himself the wholesome warning in the lines of Lucretius:

> Sed quia semper aves quod abest, praesentia temnis,
> Imperfecta tibi elapsast ingrataque vita.

He did not let his life be spoiled by longing for what is not and despising what was given to him. A more constant source of discontent was the Cambridge climate, especially the winter. Glover always found the Lent term a trial to the flesh and spirit. In August 1931, on a rainy day he wrote, 'I might stay in Cambridge moderately contented with the place, if less rain, more sun, fewer dogs and some other changes, including more friends. I had more friendship at Queen's.' He did not really lack true friends in Cambridge, but naturally death and sometimes retirement made gaps in the circle. Glover felt bereavement deeply. The comparatively early death of James Adam in 1910 was a great grief to him. The seemingly premature ending of the career of W. H. D. Rivers likewise affected him. But where grief was not aggravated by this kind of circumstance, he felt the loss of old friends like John Skinner and W. E. Heitland. As time goes on he has fewer friends to walk with. Joseph Larmor's decision to return to Ireland when he relinquished his professorship was a real blow to Glover. He writes to Larmor in 1935; 'I wish you were visible in the old rooms. I should be less cross and less "irritabrittle" as my young sister-in-law once put it. I am a good deal alone and 66.' Foakes-Jackson was on the other side of the Atlantic. But if he missed some of his earlier friends, he had many in Cambridge, as he realized when on his retirement S. C. Roberts arranged a select dinner-party in his honour in St John's combination-room. Outside Cambridge he was secure in the friendship of J. C. Carlile, with whom he frequently stayed in Folkestone as well as of Charles Brown and W. B. Selbie.

Beside the loss of friends, a more serious source of depression was the sense that the causes for which he most cared were on the defensive, if not in danger of defeat. He had returned from Canada to Cambridge at the time of the Liberal revival, a revival not just of the Liberal party in politics, but of some real magnanimity as seen in Campbell-Bannerman's courageous settlement of South Africa after the Boer War, and of Liberal progressive ideas in other directions. But after the war of 1914–18, the Liberal party was divided and shattered as a power in politics and liberalism in a wider sense was discounted. Glover felt that all he cared for in politics had suffered a setback. The British people were ceasing to believe in liberalism and ceasing to realize the possibilities and responsibilities of the Empire or Common-wealth. The spirit of independence and the Puritan discipline on which it thrives were both on the decline. Nonconformity was losing its grit and its grip, or so it seemed to Glover. For the most part his attachment to traditional forms of Puritan asceti-cism was a matter of preference rather than conviction. He did not disapprove of cards, dancing, and theatre-going on prin-ciple. In his undergraduate days he played whist and on occasion attended a dance. He never really cared for dancing, but he sometimes regretted that he had lost all interest in cards. The theatre took next to no part in his own recreations and culture, and he was rather sorry that his family did not adhere to the Bristol home tradition in this matter. The one point on which he was strict in both theory and practice was in his rigid teetotalism. He was a non-smoker but this was a matter of taste rather than principle. He disliked my Lady Nicotine but he did not regard her with the abhorrence which many good Americans entertain for her. But generally he felt that the younger genera-tion of Free Churchmen were less stalwart than their predecessors. The Nonconformist conscience no longer counted in politics. The Independents were losing faith in their principles and in their future. The prospect filled Glover's mind with profound misgivings. In theology, he sensed that the main tendencies were moving away from the interest in the Jesus of history which meant so much to him, and with this decline of interest went a tendency to exalt institutions above persons, and dogmas above experience. He regretted also the tendency to emphasize the Hebraic element in Christian origins and to discount the contribution of the Greeks. Glover was an impenitent Hellenist. He was sometimes less than just to Jewish ways of thinking, and the growing influence of Old Testament studies disturbed him. He thought it a pity that successive principals of Regent's Park College were Old Testament scholars. His own book, *The Jesus of History*, was being neglected partly because he took too little account of the Jewish and Old Testament background.

It was not only in the sphere of Church life that Glover felt and deplored the decline of Independency. In the university, too, he was out of sympathy with the reforms in the 'twenties which strengthened the authority of Central Boards of Control, diminished the sovereignty of colleges and menaced, as he thought, the independence of the individual lecturer. He was out of sympathy too with the growing predominance of natural science in university education. A race of scientific specialists would lack the fundamentals of a true education. They would never attain the universal point of view which should be a university's chief gift to her sons and daughters. Glover as he watched the diminishing share of the Classics in education found himself standing like Ajax, defending the retreating Greeks, and he feared the retreat would end in a rout. He was convinced that scientific humanism was no substitute for classical and Christian humanism, yet the tide seemed to be setting steadily and almost inevitably in the direction of the former. It is no wonder that, in his closing years, Glover often felt that everything he cared for was imperilled, if not doomed to be lost.

If anything was calculated to confirm his fears, it was the outbreak of the World War in 1939, the year of his retirement. Yet in spite of war-time anxieties—and with two sons in the armed forces, Glover could not escape anxieties—in spite of dangers at home, in spite of renewed sorrows for the loss of friends and pupils, and in spite of ill-health which dogged him towards the end, the three or four years of his retirement were a time of comparative tranquillity. Perhaps indeed the outbreak of war helped to reconcile him to retirement. He did not feel too old at seventy, and when eight of his pupils took firsts in the Classical Tripos in his last year, he would have been glad to continue. But the war would have put a period to his work as a classical lecturer in any case. He retained his rooms in college, and to keep in touch with the college he loved, while free of responsibility, was a real pleasure. He had time to take stock of his unpublished material and to prepare the selection of essays that appeared under the title, *The Challenge of the Greek*. Above all he could indulge in the delights of recollection, which resulted in his charming *Cambridge Retrospect*. As he called to mind all that Cambridge had given him as undergraduate and don, as he remembered his good friends—the pen-portraits of the members of St John's high table whom he knew best and to whom he owed most are among the most delightful feature of the book—all his irritations and resentments fell away and he was filled with thankfulness for a life spent in Cambridge. Perhaps too he realized as many of his friends realized, that he had made a finer contribution to the life and thought of his time by what seemed a division of his interests, that the combination of preacher and scholar had meant more to his contemporaries than either alone could have done, and that for this reason the disappointment of his academic ambitions may have been, to use a Quaker phrase, in right ordering.

The war brought with it claims on Glover's resources to which he gladly responded. Cambridge was regarded as a comparatively safe area and many colleges from London sought refuge there. Accommodation in Cambridge was strained to the limit, and as 67 Glisson Road was a large house, and as most members of the family were away, the Glovers opened their home to more than one homeless student. What it meant to be billeted with the Glovers is well described in this letter from a London student, Miss Shaw:

All my reminiscences are very slight, I am afraid, but his attitude to me does, I think, help to give an insight into one facet of his charming character. I was a student of London University when my college was evacuated to Cambridge during the war, and spent the whole of my three-year course billeted in Dr Glover's house; I was there at the time of his death. Living in someone else's home as an unwanted guest could, I am sure, be very difficult, but both Dr and Mrs Glover spared no pains to make me feel happy and comfortable. Dr Glover had at that time partly retired from college life, though he still occasionally went down to St John's by an early bus; when I was reading Latin for my intermediate examination, he gave up an hour of his time every Saturday morning to read Virgil with me, and I remember many happy hours talking to him in his study. There was never any sense of a great and brilliant man condescending to a young girl; he was always ready to meet me on an equal ground, and discuss seriously with me any subject that came up. I think he hated the exaggerated deference which some people showed towards him.

Doubtless Glover was the more ready to give up an hour to a young student, since she was reading Virgil. But he was equally ready to help a young minister[1] to read his Greek

---

[1] The Rev. H. W. Chapman, minister of the Baptist Church at Ashdon, Essex.

Testament. He had now more leisure for reading old favourites, *Don Quixote* or the *Odyssey*, Cowper's letters or Boswell's *Johnson*. He also had more leisure for visitors. Anyone from Canada, especially from Queen's, would be sure of a welcome. Old pupils would drop in, often bringing wife or husband to be introduced to him. College friends and a wider circle of Cambridge friends would be among his callers, helping to call forth and check some of the reminiscences which appeared in *Cambridge Retrospect*. But as time went on, he found his strength declining. He liked to go daily to his college rooms but in the course of 1942, it was becoming a tiring affair. He could face the prospect with equanimity and even humour.

In the early spring of 1943, he had to see his doctor as he was so painfully tired. He was ordered to spend three weeks in bed, to rest a tired heart, and he would have to be content to go much slower than before. Fortunately his daughter Anna, herself a qualified doctor, was at home during the last six months of her father's life and was able to look after him. He submitted to an irksome regime with great patience, and although he was worse before he was better, he made a partial recovery. He was able to see visitors again, though naturally some limit had to be put both on the numbers and the length of such visits. He had the great joy of seeing *Cambridge Retrospect* through the press and of learning that the first edition sold out within forty-eight hours.

As is usual with cardiac trouble, the end came suddenly. On the morning of 26 May he had been looking through his correspondence and had been particularly pleased with a letter from Canon Raven saying how much he had enjoyed *Cambridge Retrospect*. A little later in happy mood, he died while conversing with the nurse who came in daily to help him.

Throughout the period of weakness and up to the hour of his death, his mind did not fail nor become clouded. His affections were undimmed, and his welcome to all who visited him or had to do with him was warm and vivid. His faith stood the test of illness, and was a solace to him in many wakeful nights and long-drawn days. A treasured saying of his father's may have been often in his mind. 'So we move towards the great unknown which will be, however, full of God. May we be fit for either world!'

POSTSCRIPT

The author of a book, if he is any good at all, knows as well as any critic—sometimes much better, what its defects are. But the time comes when it should be published, defects and all. If you nurse your book too long, it becomes an encyclopaedia—or it grows heavy and tame, like other old men—you smooth down too much, qualify too much and the book loses vigour and interest. Polybius seems to have written his History for decades. Don't you! The book will be better for not being improved. Just imagine yourself improved by the removal of all your nodosities, angles and oddities! It makes one think of J. B. Priestley's description of the well-scrubbed American from whom all vestiges of character were eliminated. Quintilian said the same of books; you can correct the life out of them.

It is time for me to heed this wholesome lesson in authorship contained in a letter from Glover to his son Richard. This book has been too long on the anvil, and I must let it go, defects and all. The years I have been engaged on it have not been spent mainly in sandpapering and like refinements. I might say of this book what Augustine said of his *City of God*. 'Some years passed over my head, before I could compile and finish the whole frame of this worke, *by reason of many intercedent affairs, whose impatient haste of quick expedition would admit no delay*.' But the wealth of material at my disposal has also delayed the completion of my task. Glover kept diaries from a very early age, and I think I must have read nearly two million words of diary.

He used a Scottish commercial diary, in which the Sundays occupy a place of honour from pages 41 to 60, and then each week has its allotted two pages, three days to a page, ten lines to a day. With his abbreviations and clear small writing, Glover seldom wrote less than one hundred words a day. The record of the day's doings is so detailed and comprehensive as almost to suggest Milton's concern to present his true account of the spending of time and talent. Glover notes the text and subject of almost every sermon he hears, and he was a twicer, a regular attender at public worship both morning and evening. He furnishes the same details, when he is preacher, as he often was. He records the names of all who visited him or whom he visits; of all who walked with him, and walking became his one recreation; of all whom he met in hall and combination room or at feasts and dinner parties. The books he read, and the books he bought, are regularly entered. Bills paid, royalties received, investments made are all set down. Anniversaries of births, marriages and deaths are constantly recalled. Amid a mass of detail, significant only as a revelation of habit, there are scraps of conversation, sentences from letters, comments appreciative or critical on his books or on his lectures and sermons. Through the series can be traced his antipathies and prejudices, his friendships and enthusiasms, his disappointments and sorrows, his successes and joys, his anxieties and his doxologies. To read the whole series is to get a new impression of the man himself and since it is doubtful whether anyone will read the whole series after me, I have tried to convey that impression correctly.

Besides his regular diaries, Glover left a number of commonplace books, to say nothing of special travel-diaries. If a man may be known by his quotations, here is another way in which Glover revealed himself. The collections of letters and printed papers which I have examined are also considerable in extent. A number of correspondents sent me reminiscences or lent me letters. With such ample resources for its making, the book should be much better than it is.

While I cannot expect that my portrait of Glover will satisfy his friends and my informants I must, before I lay down my pen, thank all those who have helped me to complete the book. I cannot mention by name all who sent me reminiscences. Indeed some insist on remaining anonymous. But I hope that all, named or unnamed in the text of the book will realize how much I owe them, and will accept this inadequate but grateful acknowledgement of my debt to them.

Two particular obligations must not be passed over in silence. Dil Calvin, one of Glover's closest friends, generously passed on to me a selection of his letters and a bundle of impressions and recollections without which I could not have hoped to picture Glover in his Canadian setting. It is a great grief to me that Dil Calvin has not lived to see the book in print, for his contribution to it has been invaluable. Then I cannot say how much

I am indebted to Mrs Glover and the members of the family, and also to Miss D. F. Glover, his younger sister. Not only have all of them saved me from many blunders and given me every assistance, but they have also been most patient with a dilatory author.

As I let the book go, I think of many things which I should have liked to include and perhaps ought to have included. I could have spoken of the happiness that came to the Glover family circle through the marriage of Anna, then a major in the R.A.M.C. to Colonel (now Brigadier) E. W. Wade in 1940, and a year later of Robert to Miss Jean Muir, whom he met when they were both undergraduates at Oxford. It is interesting to record that Glover's eldest grandchild, Richard's elder son, was born a few weeks before his grandfather's death. Glover's devotion to his father and his father's memory might have been more fully illustrated. I should have mentioned the bust of his father which he presented to the Baptist Church House in Southampton Row. It stands appropriately in the visitors' reception room. Glover would have liked it to stand on the stairs, facing or perhaps I should say, outfacing the colossal statue of Spurgeon which dominates the entrance hall! A further tribute to his father's memory is embodied in the collection of some 300 books on American history which he presented to the library of the University of Bristol. With his interest in books, particularly secondhand books, I might have associated his liking for old furniture and cloisonné-ware. It was a great satisfaction to him that his treasures in this kind as well as his library came through the bombing raid of 1940 unharmed. Somewhere I should have found room for an allusion to the dinner he promoted in honour of the bookseller David. But it is too late to repair omissions of this sort.

When in response to Mr S. C. Roberts's suggestion I undertook to write this biography, I did not realize how difficult it would be and how long it would take. But I am glad I did not decline the task. It has been a privilege to come to know more intimately one whose friendship has always meant much to me. It has seemed to me well worth while to remind the present generation of the work of a Christian classical humanist, whose contribution to the defence and illumination of some vital elements in our European heritage is certainly of more than passing interest. Writing to his father in 1899, Glover said, 'I am reading R. W. Dale's life by his son, A.W.W.D.... It has wakened in me a desire to read some of the books of R.W. which is, I suppose, part of a good biographer's function.' Whatever the defects of this essay in biography, I hope at least that it will pass this test and will waken in many readers the desire to read some of the books of T. R. Glover.

Appendix

ENGLISH RENDERINGS OF THE LATIN QUOTATIONS

(*a*) *The description of Canada* (p. 133)

Canada, the foremost of all British colonies, strong in the association of two peoples, distinguished in both war and peace, mighty producer of the fruits of the earth, mighty breeder of men, to be loved for the wonderful beauty of mountains, rivers, lakes and plains, as well as for all the pleasing delights of sun and snow.

(*b*) *The letter to the University of Oxford on the death of Viscount Grey* (p. 134)

Most honoured sirs, since death has robbed you of your Chancellor, full of years indeed though not yet worn out by old age, we would like you to know with what sorrow we along with countless thousands of your fellow-countrymen feel the loss of one who through so many years took his part in public life with honours untarnished, and who for so long guided the ship of State through the rocks and whirlpools of foreign affairs. It is a joy to remember the absence of ambition, the honours unsought but accepted, the life entirely dedicated to the fatherland, for though weighed down with bereavement and loneliness and semi-blindness he would set his sorrows on one side, if only he could succour Britain in distress. Nor did he only discharge these responsibilities of public life, but he was distinguished also for simpler virtues. A lover of birds and of our national poet, he liked to spend his leisure amid mountains and lakes, not without the companionship of books, being equally devoted to two arts, absorbed in fishing as in reading, yet ready to abandon these pure pleasures if his country called, if the cause of justice needed a defender. We have seen in him the true model of a gentleman, a citizen, an Englishman, so perfect indeed that no one outshines him among our contemporaries. With you we mourn his loss, and yet, as Cicero says, while this our State endures, it will rejoice that he was born.

INDEX*

Achilles, 112
Adam, J., 67, 146, 217
Adcock, F. E., 169, 170, 196
Aeneas, 74, 75, 76
Aeschylus, 26, 43, 112, 113, 198
Afrahat, 28
Aldis, W. S., 66
Alexander, x, 172, 186
Alexandria, 173
Alington, C., 139
Allbutt, Sir C., 108
Allenby, General, 132
Ancient World, The, 195, 201, 204, 205
Angell, Norman, 125
Angus, C. F., 87, 96, 102, 103
Angus Lectures, 92, 93
Anstey, F., 22, 192
Arnold, Edward, 73
Arnold, Edwin, 8
Arnold, Matthew, 80
Aryo-Samaj, 104
Asquith, Earl of Oxford and, 41, 62, 63, 76, 117
Assiniboine Red Indians, 177
Athens, 116, 196, 201
Aubrey, M. E., 22, 91, 149, 150, 157, 159, 160, 163
Augustine, St, 4, 52, 54, 56, 156, 166, 222
Augustus, x, 74, 75, 187

Bacon, B. W., 184
Bacon, L., 177
Bailey, C., 133
Baker, H. F., 145
Baldwin, Earl, 142
Balfour, A. J., 130
Bangor, 199
Baptists, 30, 91, 152, 158, 178, 184, 185
Baptist Union, 10, 65, 92, 149, 150, 153, 155, 156, 157, 159, 161, 169, 171
Barisal, 102
Barnes, E. W., 109n.
Bartlett, W. H., 208
Baslow, 88

Bateson, W., 27, 67, 145
Beatrice, Infanta of Spain, 198
Bedford College, 63
Bell, C. K. A., 106
Bell, Dr, 29
Beloch, 40
Benians, E. A., 61, 135, 144–6
Bennett, Arnold, 116
Berkeley, Cal., 113, 169, 172, 174ff., 202
Bernard of Clairvaux, 155
Besant, Mrs A., 104
Bevan, A. A., 28
Bevan, Edwyn, 79
Bhakti, 103
Birrell, A., 76
Blomfield, W. E., 66
Bodkin, T., 206
Bonar, H., 51
Bonar Law, 117
Bonney, T. G., 103, 108, 145
Borstal, 168
Bosanquet, R. C., 22
Boswell, 111, 221
Botha, General, 118
Bowell, Sir M., 36
Bradley, A. C., xii
Brahmo-Samaj, 104
Breuil, the Abbé, 130
Bristol, xi, 1ff., 9, 10, 14, 15, 24, 123, 142, 170, 198, 224
Brown, Charles, 150, 162, 184, 185, 217
Brown, C. R., 144
Brown, W. L., 29
Browne Medal, 26
Browning, Oscar, 22, 170
Browning, Robert, 4, 177, 189, 216
Bruce, The Hon. W., 139
Buchman, Frank, 178, 182–4
Buddha, 8
Bunyan, John, 83, 85, 112, 158, 189
Burkitt, F. C., 28, 34, 95, 141
Burnand, E. C., 22
Burns, Robert, 205
Butler, Montague, 147
Butler, S., 198

* I am indebted to Mrs Glover and Miss Janet Glover for undertaking the labour of compiling the index. H. G. Wood.

www.ingramcontent.com/pod-product-compliance
Ingram Content Group UK Ltd.
Pitfield, Milton Keynes, MK11 3LW, UK
UKHW010338140625
459647UK00010B/687